REPREHENSIBLE

REPREHENSIBLE

POLITE HISTORIES OF BAD BEHAVIOUR

MIKEY ROBINS

**SIMON &
SCHUSTER**

London · New York · Sydney · Toronto · New Delhi

A CBS COMPANY

REPREHENSIBLE: POLITE HISTORIES OF BAD BEHAVIOUR
First published in Australia in 2020 by
Simon & Schuster (Australia) Pty Limited
Suite 19A, Level 1, Building C, 450 Miller Street, Cammeray, NSW 2062

10 9 8 7 6 5 4 3 2 1

A ViacomCBS Company
Sydney New York London Toronto New Delhi
Visit our website at www.simonandschuster.com.au

© Mikey Robins 2020

All rights reserved. No part of this publication may be reproduced, stored in a retrieval system, or transmitted in any form or by any means, electronic, mechanical, photocopying, recording or otherwise, without prior permission of the publisher.

 A catalogue record for this book is available from the National Library of Australia

Cover design: Luke Causby/Blue Cork
Cover image: *'Le Discret (The Secret)'* by Joseph Ducreux (1735–1802)
Typeset by Midland Typesetters, Australia
Printed and bound in Australia by Griffin Press

 The paper this book is printed on is certified against the Forest Stewardship Council® Standards. Griffin Press holds FSC® chain of custody certification SGS-COC-005088. FSC® promotes environmentally responsible, socially beneficial and economically viable management of the world's forests.

For Laura

CONTENTS

Introduction 1

Chapter One: **The Problem with Power** 5

Chapter Two: **Misbehaving Royally** 47

Chapter Three: **Feuds, Fights & Insults** 99

Chapter Four: **Wayward Geniuses** 153

Chapter Five: **Vanity Not-So-Fair** 203

Chapter Six: **Scoundrels, Both Dirty & Rotten** 245

Suggested Reading 303

Acknowledgments 311

Introduction

It sometimes feels that we live our lives in a state of constant outrage. Our leaders might have feet of clay, but it seems those feet have stepped in something much more awful than clay. The news cycle appears to have the same attention span as a goldfish with a Red Bull addiction, and then everything is amplified through the viperous echo chamber of social media. By the time you switch off the telly or mobile device and angrily climb into bed you have actually forgotten what it was that made your blood boil over your morning coffee.

We are under a bombardment from all of our screens, all of the time, reminding us with one click just what a dreadful time we are living through.

But here is one tiny, comforting thought: *we've always been appalling.* Not all of us, not all the time, but appalling behaviour runs through our history right alongside great art, soul-stirring music and methods for preserving fish – and we are *really* good at preserving fish.

I'm not talking about the great and serious crimes against humanity that we deal with on a generational basis. This is a 'polite' history of bad behaviour. I'm interested in our more venal, ridiculous, sometimes far-reaching and often private and petty transgressions. Now I understand that 'polite' is an extremely subjective word. I'm guessing that my interpretation may not match up with some people's idea of taste or propriety.

I can live with that.

I'm not saying that there *aren't* episodes in this book that some people will find raunchy, prurient or just downright filthy. And there are a few sad and tragic deaths, but my area of interest is the serial scoundrel as opposed to the serial murderer. I find fascinating the pompous and proud, the foibles of the powerful, the particular peccadilloes of some of our greatest leaders, thinkers and writers. And there are more randy royals than you can shake a sceptre at.

Sometimes it's the ridiculous and reprehensible that give us a window into our perception of what is grand, beautiful and true. These castles in the sky are often built on the shifting sands of our folly. And that's often where all the fun stuff happens.

For those of you with delicate sensibilities, may I suggest you approach this book as you would a heated spa bath in a hotel you've never stayed in before. Maybe dip in and dip out until you're ready to settle in.

For readers with sterner stomachs, may I suggest that you use this book for another, dare I say, *reprehensible* purpose? As I said before, we do live in an age of constant outrage.

So, just for fun (and if you're of legal drinking age, of course), maybe this book could serve as a drinking game. Any time you

Introduction

come across any sort of reprehensible activity that reminds you of our more morally culpable world leaders (and one orange-tinted leader in particular), take a sip of your favourite tipple.

Just don't say I didn't warn you.

Chapter One:
THE PROBLEM WITH POWER

When I was a high school history student studying the American Revolutionary War, my favourite of the Founding Fathers was always Benjamin Franklin. To me, he epitomised all that was outstanding in a person close to the many levers of power. He was a *true* man of power.

Franklin had an enlightened and inquisitive mind, a warm and charming commonality (as could be witnessed in the annual *Poor Richard's Almanack* which Franklin published from 1732 to 1785), as well as being a beacon for democracy and personal liberty. All of this seemed to emanate from the portraits of his cherubic face – a face framed by the bifocal spectacles that we'd been told he'd actually invented himself.

Or, as one of his many biographers, Albert Henry Smyth, wrote in 1907, 'It is no use blinking the fact that Franklin's animal instincts and passions were strong and rank, that they led him to the commission of deplorable errata in his life, and that the taint of irredeemable vulgarity is upon much of this man.'

Albert Henry is obviously being quite judgemental here. Let's face it, any use of the word 'taint' is often wrapped up with finger-wagging of one kind or other. But, sadly, the truth remains: Franklin was not the benign, avuncular figure I had imagined him to be when I was a lad.

Chances are he fathered quite a few illegitimate children, including a son, William, whom he conceived with his maid Deborah. (William was raised as a Franklin and eventually became governor of New Jersey.) Thomas A. Foster, the historian and author of *Sex and the Founding Fathers: The American Quest for a Relatable Past*, puts the number of illegitimate children at fifteen, and in these matters I'm always willing to err on the side of the larger number.

Franklin, during his time in London, was associated with Francis Dashwood, a most reprehensible rake and founder of the infamous Hellfire Club. Whether or not Franklin actually partook of the orgiastic indulgences of the club is up for debate, but what is better known is that Franklin did have a wide and extensive knowledge of the brothels of London, and Paris, and his hometown of Philadelphia . . .

Even when he was in his seventies and living in Paris he was still conducting trysts like a man of considerably more youthful vigour and, dare I say, judgement.

I know that duplicity between the public persona and the private person is one of the traits of those who seek and then wield power. But in Franklin's case it's just so wantonly observable. As another biographer, Carl Van Doren, wrote, 'In his morning litany he could pray to be kept from lasciviousness, but when night came lust might come with it. He went to women hungrily, secretly and briefly.'

Indeed, Franklin was a man of many passions, some beyond liberty and libertarianism. He is, after all, the only person in the world to be inducted into both the US Chess and the International Swimming halls of fame. And that's got to count for something.

No matter how flawed these people of power are, it is a simple fact that ever since we've been gathering together in communities we've needed leaders to help us save ourselves from ourselves.

During my research I came across 'The Problem with Power', also known as episode 110 of *He-Man and the Masters of the*

The Problem with Power

Universe, where Man-at-Arms aka Duncan speaks these wise words:

> I want to talk to you today about safety. Accidents don't just happen to other people. They can happen to you too. But you can do some things to help prevent accidents from happening. Using a safety belt when riding in a car can save your life and prevent you from being seriously hurt. Now I know you've been told never to play with matches, because if you do you are playing with fire. And fire can burn your toys, your home, your family, you. So use your common sense and think about what you're doing; it's better to be safe than sorry.

Well said, Duncan, and that's exactly what our lawmakers and those we put in power are simply doing for us, right? Saving us from not wearing our seat belts or playing with matches. The laws they make are surely just an example of 'common sense'? I wish that were the case, Duncan. If only some of the learned and powerful had spent less time in class and more time watching *He-Man and the Masters of the Universe*, we would all be so much better off.

Some laws are the result of prejudices or religious beliefs that often changed in accordance with whichever way the theological wind was blowing, and some just plain boggle the imagination.

However, while we're on the topic of mind-boggling legislation, let me just clear up one particular myth, especially for any expectant mothers planning on visiting the United Kingdom: it is not legal for a pregnant woman to urinate in a policeman's helmet! There is a popular belief that members of the constabulary are obliged to help an expectant woman if she desperately needs to take a whiz, but despite internet and newspaper articles to the contrary, she should *never* expect to relieve herself in a bobby's helmet. It is only ever legal if you are an Australian cricket fan and you are in England during the Ashes test series . . . (Actually, you might want to fact-check that.)

Sometimes the elite like to exercise their power, and not just through laws, particularly if they sense that society is changing in ways that they perceive as threatening towards them. To put it in sociologist terminology, 'They can scratch when they are cornered.'

In such times, those in power might spread ridiculous rumours or bogus theories that they hope will thwart social change or, even better, send society back to a time when they felt their grip on power unchallenged.

One of the more bizarre incidents involving such a dreaded fear of change is illustrated in the next story, where bikes, women's rights and trouser technology become strangely intermingled.

Get On Your Bikes and Ride

Towards the end of the nineteenth century the patriarchy came under attack from an underestimated weapon. It wasn't the growing calls for suffrage and higher education, nor was it the rise of

The Problem with Power

the unions among the factory women. No, it was something far more benign that scared the men who feared change . . . It was the bicycle.

In 1896 *Munsey's Magazine* wrote, 'To men, the bicycle in the beginning was merely a toy, another machine added to the long list of devices they knew in their work and play. To women it was a steed upon which they rode into a new world.'

I think it was the actual act of *riding* that upset male society the most. Riding a bike in a Victorian dress would have been virtually impossible, and women would valiantly try to keep their skirts from blowing up in the wind or being swept to one side – or, even more dangerously, from getting caught up in the pedals or wheels. The riding was made even more dangerous as the women would also have to dodge the abuse, and sometimes rocks, hurled at them by sanctimonious passers-by. And as for wearing trousers, forget about it – *that* was never going to happen.

However, several ingenious folks did come up with the solution of the convertible skirt. A dress that had a hidden internal system of pulleys, loops and buttons that a woman could engage to make her cumbersome dress something less life-threatening when she wanted to ride her bike.

Another solution would have been for the men of the era to grow up just a little bit, but instead they legislated against female riders. A woman riding a bike had to endure many more stringent and sexist instructions than her cycling brothers, who had virtually no rules applied to them. One particularly patronising instruction can be found in the 1895 publication the

New York World, which advised female riders, 'Don't refuse assistance when going up a hill.'

However, the most insidious attempt to stop the throngs of middle-class and wealthier women from taking up the healthy activity of cycling actually came from the medical profession. They warned of the terrifying female-only condition called 'Bicycle Face'.

The *Literary Digest* of 1895 printed this ridiculous warning: 'Overexertion in the upright position on the wheel, and the unconscious effort to maintain one's balance tend to produce a wearied and exhausted bicycle face.' It continued by saying the female rider would have these symptoms: 'Usually flushed, but sometimes pale, often with lips more or less drawn, and the beginning of dark shadows under the eyes, and always with an expression of weariness.' Other journals told how female riders would experience facial changes, 'characterised by a hard, clenched jaw and bulging eye'.

Although some physicians also claimed that bicycle face could affect male riders as well, they pretty much all agreed that women were the most at risk, seeing as it required so much physical exertion to propel a bicycle as well as a good sense of balance, something apparently not associated with women at the time.

There were also stories and articles about actresses who had lost their voices due to the heavy breathing cycling required, or of famous dancers who could no longer perform, seeing as their calves had become over-developed.

Women were warned about the dangers of the saddle and the harmful vibrations that could lead to fertility problems.

The Problem with Power

Some quacks even went as far as to link a woman who rode a bike to a woman of uncertain morals. A certain Dr Garrigue wrote about the naughty saddle causing a woman to feel an 'intimate massage', which he concluded could lead to her moral downfall.

Of all of the supposed afflictions that the bicycle could inflict on women, perhaps the most ridiculous was the imagined affliction known as 'cyclomania'. This was a supposed addiction to cycling and the drug-like euphoria that riding to the point of exhaustion was thought to bring. In the 1896 guidebook *Bicycling for Ladies*, there is this warning: 'Scorching [fast and aerobic riding] is a form of bicycle intoxication. It could be spotted in a woman who rode fast and compulsively, often seeking out hills to cause greater stress on her body. One sure sign was if you spotted a family out cycling and the mother of the family was out of her "normal" place, which was riding ahead of her family. This was a woman possessed by that nasty old demon "Cyclomania!"'

Fortunately by the twentieth century all of these odious theories had been tossed into the dustbin of quackery. These days the bicycle has been almost universally embraced as both a physically and environmentally healthy mode of transport. Our main contemporary concern with bikes is not the effect they have on women, but rather what the sight of a middle-aged man in lycra has on the community as a whole. Let's be honest, lads, if you are anywhere near my shape or size, and you insist on riding your bike in tights, well, your backside just looks like two inner tubes having an argument.

Jackson's Parrot, the Original Dirty Bird

In the modern era when we think of presidential pets we often think of dogs. The Obamas had Bo; the Nixons had Pasha, Vicky and King Timahoe; the Kennedys had four dogs, including a gift from Khrushchev called Pushinka. It was said that Pushinka's mother had actually been one of the Soviet Union's famous dogs in space.

The current administration, however, is virtually pet-free (unless you count Mike Pence's rabbit Marlon Bundo and, of course, Jared.)

Yet, strangely enough – and although it hasn't been the case for more than half a century – birds and parrots in particular were beloved presidential pets.

The Washingtons had a parrot. Thomas Jefferson had a mockingbird called Dick. Ulysses S. Grant was said to own a parrot, and his one-time boss's son Tad Lincoln was the loving owner of a turkey called Jack. Teddy Roosevelt had quite a few parrots, and up until his assassination William McKinley owned a parrot that was somewhat sarcastically named 'The Washington Post'.

But perhaps the most infamous of all the White House birds was Andrew Jackson's African grey parrot, Poll.

Poll had originally been a gift for his wife, Rachel; unfortunately she passed away just before his inauguration in 1829. Poll, however, did make it to the Pennsylvania Avenue residence, where the new president became the bird's primary companion.

Let's not forget that Jackson had been given the nickname 'Old Hickory' as a tribute to his toughness and strength. He

The Problem with Power

killed a man for cheating at horseracing and took part in a terrifying number of duels. Hell, at the age of sixty-seven he beat a would-be assassin senseless with a walking stick after the man's gun misfired.

To give another clue to Jackson's nature, one of the first things he did when he arrived at the White House was to install over a dozen spittoons.

But it would seem that he did indeed dote on that Poll, spending lots of quality time with the bird. In hindsight, he probably spent too much time, considering some of the bad habits Poll picked up from his owner. You don't have to be David Attenborough to realise that adopting a bird blessed with longevity like a parrot when you are of an advanced age means that there is a fair chance the bird will outlive you. And as such, Poll was one of the guests of honour when Andrew Jackson was laid to rest in 1845. However, his stay at the funeral was brief.

The following was recorded in the writings of Reverend William Menefee Norment, who is quoted in the third volume of *Andrew Jackson and Early Tennessee History*: 'Before the sermon and while the crowd was gathering, a wicked parrot that was a household pet got excited and commenced swearing so loud and long as to disturb the people.'

He continues, saying the bird 'let loose perfect gusts of cuss words' and that the mourners were 'horrified and awed at the bird's lack of reverence'.

Poll was eventually removed – to where, no one actually knows. But I'd like to think that the ghost of Poll was secretly smiling almost one hundred and thirty years later when Nixon was forced to release those infamous tapes and the world would get its next insight into private presidential profanity.

Swears, Bears and Solemnity

I have to admit that I've always been something of a swearer. As a young Catholic lad, swearing was pretty much the only sin that I could confidently list off when going to confession. It's a sad fact that I owe my knowledge of the Stations of the Cross to the fact that I was a potty-mouthed eleven-year-old.

Years later, when I started working in radio, I even invented a character who would allow me to swear on air . . . well, almost.

Keith the Moravian Swearing Bear was a sort of agony aunt to the station's listeners. They would write in their problems and then Keith (played by yours truly) would berate them in a foul-mouthed tirade, and our poor producer would have to edit out the worst of the swear words. Only one ever sneaked through.

Hey, it wasn't highbrow but Keith did have quite a loyal following among a certain section of our audience, so much so that we released a T-shirt with a rather gruff bear on the front saying the words, 'What The F&#K Are You Looking At?' It sold quite well, and it is still with some misplaced pride that I recall seeing one of Keith's fans being escorted out of the Sydney Cricket Ground wearing that same T-shirt.

Oh, and before you ask why Keith was Moravian, all I can say is that his first script was written on the back of a beer coaster.

According to my wife, I am something of a 'sleep swearer'. I hasten to add that this doesn't mean I scream out in terror from some dark dream, but rather someone who even though sound asleep will rattle off a few swear words and then chuckle like a naughty schoolboy.

So swearing and I have had a long friendship.

These days when we think about swearing we usually think of obscene language that is meant to cause offence. This is, of course, always subjective and in accordance with the sensibilities of both the speaker and the listener. However, for a very long time this was by no means the standard definition of swearing. To understand the codifying of swearing in Tudor and Stuart England there is a fantastic essay written by Swansea University Professor John Spurr with the title '"Damn your Blood": Swearing in early modern English', which is not only a fascinating read but really captures the nature of swearing as it moved from the Middle Ages into the spoken English that we would recognise today.

He writes, 'The oaths of the Tudor and Stuart centuries, the era of Shakespeare (1564–1616), still jump out at modern readers from plays, courtroom testimonies and countless other sources. And they strike us as very different from our own bad language. Swearing – solemn or profane – was a religious issue: an oath called on God to guarantee the truth of a statement, just as profane swearing took God's name in vain.'

It would be a fair assumption that the profane would immediately enrage the good folk of town and village. But those who overused the oath of 'swearing to God' and trivialised that sacred bond were also brought into disrepute, along with anyone who expressed such an oath to back up a falsehood. The remnants of the latter are still evident in our modern-day perjury laws. However, it was never just as cut and dried as that, because over the centuries people modified these oaths in accordance with the linguistic and social fashions of the day, changing and adapting the language of oaths and profanity, something we still do today.

Spurr uses a poem from a sixteenth-century Protestant preacher to demonstrate the overabundance of oaths that were in use at the time and how they were seen as diluting and perverting the original intention of swearing an oath:

> Some swear by God's nails, his heart and body
> And some swear by his flesh, his blood and his foot
> And some by his guts, his life and heart root,
> Some other would seem all swearing to refrain
> And they invent idle oaths; such is their idle brain:
> By cock and by pie, and by the goose wing
> By the cross of the mouse foot and by Saint Chicken
> And some swear by the Devil, such is their blindness.

Laws were brought in and people were prosecuted for not only profanity but also for simply taking the Lord's name in vain. Professor Spurr tells the story of an Essex woman, Margaret Jones, who was arrested for being 'a swearer using most cursed oaths, as namely God's wounds, God's heart. When chided by her vicar, she retorted, "God's heart she should swear in spite of his teeth [God's teeth I'm assuming]: as she used much swearing, so she laid violent hands and smote the vicar . . . and then followed him, swearing, from one end of the town to the other."'

Just think, if only she'd waited for a couple of hundred years she would have found herself a beloved star in a reality television show like *Ye Olde Real Housewives of Essex* instead of up on charges before the local magistrate.

Spurr goes on to explain that the attitude towards swearing at the time was akin to 'an infection, a contagion or a flood. It was a sin that would damn the swearer's soul and might well provoke immediate punishment from on high . . . Clergy urged their congregations not only to avoid the bold oaths of the libertines [phrases that we would probably consider to be swearing], but also to be wary of "the more petty oaths of faith and troth; take heed of also cursing and taking God's Name in vain, remembering that the Lord will not hold such guiltless."'

By the reign of James the First, the monarch had brought in some laws that put the screws on swearing, codifying the attitudes towards swearing that were prevalent at the time.

When a sailor by the name of Robert Abbot let loose a blue streak, he was fined for six oaths of 'by God' and six curses of 'damn your blood'. It is interesting to note in the latter charge for 'damn your blood' that we have an intersection between what we would consider to be two different strands of cursing. Firstly, the act of laying a curse and, secondly, that of using a curse as a swear word.

Reprehensible

These two strands, which would be regarded as completely different in the modern world, were far more intertwined and inseparable for centuries.

So it appears that swearing was as complex an issue back then as it is now, and laws regarding swearing were and still are virtually useless. As we've become a secular society the inherent nature of swearing has obviously changed – language and morals are both fluid by nature.

Plus, we all know how bloody good it feels to let off a loud burst of purple language when the mood or the occasion takes you. And let's not forget people who use euphemisms like 'shoot', 'fudge' or 'fiddlesticks' – these people are in their own way still swearing. It's just that they have set the bar so much lower than the rest of us.

Of Course They Banned Christmas

In 1659 the Puritan government of the Massachusetts Bay Colony put a bit of coal in everyone's stocking by passing the following law:

> For preventing disorders arising in several places within this jurisdiction, by reason of some still observing such festivals as were superstitiously held in other countries, to the great dishonor of God and offence of others, it is therefore ordered by this Court and the authority thereof, that whosoever shall be found observing such days as Christmas or the like, either

by forbearing of labor, feasting, or any other way, upon such accountants as aforesaid, every person so offending shall pay of every such offence five shillings, as a fine to the county.

The concept of not celebrating Christmas or Easter – or Whitsunday, for that matter – comes from that fun old Puritan maxim, 'They for whom *all* days are holy can have no holiday.'

The Puritans had always looked a bit askance at Christmas; they saw it as a bit too much of a coincidence that it fell on the same day as the pagan Roman holiday of Mithras, right in the middle of the extended Roman booze and food (and associated hanky-panky) festival known as Saturnalia.

They thought that it was an act of spiritual weakness that Pope Julius I had arbitrarily chosen 25 December as the birth date of Christ as a way of co-opting pagans into the Christian faith. (The Puritans believed that Christ had been born sometime in September.) But mostly they hated Christmas because it was by medieval times a great excuse for drinking and partying. (Some things never really change, do they?) The sixteenth-century clergyman Hugh Latimer wrote, 'Men dishonour Christ more in the twelve days of Christmas, than in all the twelve months beside.'

It was the English Puritans who abolished Christmas as a holiday in 1645, but it was the even more zealous devotees in New England who would actually go so far as to ban the holiday and make its celebration an actual crime.

By 1660 Christmas had been officially reinstated in England, but it was still banned in Massachusetts well into the 1680s. In fact, when in 1686 Sir Edmund Andros, the governor of the

Reprehensible

colony, attempted to hold a Christmas celebration in the Boston Town Hall, he had to do so under heavy armed guard. And even as public support grew for reinstating the holiday and rolling out the old eggnog, the Puritans of New England grimly held on to their anti-Yuletide grumblings.

Cotton Mather, a leading churchman of the district, told his flock in 1712, 'The feast of God's nativity is spent reveling, dicing, carding, masking, and in all licentious liberty . . . by mad mirth, by long eating, by hard drinking, by lewd gaming, by rude reveling!' Even for someone from a large Catholic family, that sounds like a pretty boisterous Christmas.

Let's not forget that Cotton Mather was also one of the bastards who went around persecuting anyone he perceived to be a witch, and whose book *Memorable Providences* laid much of the theological groundwork for the Salem witch trials. Although he himself claimed to have never attended the trials, his pamphlets and sermons spoke of them in glowing terms and helped fuel the witch hysteria that grasped that region of America in the early part of the eighteenth century.

This attitude persisted through much of the eighteenth century. Those who partied hard on Christmas were looked down upon as not showing appropriate piety, the same way my grandmother would fly off the handle if someone dared spell Christmas as 'Xmas' – trust me, that was one card-buying mistake you only ever made once.

In America, a much more relaxed change in attitude to Christmas began to grow after the 1823 publishing of Clarke Moore's 'A Visit from St Nicholas' (more popularly known as

''Twas the Night Before Christmas'). In 1863, Alabama became the first US state to make Christmas Day a holiday, but the good folk of New England defiantly held on to their Puritan-based beliefs. Up until the 1850s, Christmas Day would find places of business and schools still open and operating. However, there was a mood for change. The poet Henry Wadsworth Longfellow noted in 1856, 'The old Puritan feeling prevents [Christmas] from being a cheerful, hearty holiday; though every year makes it more so.'

By the time President Ulysses S. Grant declared Christmas a national holiday in 1870, the pious folk of New England had shed their inner Scrooge and were ready to embrace the fine traditions of Christmas, like a good meal, great company and arguing over whose year it was to give Great-Uncle Phil a lift home.

For Whom the Bell Really Tolled

If you were an American field or factory worker in the 1830s your life was pretty grim. There was no such thing as collective bargaining; there existed virtually no workers' rights. In fact, there was not a lot to really look forward to other than back-breaking work for a subsistence wage. However, if you lived in one of the many towns or cities where the town hall bell rang out loudly at both 11 am and 4 pm, you could at least look forward to downing tools and enjoying 'grog time'.

Think of it as a late-morning and afternoon tea break, without the tea and without the biscuits.

Moreover, the 1830s was the high-water mark (or low, depending on your perspective) of alcohol consumption in the modern history of the Western world.

By the 1820s, whiskey was cheaper than beer, wine, coffee, tea or milk. People mistrusted water because it was pretty filthy and disease-riddled, so when that bell tolled, time was taken out of the workday to have a shot or two. And if whiskey wasn't available, another popular choice of the day was hard cider – cider that had been fortified with the addition of pure alcohol to extend shelf life as well as increase potency.

To put this in perspective, the annual alcohol intake of a present-day American is almost one-third of what was consumed by most adults in the 1830s.

You probably started the day with a drink; you had some more with lunch, then a tipple after work and more with dinner. Why not stay at cruising altitude with those two sanctioned drinks to split up your miserable workaday existence?

Englishman Frederick Marryat, a distinguished naval officer, shed light on American swill power with this often used quote from his 1837 book, *A Diary in America*:

> I am sure the Americans can fix nothing without a drink. If you meet, you drink; if you part, you drink; if you make an acquaintance, you drink; if you close a bargain, you drink; they quarrel in their drink, and they make it up with a drink. They drink because it is hot; they drink because it is cold. If successful in elections, they drink and rejoice; if not they drink and swear; they begin to drink early in the morning,

they leave off late at night; they commence it early in life and they continue it, until they soon drop into the grave.

And once that grave had been filled, I am going to assume everyone went back to the tavern for the wake. It's the basic circle of life, with a bourbon chaser.

You Can't Put That in Your Sat Nav

Most of us know that for centuries many streets, lanes and alleys, particularly in Great Britain, got their names from the business conducted in that area. London's Pudding Lane is often cited as one of the most famous examples.

Actually, it's not *strictly* true. Pudding Lane does get its name from puddings, but just not puddings as we know them today. 'Pudding' was a medieval word for animal offal, and it is thought that the name came from the bits of unused animal stomachs and rotting intestines that would slide off carts transporting discarded waste from the butchers in Eastcheap to barges down by the Thames. So it seems that Pudding Lane got its name from filth rather than sweet baked treats.

But that aside, streets like Candlewick, Milk and Bread Street are more accurate examples of what I'm talking about. So you would naturally assume that a place named Grape Street or Grape Lane might indicate that taverns or wine merchants – or maybe even a fruit market – would have been located in that area.

Reprehensible

I'm afraid not.

The tradition of naming thoroughfares according to the activity most closely associated with it – no matter how venal that activity was – dates back to the Norman expansion through Britain. In a time before sanitation, for instance, certain streets, usually located near taverns or markets, became places well known for people to relieve themselves. So it was not uncommon for many of Britain's towns to have at least one Pissing Lane, or a Shitburnlane. And who could pass up renting a property on Stynking Alley or Foul Lane?

The rise of the Puritans saw to it that all vulgar placenames associated with unmentionable activities were given a good scrubbing and replaced with euphemisms. Victorian town planners later corrected any of those that may have slipped through the net.

So what are we to make of Grape Lane?

Like the previous placenames, it's coded language that points to some rather more primal sort of hanky-panky going on in that street. 'Grape' was the sweetening of the word 'Grope'. (Actually, if I'm completely frank, it was a sweetening of 'Gropec#nt', and this charming phrase had its original derivation in the Old Saxon.) This meant that there were either brothels or just plain sex in the street that could be purchased in this location. Other names for such streets were Codpiece or even Whores-Lie-Down, both of which would later be cleaned up as Coppice and Horslydown respectively.

In a rather bizarre moment, a petition was submitted to the British Parliament in 2012 asking that, for the sake of preserving national heritage, all streets and lanes that had once been called such things as Gropec#nt be restored to their original names, in all their offensive glory. The petition was rejected, with the reasoning that the UK Government was not responsible for street names and the issue was a matter for local authorities.

Personally, I would love to find a town in England that has an intersection between a Grape Lane and Horslydown Street – I bet it's got a bank on the corner.

A Banquet of Chestnuts

Of all of the stories of debauchery and intrigue that surround the period when the Borgias ruled the Vatican, there is none more salacious or disputed than the infamous 'Banquet of Chestnuts'.

Rodrigo Borgia had become Pope Alexander VI in 1492, using his wealth and power, as well as some rat cunning and backstabbing (sometimes literally), to rise to this exalted position. He also brought the rest of the family with him, including his son Cesare and his famous daughter Lucretia, both of whom acted not only as advisers but also as their father's eyes and ears within the papal court. They were also first-rate schemers in their own right. Lucretia, as it is often pointed out, was perhaps more famous for being sinned against than for sinning. However, her family did use her youthful grace and beauty to install her in three political marriages. Suffice to say there was never any need for a divorce court in the two marriages that met an untimely end.

Reprehensible

There is one school of thought that Cesare organised the 'Banquet of Chestnuts' not solely for a bit of bacchanalian fun, but also as a way of placing some of the most powerful cardinals into compromising positions (well, quite a few different positions) that he could later blackmail them with.

The most cited and most lurid account of the event comes from the writings of the Alsatian-born Johann Burchard, who had risen from a humble priest to be a gifted chronicler for several popes, as well as the papal master of ceremonies for some.

However, even though he was extremely powerful at the time of Alexander VI, he was by no means a fan of the Borgias and their ways of getting things done.

This is from his diary:

> On the evening of the last day of October, 1501, Cesare Borgia arranged a banquet in his chambers in the Vatican with fifty honest prostitutes, called courtesans, who danced after dinner with the attendants and others who were present, at first in their garments, then naked. After dinner the candelabra with the burning candles were taken from the tables and placed on the floor, and chestnuts were strewn around, which the naked courtesans picked up, creeping on hands and knees between the chandeliers, while the Pope, Cesare and his sister Lucretia looked on. Finally prizes were announced for those who could perform the act most often with the courtesans, such as tunics of silk, shoes, barrets and other things.

Before you start wondering, a barret was some sort of cap, which does nothing to make this story any less weird.

For centuries this account by Burchard has been heavily disputed, although there are two other sources indicating that at the very least some highly inappropriate hijinks did indeed go on in the Vatican on that particular night.

Then there is the undisputed fact that the Banquet of Chestnuts featured in the Neil Jordan television series *The Borgias*, which like the rest of the series is not short on sumptuous sets and costumes (well, for as long as those costumes stay on). I've always found that when it comes to disputed historical events, I tend to lean in favour of the versions that feature Jeremy Irons.

Some Arcane American State Laws

No great democracy believes in the sanctity of an individual state's right to create legislation as much as the United States of America. This can have profound, tragic and, in the case of the below legislation, often ridiculous results.

Although most of these laws are obviously arcane, we are still left with two burning questions: Firstly, even though they are virtually never enforced, why are they still on the statute books this far into the twenty-first century, and secondly, what sort of bad behaviour caused the wise and the good to sit down and devise these laws in the first place?

Reprehensible

ALABAMA: It is illegal to wear a fake moustache in church, as it might cause 'unseemly' laughter.

ALASKA: It is illegal to wake a sleeping bear so that you can take its photo. However, if you have a gun instead of a camera, you can kill it awake or asleep.

ARIZONA: You can't hunt camels, or keep donkeys in bathtubs, but you must give a thirsty person water if they ask you for it. And, most importantly, you are limited to no more than two dildos per household.

ARKANSAS: You can't keep alligators in your bathtub. (What is it about Americans keeping animals in bathtubs?)

CALIFORNIA: If you're a woman, apparently you can't drive your car while wearing a housecoat, although I don't think anyone has actually owned a 'housecoat' since the second season of *Bewitched*. Also, if you are a pet owner, you can really get into trouble if any animal under your control copulates within 500 metres of a tavern, a school, or a place of worship.

COLORADO: You can't mistreat rats. Also, it's illegal to lend a vacuum cleaner to a neighbour. And don't even think about engaging in any sort of acrobatics that might scare a horse.

CONNECTICUT: Another state that hates gymnastics; it's illegal to walk across the street on your hands.

DISTRICT OF COLUMBIA: If you have small children, don't ever let them throw stones unless you want to wind up in court.

DELAWARE: It is against the law to attempt to pawn a wooden leg.

FLORIDA: Farting after 6.00 pm is prohibited, as is singing in a swimsuit. Unmarried women may not parachute on a Sunday,

The Problem with Power

and it is illegal to have sex with a porcupine. (Do you really need a law for that one?)

GEORGIA: It is illegal to carry an ice-cream cone in your back pocket on Sundays, and all sex toys are banned. I can't help but think that these two laws are related.

HAWAII: Hawaiian people are very easy-going, but don't let them catch you putting pennies in your ear.

IDAHO: All boxes of candy given as a gift should weigh more than fifty pounds. Way to go, Idaho!

ILLINOIS: The official language of Illinois is not English but rather something called 'American'.

INDIANA: It is illegal to go to the theatre, the cinema, or ride a streetcar within four hours of eating garlic. Also, bathing in winter is prohibited.

IOWA: Kisses may last up to but not exceed five minutes. Also, it is illegal for any venue to charge patrons to see a one-armed piano player.

KANSAS: You can't shoot rabbits from the back of motorboats (that's you in the boat, not the rabbit), and you must never use mules to hunt ducks.

KENTUCKY: A woman may only appear in a swimsuit on a highway if she is in the company of two police officers. Preferably, these officers should be armed with clubs.

LOUISIANA: It is illegal to gargle in public.

MAINE: If you don't have your Christmas decorations down by 14 January, you will *so* find yourself on the 'naughty' list.

MARYLAND: It is against the law to take a lion into any theatre.

Reprehensible

MASSACHUSETTS: It is illegal for a couple – even a married couple – to sleep nude in a rented room. Also, men need a licence to grow a goatee.

MICHIGAN: A woman's hair is considered her husband's property, and she cannot cut it without his permission.

MINNESOTA: It is illegal to enter this state with a duck or chicken on your head. And any woman who impersonates Santa Claus could face up to a month in jail.

MISSISSIPPI: You can be arrested for walking around fully clothed with an erection.

MISSOURI: Oral sex is illegal – which is somewhat ironic considering that Missouri's motto is 'The Show-Me State'.

MONTANA: Sheep must be chaperoned if they are to ride in any sort of vehicle. And unmarried women are banned from fishing alone.

NEBRASKA: You can be fined if your child burps during a church service.

NEVADA: Whatever you do, never take your camel out onto the highway.

NEW JERSEY: It is against the law to frown at a police officer or slurp soup.

NEW HAMPSHIRE: You can't tap your feet, nod your head or any other physical manifestation indicating that you are moving along to the beat of any music you may hear in a tavern, cafe or restaurant.

NEW MEXICO: Women may not appear unshaven in public. (I'm starting to notice how many of these laws seem to restrict women from doing things.)

NEW YORK: It is against the law to throw a ball at someone's head just for fun. You shouldn't speak in an elevator (here, here to that!), and flirting will risk you a $25 fine.

NORTH CAROLINA: There is a $2000 fine for being in possession of a lottery ticket. You also can't charge for fortune telling (but I'm guessing you already knew that). It is illegal to sing off key or plough a field with an elephant. God only knows the punishment for doing both at the same time. And any meeting is illegal if the participants are wearing costumes, so you're going to have to have your 'furry convention' in another state.

NORTH DAKOTA: It is against the law to serve beer and pretzels together. Owners of any bar that does so can find themselves in big trouble, just like how you'll never find me in North Dakota.

OHIO: It is illegal for more than four women to share the same house. (This 'woman issue' is really getting to be a pattern.)

OKLAHOMA: You can get busted for 'making faces' at a dog.

OREGON: You must bathe covered from neck to knee in clothing. Okay, this one is completely being ignored, I hope.

PENNSYLVANIA: This law goes back to the start of the last century: 'Any motorist who sights a team of horses coming towards him must pull well off the road, cover his car with a blanket or canvas that blends in with the countryside, and let the horses pass.'

RHODE ISLAND: Sensibly enough, it is illegal to bite off another human's leg. Somewhat less sensibly, it is also illegal to throw pickle juice at a trolley.

SOUTH CAROLINA: If a chap proposes to an unmarried woman, he is required by law to see that the wedding takes place.

This means that once you propose, there is legally no backing out. The law doesn't mention what happens if a man proposes to a married woman – maybe that sort of thing just doesn't happen in South Carolina.

SOUTH DAKOTA: It is against the law to fall asleep in a cheese factory.

TENNESSEE: You must never catch a fish with a lasso. I reckon if you can catch a fish with a lasso, move to a state where it *is* legal, because you are going to make a fortune.

TEXAS: You cannot, under any circumstances, sell your own eye. Nor may you take more than three sips in a row from a beer while standing. But you are legally allowed to own up to, but no more than, six dildos. Take that, Arizona.

UTAH: It is strictly against the law to fish from horseback, so if you are one of those lasso fisher-folk from Tennessee, may I suggest that you avoid Utah also.

VERMONT: You are obliged by law to take, at the very least, one bath a week. And if you have just one, it is preferable that you bathe on a Saturday night.

VIRGINIA: It is illegal to have sex with lights on. (So that's how the state got its name!) Also, you can't hunt on a Sunday unless your game is raccoon, and even then, there is a 2.00 am curfew.

WASHINGTON: Lollipops are forbidden, and it is also illegal to pretend that you come from money.

WEST VIRGINIA: It is illegal to fall asleep on a train, but bestiality is okay as long as the animal weighs less than forty pounds.

WISCONSIN: It is illegal to kiss on a train.

WYOMING: Women must be at least two metres away from the bar at any establishment that they might be drinking in. And for some reason known only to them, the good folk of Wyoming are forbidden from photographing rabbits from January through to April. I'm assuming it has something to do with the mating season, but you'd probably have to ask someone from West Virginia to know for sure.

Mummy Issues

There is a thought among some psychiatrists that the actions of most successful men are in some way an attempt to seek the approval of their mothers. There may be some truth to this, but surely being considered a Founding Father of a nation would help settle any 'making mummy proud' issues once and for always.

Apparently not.

George Washington had always had a difficult relationship with his mother, Mary Ball Washington. His father had died when he was young, and his mother never remarried, wanting to make sure that her late husband's lands would stay available for her children to inherit. Some say she was formidable; others say she was terrifying. George's cousin once described her with the words, 'I was ten times more afraid of her than I ever was of my own parents.'

So disparaging was she of her son's achievements that during the Revolutionary War some French officers who were garrisoned

Reprehensible

near Mary, who would often move in the same circles, were convinced that she was secretly a loyalist supporter of King George III of England.

It seemed that as Washington grew into manhood there was nothing he could do to subdue his mother's often stated sense of disappointment.

This goes back to 1755 when George was serving in the Royal Army in the backwoods of Pennsylvania fighting the French. His mother wrote to him, asking if he could procure for her a servant and (I'm not making this up) some butter.

We actually have his reply: 'Honoured Madam . . . sorry, it is not in my power to provide you with a Dutch servant or the butter you desire. We are quite out of that part of the country, where neither are to be had, there being few or no inhabitants where we now lie encamped, and butter cannot be had here to supply the wants of the army.'

Suffice to say, his letter was not well received.

This sort of behaviour would be repeated over twenty years later, when, in the final desperate months of the War of Independence, word reached Washington that his mother had written to the House of Delegates, pleading for money and hinting that her son was a less-than-generous child. Although in mid-battle and dealing with the traitorous actions of Benedict Arnold, George pleaded to the House not to furnish his mother with any funds. He had bought her a house and rented her farmland. He had already 'answered all her calls for money'. He and his other four siblings, he wrote, would 'divide the last sixpence to relieve her from real distress. This she has been repeatedly assured of by me.'

The Problem with Power

But like all overbearing mothers, Mary Washington managed to have the last word. In 1789, George rushed to her bedside – and not only because she was gravely ill. He had some very important news. This was the contemporary account of what would prove to be their last meeting:

George: Guess what? They want me to be president.
Mother: I'm dying.
George (overcome with sadness): Well, as soon as I am settled in New York, I shall come back and . . .
Mother: This is the last time you'll ever see me. But go do your job. *That's more important.*

However, many years later the story would be retold by Washington's step-grandson, George Washington Parke Custis, who wrote of how Mary Ball had sent the first president off with these stirring, fictitious words: 'But go, George, fulfil the high destinies which Heaven appears to have intended for you; go my son, and may that Heaven's and a mother's blessing be with you always.'

This was one battle that George Washington was never going to win. It paints Mary Ball as the doting mother, sacrificing her own comfort for the good of her son and the nation. Even from the grave she manages to get the last word.

Reprehensible

Anthony Comstock: Patriot, Puritan, Nutjob

Like many people of his generation, Anthony Comstock found his personal sense of destiny and first taste of notoriety in the 1860s, in the American Civil War. It was during this period that he earned a tall reputation for not only castigating but actually *prosecuting* any soldiers under his command whom he considered to have used foul or bawdy language – much to the chagrin of Comstock's superiors, who needed as many boots on the ground as possible. To them, swearing or not swearing was a completely secondary issue. He also performed a daily display of pouring his whiskey ration on the ground in a vain attempt to inspire his troops to join him in sobriety. It made him a figure of ridicule.

After the war, he got a job in New York as an administrator for the YMCA. (If only we could get the Village People to travel back in time!) While there, he prosecuted two men for peddling pornography, and thus his career as an extreme moraliser got off to a flying start.

But not everyone was a fan. So disgruntled was one of the chaps that he had prosecuted that the man slashed Comstock's face with a knife – an act that no doubt added credence to Comstock's already firmly held sense of self-righteous zeal against the reprehensibles.

National fame came after Comstock attacked the well-known feminist, free-love advocate and first woman to run for president, Victoria Woodhull. Woodhull had written an article describing an affair between the puritanical preacher Henry Ward Beecher and a female member of his congregation. Beecher had constantly preached against Ms Woodhull and her libertarian views, and she was merely pointing out the preacher's hypocrisy.

Comstock, seeing a fellow beacon of virtue under attack, launched his own *counterattack* against Victoria Woodhull. (Sound familiar?) He prosecuted her for obscenity – not for any of her other provocative writing, but simply for the details she had included in her article about Preacher Beecher.

Woodhull was eventually let off on a technicality, but the case had the unfortunate effect of giving Comstock a national platform, as well as important political backing. With these two forces at his back, he set about his next pet project – the ominously titled 'New York Society for the Suppression of Vice'. It's always a red flag when you see the word 'suppression' in any organisation's title, no matter what your beliefs may be.

Through this organisation's agitation, he convinced Congress to pass the 1874 Comstock Law, which forbade sending 'obscene, lewd and lascivious material' through the mail. Bear in mind that, as far as Comstock was concerned, 'obscene, lewd and lascivious' not only meant pornographic images but any material that he considered to contain a moral threat to the age. Included in this unholy trinity was any information about birth control or biological books that represented anatomically correct descriptions about how human beings procreate. At the risk of repeating myself: SOUND FAMILIAR!?

On the back of his moral crusade, twenty-four states restricted access to information regarding contraception, including in Comstock's home state, which came up with a law that could see a married couple imprisoned for up to a *year* for using birth control. For years, medical students were denied access to basic textbooks on human anatomy, particularly any involving descriptions or depictions of reproductive organs.

So broad and arbitrary were these rules that in 1895 an editorial in *The New York Times* complained of 'Comstockery', a word they invented to describe 'censorship because of perceived obscenity or immorality'. This word was later re-used by George Bernard Shaw when, in 1905, Comstock successfully campaigned to have his play *Mrs Warren's Profession* shut down on Broadway because its protagonist is a former prostitute and brothel madame.

Shaw wrote, 'Comstockery is the world's standing joke at the expense of the United States. Europe likes to hear of such things. It confirms the deep-seated conviction that America is a provincial place, a second-rate, country-town civilization after all.'

Comstock replied by describing Shaw as an 'Irish smut dealer'.

Comstock didn't take criticism well, as you might assume – he was something of a braggart. He liked to boast that he had been responsible for over 4000 arrests, and he was particularly proud of the fifteen people who had been driven to suicide as part of his 'fight for the young'. This earned some considerable contempt from his peers ... and the admiration of the up-and-coming J. Edgar Hoover.

But it was in his work with the US Postal Service that Comstock was free to pursue what he regarded as his most *essential* work: the war against dildos. Not that he would even call them that, of course. When talking about dildos, he would simply say that they were 'too gross to describe' and would only speak of them using the generalisation 'immoral rubber goods'.

The Problem with Power

What Comstock lacked in descriptive power he more than made up for in effort. His campaign of confiscating any sex toy sent through the mail was so feverish that it could not be measured in numbers. Suffice to say that in the year 1882 he was responsible for the seizure and destruction of some 64,836 pounds of dildos. It also goes to show just how popular dildos had become in the latter half of the nineteenth century. This is owing to two factors: firstly, the Civil War had vastly improved the industrialisation of the rubber, meaning that dildos could be quickly moulded and cast, as opposed to ... well, I'm assuming, carved?

Secondly – and sadly – the Civil War had decimated the male population, increasing demand.

Seeing as sex shops didn't exist yet, the only way you could get your 'immoral rubber goods' was through the post. That is, if you could get them past the judgemental eye of Anthony Comstock.

Fortunately, with the coming of the twentieth century, Comstock saw his influence begin to wane. As historian Andrea Tone noted, 'To be sure the leniency accorded birth control offenders may have been related to widespread loathing of Comstock, the man. Comstock's belligerence and courtroom histrionics offended judges, alienated prosecutors and prompted a steady stream of derogatory editorials, cartoons and poems in turn-of-the-century newspapers and journals.'

After his death in 1915, many of his laws were overturned, particularly his more draconian ones regarding the suppression of birth control. Eventually his views became more and more out of step with a modern, more liberal age. Comstock faded into obscurity, to the point where, if he was remembered at all, it was often as an object of ridicule – which is a far cry from the vision he had of himself and his divine vocation.

He once described himself as 'the weeder in God's garden'.

Ulysses S. Grant: General and Gymnophobe

Ulysses S. Grant was a towering military figure, a wonderful memoirist and a pretty so-so president, but there are more than a few quirks to his personality that bear some investigating. Obviously, there was his well-documented struggle with alcohol. It has often been stated that inactivity was his greatest inducement to drink, a habit that was first noticed not only at West Point Military Academy but also later during the Mexican–American War of 1846. Grant was by no means a lazy man, but when not fully engaged by an activity he found interesting, he would often reach for a bottle. Regardless, he still managed to emerge from that war with two promotions and a bright military future. This problem with the drink was always at his heels, including a threatened court martial over being drunk on duty.

He also smoked over twenty cigars a day, a habit that barely made a dint into the estimated *ten thousand* boxes of cigars that grateful citizens had sent him both during and after the Civil War. It would, however, result in the tongue and throat cancer that would eventually kill him.

What is less known is that his real name was Hiram Ulysses Grant. Not surprisingly, he dropped the Hiram as a youth because he did not like having the initials H.U.G. He would be known for the rest of his life as Ulysses – except from his father, who nicknamed him 'Useless'. (Grant's father had more than enough of his own personal issues.) Also, the 'S' in the middle of his name stands for nothing. It was a simple clerical error made at his enrolment at West Point, and it just sort of stuck.

It is also somewhat peculiar that the man who presided over some of the bloodiest battles in American history was himself extremely squeamish at the sight of blood, so much so that he insisted all his meat be cooked well done. In fact, he liked his meat burnt. This was true for all meats, with the noticeable exception of chicken, which he completely refused to eat under any circumstance. As he explained to his cooks, 'I could never eat anything that went on two legs.' Also, his favourite breakfast was cucumbers soaked in vinegar. I'm not judging, but this does seem unnecessarily spartan.

However, one of Grant's oddest traits was that he was a confirmed gymnophobe or, as fans of the sitcom *Arrested Development* would say, he was a 'never-nude'. Rumours about Grant's compulsive need to never be seen naked first surfaced during the Civil War, where it was observed that, unlike all of the other soldiers, regardless of rank, Grant chose to bathe in private. He took his baths inside a specially constructed tent, as opposed to going tackle-out in plain view of all and sundry.

However, this inclination seems to pre-date the Civil War. Grant would actually brag that since childhood no one had seen him naked. And, yes, I know 'brag' does seem like an odd choice of word, but that's how his contemporaries described it. He bragged about how he had concealed himself from nurses and doctors, from other soldiers at West Point, even hinting that Mrs Grant had never actually seen him fully in the buff. Considering that the Grants had four children, this must have meant quite a bit of clothes-on behaviour. So maybe their relationship was steamy if a bit, shall we say, 'visually restrained'.

Leviticus Warned You

On 7 September 1642, Thomas Granger became one of the first people hanged in the American colonies. Considering the group of Puritans he ran with, and the crime he was convicted of, it's surprising he ever made it out of the mouth of the River Thames. His offence and subsequent plight was documented in Governor William Bradford's diary, *Of a Plymouth Plantation*: 'He was this year detected of buggery, and indicted for the same, with a mare, a cow, five sheep, two calves, two goats and a turkey.' He then goes on to add, 'Horrible it is to mention, but the truth of history requires it.'

It was with the mare that Granger was busted, and bizarrely enough his trial involved going around the village identifying the other animals with which he had transgressed. Apparently the horse, the cow and the calves were pretty easy to identify, but he confessed that he couldn't be certain about the sheep and goats, and he wouldn't even hazard a guess as to which turkey he had been with.

This was described at the time as engaging in a 'lewd practice' with the poor animals. And I do mean poor animals because their identification was not only to support the prosecutor's case in court, but also to bring the Plymouth Colony into line with Leviticus 20:15 from the Bible: 'And if a man lie with a beast, he shall surely be put to death; and ye shall slay the beast.' (You know those Puritans loved their Leviticus.)

Not only did the colonists kill the animals in front of Granger, but they then swiftly buried them, just to make sure that no one from the village would even think about cooking up one of the defiled beasts.

The good folk of Plymouth were particularly proud of this judgement. They made sure that everyone knew the sacrifice they were making by burying perfectly good food in the hardscrabble existence that was life in the colonies at the time.

Oh, and they also had no qualms about hanging a seventeen-year-old boy for bestiality. Not that Thomas was a novice to the shameful act – he would say that he had been introduced to the practice by an elder farmhand back in England a few years before. It was a time he was said to have recalled with great fondness, which was probably not the best tack to take when on trial for zoophilia.

Granger's reprehensible act, as well as an outbreak of general immorality, even caused Governor Bradford to think that the Pilgrim's strident moral codes might actually be the cause of the deviant behaviour. He wrote:

Reprehensible

It may be in this case as it is with waters when their streams are stopped or dammed up; when they get passage they flow with more violence, and make more noise and disturbance, than when they are suffered to run quietly in their own channels. So, wickedness being here more stopped by strict laws, and the same more nearly looked unto. So, it cannot run in common road of liberty as it would, and is inclined. It searched everywhere, and at last breaks out where it gets vent.

Wise words indeed, but sadly too late for the turkey.

Chapter Two:
Misbehaving Royally

Let's be honest, royal scandals just aren't what they used to be. Take the British Royal Family, for example. For centuries people have plotted, seduced, battled, bribed, beheaded and committed countless crimes to either seize the throne or at least increase their access and influence over it. But the greatest scandal involving the Royal Family these days is one young couple trying to get as far away from that throne as they possibly can. And who can blame them.

I'm talking about Harry and Meghan, who have thrown the tabloid press into a frenzy with their decision to step down as senior royals. There have been countless column inches devoted to besmirching their decision, as if their course of action was the worst thing that any royal has ever done.

Yet oddly enough in all that vindictive editorialising I have not once come across the words 'chopping block'.

I have to confess I am not an avid 'royal watcher' and only ever read magazines that gush royal reportage when I am in a doctor's or dentist's waiting room. As such I only first became aware of the fractious nature of the relationship between the press and Harry and Meghan when the tabloids flew into full-tilt hubris after the birth of their child Archie. When the young couple announced that the christening of their newborn son would be a 'private affair' the press went berserk.

There were cries of outrage: why wasn't the whole royal press gallery allowed to photograph every millisecond of young Archie getting his baptismal dunking? *What a dreadful break with protocol! Who do these young royals think they are? Oh sure, they want publicity when it suits them! This is a right royal baby scandal!* And so on.

Reprehensible

You want to know what a right royal baby scandal looks like? Let's go back to 47 BC, when Cleopatra made her way into Rome with her baby in her arms – the baby she had named 'Caesarion' in honour of the man she claimed was the father, the one and only Julius Caesar.

Caesar denied this at first, even getting his friend Gaius Oppius to distribute a pamphlet among Rome's elite to refute Cleopatra's paternity claim. However, Caesar would be dead within four years. Mark Antony, who had by now shacked up with Cleopatra, recognised the lad's lineage. This got the statesman and military leader Octavian pissed off and, well, the next thing you know there are two years of dreadful civil war, ending with fortunes lost and too much blood spilled all round – apart from Octavian's, who became Augustus Caesar, the first Roman emperor, and kicked off 200 years of peace known as the Pax Romana. For the other major players, including the poor lad Caesarion, it would only end in death.

While we're on the topic of Prince Harry, let's not forget that as a younger man he was often chastised in the press for partying too hard. In fact, at the age of seventeen, he admitted to his father that he had tried marijuana on more than one occasion. The palace's solution was to pack him off to rehab for a day! According to a spokesperson from St James's Palace, it was a way 'to learn about the possible consequences of starting to take cannabis'.

Talk about scared straight!

Then there were the tabloid headlines and screaming front pages that showed Harry and his mates playing a bit of nude

Misbehaving Royally

billiards in a Las Vegas hotel. This caused Harry to release a statement: 'At the end of the day, I have probably let myself down, I let my family down, and I let other people down. But it was probably a classic example of me probably being too much army and not enough prince. It's a simple case of that.'

If you want a 'classic example' of young boofheads acting up with serious consequences, you can't go past the 1380 royal ball held to celebrate the wedding of a beloved member of court, where a young King Charles VI of France was part of some tomfoolery that ended tragically.

Charles and four of his idiot friends decided to put on costumes made of shaggy cloth and wool and 'entertain' the crowd by drunkenly dancing around as 'wild men'. This performance, however, was short-lived. Charles's brother, the Duke of Orleans, who was completely wasted, knocked over a torch, igniting the wild men's costumes. In their panic, they kept running back into each other, which of course only served to help spread the flames.

Charles was rescued but the other four burned to death. When news of the tragedy spread to the local citizenry there were riots – not in response to the loss of life but because the good folk of France had endured just about enough of Charles's wasteful spending on extravagant events.

That's the sort of episode that not even the best public relations department can easily gloss over.

Then there was the suspicious death of William II of England, who died from what was described as an accident while hunting in the New Forest in August of 1100. The problem with this version of events was that William was a pretty dreadful king and was roundly disliked by most of the nobles in court. Plus, the person who admitted to *accidently* shooting the fatal arrow right through the monarch's heart was Walter Tirel. Tirel was recognised as being one of the most gifted archers in the land. Plus, they hastily exited the forest, leaving the king's body behind.

Imagine if Walter Tirel had to endure the same scrutiny that surrounded the countless and ludicrous conspiracy theories that surfaced after the death of Princess Diana? First, there was the rumour that Prince Philip had been behind the car accident in the tunnel, making sure that Diana died before she could get engaged to her Muslim boyfriend, Dodi Fayed, or give birth to Dodi's child. According to this conspiracy camp, Diana was pregnant at the time.

There were still others who claimed that, not only did Prince Philip order Diana's death, but he did so in his role as the leader of an ancient Egyptian order of vampires dating back to the time of the pharaohs.

These crackpots exist, as do those who are convinced that Queen Elizabeth II is actually a shape-shifting lizard, a descendant of a long line of humans who mated with reptilian folk from another planet. This would be laughable – actually, it *is* laughable – but what is more worrying is the 2016 article in *The Guardian* that stated around twelve million people in the US believe interstellar lizards in 'people suits' rule their country. And, yes, Liz is the head lizard.

Then there are those who dismiss such talk as nothing more than ridiculous ranting from the lunatic fringe. *They* believe that instead of the queen being a shape-shifting alien or Prince Philip being an ancient vampire, the two aged monarchs are nothing more than Satan-worshipping cannibals. Their evidence being the large (and completely false and undocumented) number of children who seemed to go missing whenever they went somewhere for a state visit.

Then there are those scoundrels who claim that Pippa Middleton wore prosthetic buttocks so she could upstage her sister when she married Prince William.

I wish I could say I was making that up . . .

Also for anyone wondering why I haven't mentioned Prince Andrew, well to be perfectly honest, I couldn't actually write anything that would be more outrageous and ridiculous than his own now infamous interview with the BBC.

However, for centuries our obsession with royal families and dynasties had a far greater importance than just selling magazines and feeding lunatic conspiracy theories. For millennia, the fate of nations was in the hands of their ruling families. This is why they were such good fodder for plays and literature. Think about Robert Graves's *I, Claudius*, or Shakespeare's history plays, and let's not forget the recent television series *The Crown*. These managed to show the family-based drama we can all relate to, yet this drama had the extra intensity of having massive political ramifications. In earlier times, the royal family was basically a soap opera – a soap opera that could take your land or send you off to war.

So why are we still so obsessed with royalty in these days of modern constitutional monarchies? Dr Donna Rockwell, a clinical psychologist, explained her theory in *Glamour* magazine:

It's comforting to see a structure where that structure seems to create a semblance of order . . . So in the same way, I think when an adult is feeling a sense of inner chaos, it's comforting, even neurologically speaking, to observe something of structure.

We see structure and we feel comforted. So it is actually a neurological response of relaxation that occurs in us seeing the queen, and the [grand]daughters-in-law, and the line [of heirs].

So the royals have gone from being the rulers of the masses to being the Xanax of the masses.

But, I'm pleased to say, this wasn't always the case . . .

So That's How You Catch 'em

For years historians have argued over the duration of Pharaoh Pepi II's reign. Some say it was a virtually impossible ninety years, others a lesser but still amazing sixty-five years. However, they do agree on one fact: it was far too long.

Pepi II oversaw the decline of the Sixth Dynasty. Its economic, spiritual and political erosion pretty much parallels his estimated time in power. This can be put down to several factors: in-court intrigues, mismanagement of the Egyptian civil service, droughts and, well, just the simple fact that Pepi – also known as King Neferkare – had more than just a few peculiarities of his own.

Misbehaving Royally

First, he had many wives – nothing unusual about that. However, we also know that these wives, Neith, Iput II, Ankhesenpepi both III and IV, were his half-sisters. Plus, he was also probably married to another relative, who may have been his full sister, Udjebten. And that's just the ones that are well documented. Even by Ancient Egyptian standards these shenanigans were more than just a little bit creepy.

Plus, he also seems to have had a somewhat unhealthy obsession with pygmies. Upon hearing that Harkhuf, one of his emissaries to Nubia, had captured a pygmy, he wrote him a rather expansive letter that Harkhuf would later record in posthumous recollections of the pharaoh:

> You have said that you have brought a pygmy of the god's dances from the land of the horizon dwellers, like the pygmy whom the god's seal-bearer, Bawerded, brought from Punt in the time of King Isesi. You have said to my majesty that his like has never been brought by anyone who went to Yam previously. Come north to the residence at once! Hurry and bring with you this pygmy, whom you brought from the land of the horizon dwellers live, hail and healthy, or the dances of the god, to gladden the heart, to delight the heart of the King Neferkare who lives forever!

He continues giving specific instructions for the care of the poor captured pygmy:

> When he goes down with you into the ship, get worthy men around him on deck lest he fall in the water. When he lies

down at night get worthy men to lie all around him in his tent. Inspect him ten times a night!

My majesty desires to see this pygmy more than the gifts of the mine-land and of Punt! When you arrive at the residence and this pygmy is with you live, hail and healthy, my majesty will do great things for you, more than was done for the god's seal-bearer, Bawerded, in the time of King Isesi.

So, in hindsight, it's a fair observation that Pepi really had a thing for pygmies.

His other obsession was food. He was a prodigious eater, who would break his day into brief work periods that would straddle his rather long and indulgent feasts. The only thing he hated about these feasts was the constant hassle of having to shoo flies away from his food. To this problem he devised a rather bizarre solution.

Before each meal started several slaves would be brought into the dining area (either inside or out, as Pepi loved a picnic) and they would then be stripped naked and covered in honey. The poor slaves would then walk around serving as living, breathing fly-strips, keeping the annoying insects away from the pharaoh's meal.

You know what, by 2164 BC it was probably time for the Old Kingdom to start winding down anyway.

Here Comes the Sun King

By the year 1653 Anne d'Autriche found herself in a bit of a pickle. Her husband, King Louis XIII of France, had passed away just over a decade before. Her son Louis XIV was on the brink of manhood, approaching his sixteenth birthday. Her hold on power relied primarily on Louis being able to prove that he could easily produce an heir to the throne. This would lock him in place as the rightful ruler and with that guarantee her position as one of the most powerful women in Europe.

However, Anne worried that her son might take after his father when it came to prowess in the bedroom. Louis XIII was rumoured to have been gay – or maybe he was just plain uninterested – either way, Anne had made no secret that as a lover her husband had been, even at his most earnest, nothing short of underwhelming.

So like any concerned mother she consulted the family's clergyman, Cardinal Mazarin, and the two of them scoured the court to find a woman that young Louis could cash in his V plates with. The right candidate should be not overly ambitious, free of disease yet skilled in the bedroom arts, trusted . . . and for some reason they decided that this lucky candidate should not be a great beauty.

For these reasons they soon settled on Catherine-Henriette Bellier, who was also known as 'One-Eyed Catherine', for the obvious reason that she had only one eye.

She was trusted by Anne. *Tick.* She was happily married, and yet had also conducted an affair with the Archbishop of Sens.

Reprehensible

Tick. She was described by a contemporary as 'ugly as ugly can be'. *Tick.* And she was, for someone of her time, remarkably disease-free, which is always a good thing, especially when you are 'breaking in' the nation's number-one son and heir. *Tick and tick.*

Oh, and she was almost twenty-five years older than young Louis, so there was no chance of any adolescent passions being inflamed to a dangerous level.

And so one autumn afternoon Louis was led into his bedroom to find One-Eyed Catherine waiting, lying naked on his bed. His mother as well as the rest of court held their breath to see if Louis would rise to the occasion.

And did he ever – he took to sex like a duck to water, validating Catherine's skill and passion as a tutor. In fact, this would not just be a one-off introductory lesson. Louis would continue to visit her for years to come, sometimes multiple times a day.

For her services to King and Country, Catherine was given a considerable sum of money, two townhouses in Paris and the Hôtel de Beauvais, just near the Louvre, as well as the title Baroness de Beauvais.

Years later the royal architect Antoine Le Pautre, Catherine and her husband along with Queen Anne d'Autriche, would stand on the balcony of that hotel and gleefully wave to King Louis XIV as he made his wedding procession through the streets of Paris, both women content in the knowledge that the young royal would be capable of performing his matrimonial duties.

Which he did, and then some.

Oh, and by the way, his wife, Marie-Theresa, was also his first cousin, the marriage having been arranged to ratify a peace treaty. Louis and Marie-Theresa did, however, fall in some sort of love and managed to have six children together – one less than the number of children Louis created with Madame de Montespan, his second 'wife' . . . but more on that a bit later.

Louis would go on to have many more children with well over a dozen other women – and they are just the well-known ladies of status we know about. He even had an affair with Henrietta of England, who just happened to be his brother's wife. Plus there were countless other women to be found, either in court or working on the grounds, for the randy monarch to amuse himself with. He did, however, return to his wife's bed every night. Lovers were apparently for the daytime; the queen was for the nighttime.

It would also seem that the queen was more than capable of dealing with Louis' infidelities. Françoise-Athénaïs de Rochechouart, Marquise de Montespan was not only Louis' lover for over a decade but lived in an apartment in Versailles on the very same floor as the queen. Mistresses would often travel with the king and queen, and Louis would openly and lovingly support his illegitimate children, paying for their education and organising their marriages so they would end up with titles.

And speaking of children, Louis had a particular obsession with watching his partners give birth. Sure, it's perfectly right for the father of a baby to be present, if so desired by the mother, at the birth of a child. It's another thing entirely for the father to prefer a birthing position and design a special bed just so he could get a better look at what was going on.

Louis would lose Marie-Theresa to a sudden illness in 1683. He was only forty-four years old and certainly not prepared

Reprehensible

to spend the rest of his life alone – well, what passed for being alone in the Sun King's world. And if you ever wondered how he got the moniker 'Sun King', he simply gave it to himself – sort of a historically more successful version of the *Seinfeld* episode where George wants everyone to call him 'T-Bone'. He was the most eligible and powerful widower in the world at the time, and subsequently brought up for consideration the vast array of attractive and regal young princesses to be found in Europe.

Then he reflected.

His son had given him a three-year-old grandson and, with his daughter-in-law pregnant again, it looked like matters of lineage were well in hand. He didn't need to make any more alliances; his power could not be increased by any union. So Louis XIV did probably the most scandalous thing imaginable at the time: he married for love and companionship.

The woman in question was the governess to several of his bastard children – Madame de Montespan. And Louis' family and friends were not the least bit happy about it. His son had a meltdown, but nothing compared to the reaction of his war minister, Louvois, who apparently proclaimed, 'Oh, Sire! Has your Majesty really considered this? The greatest king in the world covered in glory, to marry the widow Scarron. [She had been married to a poor poet called Scarron.] Do you want to bring dishonour on yourself?' The good minister then dropped to the floor and really let loose: 'Sire, pardon the liberty I take. Relieve me of all of my posts, throw me into prison, but I will never look upon such an indignity.' Which I guess is the seventeenth-century version of, 'Are you one hundred per cent sure about this?'

The marriage took place in secret in either late 1683 or early 1684, no one can say for sure, which I guess is a central part of the whole 'secret marriage' thing. Madame de Montespan, however, continued in her role as a governess, but this time from an apartment only a few steps away from the king's chambers.

Louis even gave up the adultery caper, for a while anyway.

In fact, at the age of seventy-two Louis was known to make love to his wife at least twice a day. And that was just the trysts with his wife!

I'd like to think that Catherine-Henriette Bellier would have been looking down from heaven, through her one good eye, enjoying the sight of the randy old Sun King in his twilight still getting his leg over, thinking, *Well, I started all that.*

Stinky ol' King James

Sure he brought the Scots to the party and established the Stuart dynasty and gave us an accessible translation of the Bible, but King James I (VI of Scotland) was not a person you would ever want to be caught downwind of. For a start, he rarely bothered to change his clothes, in particular his favourite hat, which he would often wear twenty-four hours a day, only discarding it once it had been worn to death. But the accounts of his habits while hunting give us an insight into this smelliest of all monarchs.

King James adored riding and hunting, so much so that when he was in the saddle he would not dismount to relieve himself

– and that goes for both number ones and number twos. But things got even weirder once a stag had been brought down. James was always first in line to cut the poor creature's throat. He would then slice into the belly and stick his hands (and sometimes even his feet) into the wound and smear blood and entrails all over himself and his hunting companions.

All that being said, at least he was a regular bather. Apparently, despite his frequent protestations against the practice, he never missed his annual bath, and I wish I could say that I was joking about that.

Royal Ticklers

Probably the first recorded use of foot tickling to get a female monarch in the mood for sex comes from ancient Egypt, where Queen Hatshepsut, who ruled from 1748 BC, would have a eunuch rub anise oil over her feet and then tickle her soles with a peacock feather until she decided that she was ready to go.

After that, we don't really hear much about the practice of foot tickling as a precursor to royal trysts until the Romanovs of Russia, and by then it had become something of the 'go to' foreplay ritual for the tsarinas, countesses and concubines that occupied the highest levels of the Russian court.

The Regent of Russia Anna Leopoldovna, who ruled briefly from 1740–41 had *six* professional ticklers in her retinue. Why six? Well, let's assume they worked in eight-hour shifts, and she liked both feet tickled, then I guess six seems to be the bare minimum that the regent required to get her into such a state of arousal that she could even begin to entertain the thought of making love to her husband, whom she was never actually that fond of. In her eyes, he was a bit on the plain side, plus she already had more than her fair share of both male and female lovers, so sex with the hubby was probably a bit of a chore. Having said that, she still kept the ticklers on a short leash (not literally, I think), for extra fun with her lovers as well.

And these were no ordinary ticklers – you couldn't just turn up with a quiver of feathers and a Handel mix-tape. It could take years of study and working your way up the ranks before you and your feathers were allowed anywhere near the feet of someone as noble as Anna Leopoldovna. You also had to be skilled in the singing of bawdy songs and telling of erotic stories; these also seemed to do the trick when getting female members of the Russian aristocracy a bit toey (pun intended).

And you had to be either a woman or a eunuch.

If you had all these skills and attributes on your CV, you could actually find yourself with a well paid, highly ranked position within the Russian court. It could actually be quite a foot in the door (sorry), as long as if, as a male tickler, you were willing to work around the whole 'eunuch thing'.

Catherine the Great also indulged in the practice of foot tickling, but to be honest, the monarch that oversaw the 'Golden Age of Russia' is going to need her own chapter when it comes to lusty exploits.

Never Complain Again About Nosy In-laws

Sure, Marie Antoinette and Louis XVI were young when they got married. He was fifteen and she a mere fourteen-year-old – even for European royalty this was a bit on the tender side. Four years after that marriage they were crowned King and Queen of France, but they were yet to produce an heir.

Marie's mother, Empress Maria Theresa of Austria, was getting increasingly concerned with not only the lack of an heir but the rumours flying around court that the marriage had not even been consummated. So she did what seemed like the appropriate thing to do at the time – she dispatched her son Joseph II, the Holy Roman Emperor, to see if the French king was accomplishing anything in regards to the important business of producing a son and heir.

The young Queen Antoinette was greatly relieved to see her beloved brother, but she did have a confession: Louis was an extremely rare bed companion, and on those occasions when he did turn up, not much was really happening between the sheets.

Actually, Joseph's investigations were (sadly for Louis) a little more thorough than you'd expect, as exemplified in this passage taken from a letter Joseph wrote to his brother Leopold. (Leopold, it seems, was just as curious as everyone else in the whole sad situation.) And, quite frankly, Joseph does not hold back:

> In his marriage bed, he has strong erections, he inserts his member, remains there for about two minutes without moving, withdraws without ejaculating, and while still erect, bids goodnight. It's incomprehensible . . . My sister does not

have the temperament for this, and together they make an utterly inept couple.

You know what, I used to feel a bit emasculated asking my brother-in-law to come over and hang some pictures (I'm no good with power tools) but at least *he* never had to write an embarrassing letter like that one.

Take Me to the River

These days monarchs perform many public duties, some of which are aligned with charities or causes they support. Then there are those random events at which a head of state is expected to turn up, and wave and smile, such as tree plantings, factory openings and hospital visits. But there are also those enshrined annual duties that are the mainstays of being king or queen in a Western democracy, such as the opening of parliament or delivering a Christmas message. These are not just part of the royal calendar, but over the years they've become punctuation points in a nation's annual history.

The Ancient Egyptians were well aware of the importance of observing the passage of the year and its seasons. At many of these occasions the pharaoh would take centre stage to demonstrate the gravity of any ceremony, just as we would expect any modern monarch to do.

Except for one event.

Reprehensible

To understand this, we need to have a quick look at the Egyptians' creation myth, which in its most abbreviated version tells of how the creator deity Atum existed in a universe all unto himself. And, well, Atum did what most men do when they are left to their own devices: he masturbated.

From his ejaculation sprang forth a pair of twin gods, Shu (the air god) and Tefnut (the goddess of moisture, dew, water and rain). So according to their cosmology, Ancient Egyptians owed their very existence to good old Atum taking a little bit of 'executive time'. Naturally, then, how would you expect to make sure the Nile, on which your lives depend, stays bountiful and fertile?

That's when it was pharaoh's time to shine.

Not all pharaohs, mind you, but many of them were expected to ejaculate into the River Nile on an annual basis to guarantee a plentiful harvest. The practice did go in and out of fashion, but it was a pretty much cherished annual event in the Egyptian calendar for centuries.

It was going to be a particularly good harvest if the pharaoh's 'seed' was abundant and could be seen floating off downstream, swept along in the flowing waters of the sacred river. For this reason, the ritual had to be observed – you couldn't just take pharaoh's word that he had performed his duty. What is not recorded is just how many observers were required. Was it one high priest, or did the whole royal court make their way down to the riverbank? Did people vie for positions? Did local bookmakers lay odds on the duration of the act? Was there a polite 'golf clap', or did the crowd go full-on 'World Cup-winning goal' when the act was complete?

No one really knows for sure, but I can bet on one thing: even just one high priest would be enough to create sufficient performance anxiety.

Victoria's Bridesmaids

When asked to think of a British royal who could be regarded as prudish and judgemental, most people would conjure up an image of dowdy old Queen Victoria. What's the famous quip that springs to mind when you of think of that monarch? 'We are not amused,' of course. There are a plethora of origin stories about the Queen using this phrase to cut someone down. Pretty much all of them are told or recorded posthumously, and most of them are in regards to a courtier telling an anecdote that Her Majesty had thought to have strayed into topics not suitable for discussion.

One such story involves her daughter Louise, who was conducting an affair with courtier Sir Arthur Bigge. This is according to official biographer A. N. Wilson, who recently told *The Sunday Times*, 'Bigge liked telling smutty jokes. He was doing this one evening and embarrassing everyone present, male and female. The Queen looked sharply down the table and declared, "Sir Arthur, we are not amused." . . . She was not using the royal "we": she meant that nobody present thought that he was being amusing.'

I might even hazard a guess that wily Victoria may have also meant the comment to pass judgement not only on the crude joke but on the broader liberties he was taking with her daughter.

Reprehensible

Then there is the theory that she never said the famous phrase at all. Some historians attribute the words to Elizabeth I, and others conclude that one or two of her children concocted the story years after Queen Victoria's death to cast their mother in a harsh, humourless, scolding light. One of the last people with a living memory of Victoria was her granddaughter Princess Alice, Countess of Athlone, who in a 1976 interview recalled, 'You know, I'm so disappointed. I asked and she never said it.'

Whether she did or didn't, the phrase 'we are not amused' is still seen as a prudish, judgemental statement from a prudish, judgemental woman.

Over the years the very word 'Victorian' has come to mean censorious and joyless. And while there is much truth to it, some of those attitudes were in fact more often found in the Queen's consort, Albert, than in the infatuated young Victoria.

Albert was by any measure, even for his time, a downright prig, quick to judge and not one to be swayed in ideological arguments.

This could have come from a deep Teutonic sense of duty and honour that he had learned from his beloved grandmother. Or maybe it came from a combination of his grandmother's influence and his embarrassment that both his father and brother were notorious philanderers who had regularly dropped their trousers in many of the great houses of Europe.

For whatever reasons, Albert's priggishness caused quite a few arguments with Victoria in the lead-up to their wedding in 1840. And the biggest sticking point was the dozen young ladies whom Victoria had chosen to be her bridesmaids.

Misbehaving Royally

Albert not only insisted that his future wife's bridesmaids be virgins, but also that their mothers were women of impeccable character and should all be free from scandal.

Victoria was fully aware that most of her friends' mothers had been members of the court in which young Victoria had been raised and many – if not all of them – had indeed partaken in dalliances, or rumours of such, with the men of the court, whom she referred to as her 'naughty uncles'.

To Albert's horror, one of the proposed bridesmaids was Lady Ida, the illegitimate child of Victoria's uncle, the late King William IV, and the actress Dorothea Jordan. This became a sticking point and threatened to ruin the whole event – that is, until Victoria's Prime Minister and beloved confidant, Lord Melbourne, took Albert aside and assured him that, if they were to apply his stringent criteria, there simply would not be a dozen eligible aristocratic young women in all of Britain.

So, with that problem solved, everything was back on track. The one last-minute change that needed to be made was that only eight bridesmaids accompanied Victoria down the aisle. This was simply because the train on her dress was too short to accommodate the full company of twelve, and even those eight were so bunched that they tripped over each other's heels. And Albert found it within himself to acquiesce by gracefully presenting each of the bridesmaids with a gift of jewellery for the event – a tradition that would endure for years.

In fact, the royal wedding of 1840 established many traditions that still exist to this day: the bride wears white, the wedding is held during daylight hours and a large iced fruitcake is served as a centrepiece or wedding cake. And, most importantly, in a tradition that is as valid today as it was then, any prospective groom with half a brain in his head should know better than to say anything – and I mean *anything* – derogatory about those women his fiancée has chosen to escort her down the aisle.

We're Going to Need More Febreze

One of the strangest pieces of bespoke furniture ever created was done so by the French company Soubrier at the start of the twentieth century. It was a one-of-a-kind *siège d'amour*, or 'seat of love', for the Parisian brothel Le Chabanais, and it was only ever intended for one client in particular: Britain's Edward VII, or Albert Prince of Wales, as he was then known. Discretion only speaks of him using it before his coronation, but he was such a randy bugger I'll take that with a grain of salt – and that's with the knowledge that he was actually sixty before he became king. I suspect that one of the reasons for Queen Victoria's longevity was her reluctance to hand her son the throne . . . the *nice* throne, that is.

The sex chair was made to accommodate the prince's considerable bulk, as well as his desire to engage with multiple partners. It's quite rococo in its design, with cushions nicely covered in green velvet, some placed where you would imagine, and others that occupy spots that seem to illustrate that old saying, 'I guess you just had to be there to get it.' It has more than its fair share

Misbehaving Royally

of handgrips and stirrups, which apparently made it easier for the Prince of Wales to take up various upright or prone positions in order to mitigate the ever-present danger that he might unwittingly crush one of the women with whom he was engaged.

However, up to this point no one has come up with a definitive theory on just who went where while whatever was happening. I may have led a sheltered life, but all I could think of when I looked at the gilded contraption was, *Well, at least one person is going to be very uncomfortable, and I bet that person is not going to be the prince.*

Soubrier reacquired the chair and posted pictures of it on the internet, which led to countless memes of people superimposing stick figures over it in an attempt to figure out just how Albert and his companions would have actually used the damn thing.

What is not in doubt was Edward's historic appetite for both food and sex.

To give you an idea of his culinary excesses, this was a man who would often start his day with an 8.30 am serving of roast chicken and lobster. His lunch would usually consist of up to eight courses, and this would be consumed only shortly after he had finished off a morning tea of cakes and his own custom-made blend of tea from Fortnum & Mason. The afternoon would be broken up by a 'light snack' of sandwiches or pies, followed by a twelve-course dinner. And don't forget about the late serving of cake taken just before bed.

Actually, one of the ways you knew that Edward was attending the opera or the theatre was that interval would be expanded to an hour just so he could fit in some good old hardcore cake scoffing.

So if that's his food indulgences, what about the sex?

For a great account of this, you need look no further than the writings of Dr Kate Lister from Leeds Trinity University who, apart from researching historical sexuality and sex work, also collates the Whores of Yore website. She describes 'Dirty Bertie' aka Edward the Caresser as 'a man of gargantuan sexual appetites, who rutted his way through available (and not so available) lady folk like a tomcat with three testicles'. And despite being married and having five children with the beautiful Princess Alexandra, he also maintained affairs with Lady Randolph Churchill; French actress Sarah Bernhardt; Irish-born aristocrat Mary Cornwallis-West; Daisy Greville, who managed to be both Countess of Warwick and an outspoken socialist; Lady Susan Vane-Tempest; Lillie Langtry, star of the stage; Agnes Keyser, with whom he had a very special bond, the prominent humanitarian remaining close to Bertie right up to his death; French soprano Hortense Schneider; and can-can dancer Mademoiselle La Goulue, whom he shared with the artist Toulouse-Lautrec – and those are the affairs that were the best documented.

According to Lister, La Goulue would even shout at him when he entered the Moulin Rouge, ''ello, Wales! Are you going to pay for my champagne?' Their dalliances were that much of an open secret.

And He Was A Gambler

Apart from his marital crimes, gluttony and lack of personal hygiene, Henry VIII was also a shocking gambler. Among a whole bunch of nicknames, few of which were flattering, he was known during his reign as 'England's Number One Gambler'. He loved shooting dice, as well as a game called 'tables' – a version of backgammon but more tuned to making wagers. And he loved cards, including the new game sweeping through Europe known as 'bragg', a forerunner to our modern game of poker.

Henry wasn't just a discreet, behind-closed-doors gentleman gambler. Rules for his privy chamber might have forbidden 'immoderate and continual playing of cards', but we can assume that Henry's definition of 'immoderate and continual' was probably the same for gambling as it was for the rest of his vices. Rest assured, he didn't restrict his gambling to just around the privy chamber.

At the time, large gambling festivals were popular all over Europe and England, and Henry was a frequent competitor. Just try and imagine Queen Elizabeth II at a televised poker contest, throwing down a tiara as she loudly challenges, 'You've been bluffing all night; we are going all in!' This might give you just some idea of the disparaging impression that many of Henry's subjects had of his gambling ways. These opinions were made even more negative because, well, Henry was what we'd call a 'mug punter' – he often entered these events thinking they could be a way of raising much needed revenue, yet in cards alone he lost over three thousand pounds (close to one and a half million pounds in today's money) in a two-year period.

Reprehensible

The low point of his gambling addiction came when Henry lost the Jesus Bells of the original Saint Paul's Cathedral over a single roll of the dice while gambling with his old friend Miles Partridge. This proved too much, even for his most devoted followers. He made a passing attempt at public contrition and Miles wasn't seen around the court as he had been. From then on, the King found it somewhat harder to find people to wager with.

He also introduced laws to make it harder for the poor to gamble. In 1541, he forbade any person with an income of less than twenty pounds per year to 'play any game for money', and he made it clear that if they needed to fill their spare time, they should instead practise archery.

It would seem that both the king and parliament had come to the conclusion that gambling was the reason behind what they perceived as a genuine lack of skilled archers in the kingdom – and the longbow was still an important weapon in the English arsenal. The reason they decided that a person's income was the yardstick for excluding them from playing games for money was simply that if they were rich they weren't ever going to give up their fun.

These games included many of the activities that Tudor England liked to wager on, such as tennis, quoits, dice, skittles and something known as 'shove ha'penny', which seems to be an overly complicated and extremely tedious game that involved sliding coins into various scoring areas on a smooth wooden board. (It's actually still played in some English pubs to this day.) All wagering on these games was banned, except for a few days in and around Christmas. That being said, according to the records of the time, these laws were enforced to the point where prosecution became difficult because the courts were clogged with offending gamblers. Eventually the population ignored these new gambling laws almost completely – as did the monarch who introduced them, who by then had much weightier issues on his mind.

Catherine the Great

First off, let's deal with the elephant (or dare I say 'horse') in the room: Catherine the Great was not crushed to death attempting to have sex with a stallion. Her death was far more mundane and prosaic; she passed away from a stroke while sitting on the toilet. Yes, she went Elvis-style; the whole horse story was concocted by some of her many enemies to posthumously sully her reputation.

Secondly, her name was not Catherine and she was not actually Russian. She was born Princess Sophie of Anhalt-Zerbst in 1729 in what is now Poland. Her family was of Prussian nobility, and although not particularly wealthy, they seemed adept at the political games of eighteenth-century Europe. Two of her cousins became kings of Sweden – Gustav and Charles XIII – but both would be eclipsed by the young woman who learned Russian and converted to Russian Orthodox. Then, in 1745, she changed her name to the more Russian-sounding Catherine and married her second-cousin and future Tsar, Peter III of Russia.

And from the start, it was not a good match.

Reprehensible

Catherine was witty, intelligent, outgoing and well educated. Her husband, well . . . he was more than just a bit odd, particularly in the bedroom, where he kept his main obsession: toy soldiers. He had a chest full of them stashed under his bed and would drag them out and play with them when no one was around. I should point out that he was very much a grown man when he did this. Look, I know that there are men who take great pride and joy in their model army collections, and fine – it's good to have a hobby. Each to their own and all that. But Peter was more obsessed than your average hobbyist. This is best demonstrated by a bizarre incident that occurred early on in the royal marriage.

In John S.C. Abbott's book *The Empire of Russia: Its Rise and Present Power*, he retells Catherine's description of one particularly disturbing visit to her new husband's rooms: 'One day, when I went into the apartments of His Imperial Highness, I beheld a great rat which had been hanged, with all the paraphernalia of an execution. I asked what all this meant. He told me that this rat had committed a great crime, which according to the laws of war, deserved capital punishment.'

The act of treason committed by the poor rat? It had knocked over some of Peter's carefully placed toy soldiers, and had even been so disrespectful as to chew off the heads of some of the men.

Peter's dog had captured the rat, at which point the future leader of Russia put the poor thing on trial and found it guilty of high treason – he actually conducted a full mock trial in his bedroom. Catherine would later recall, 'In justification of the rat, it may at least be said that he was hung without having been questioned or heard in his own defence.'

Peter would also dress up the household servants in military garb and make them endure hours of mock parades up and down the palace courtyards. He even attempted on more than one occasion to get his new wife to dress up as a soldier so he could inflict military drill exercises on *her*. Suffice to say, she politely refused.

There was always a sense of inevitable doom around this union. On one side you have a man who, when not playing out childish military fantasies, was usually to be found drunk and highly argumentative. On the other side, you have a woman who for years maintained a witty and mutually enthusiastic pen-pal friendship with the French writer and philosopher Voltaire.

No wonder she started taking multiple lovers!

One of those lovers, Count Grigory Orlov, was among the coup leaders who deposed Peter in July 1762, after which Peter mysteriously died. He was probably strangled, although strangely enough there was never a conclusive autopsy. Despite the fact that she knew a lot of the conspirators involved in his demise, and she had made no secret of her disdain for her husband, Catherine was never linked to his death. Moreover, she soon became Empress of Russia, ruling first as empress consort for a few months and then as empress in her own right for almost thirty-five years.

Some historians regard that period as a golden age in Russian history. This is a matter of one's own historical perspective, but there is one thing that we all can agree on: she was a lusty ruler.

History is littered with kings, emperors and the like with overactive libidos. What set Catherine apart was, well, she was a woman. And despite the fact that much of the libidinous legends that grew around her were either concocted or exaggerated by her

Reprehensible

detractors, including her own son, the future Tsar Paul I, there is enough in her own writings and memoirs, and recollections from her friends and lovers, to confirm that Catherine the Great was very fond of the pleasures of the bedroom.

She herself once said that she needed sex at least six times a day to make sure that she could concentrate on running such an enormous empire and deal with all the associated stress.

And speaking of enormous, the empress was something of a connoisseur of the better-endowed gentlemen of her court. One lover, army commander Grigory Potemkin, was said to have 'elephantine sexual equipment', according to an anonymous lady-in-waiting. Apparently Catherine was so enamoured of his Battleship Potemkin (sorry, I couldn't help myself) that she had it cast in porcelain so she could 'console herself' when her 'tiger' was away with the troops.

Potemkin was also so keenly aware of his role in Catherine's sex life, and just how important sex was to her happiness, that when he was away, or maybe just plain exhausted, he would suggest to her various other noblemen who could step in and do the job.

Now this is where things get a bit out of hand. There are some who suggest that Catherine may have had up to 300 lovers, others say it was no more than a scant dozen, and there are a multitude of various guesses that fall in between. One thing is for sure – they were on the whole considerably younger than the empress. This age difference would continue to widen as she aged, ensuring they were all healthy and free of disease. Catherine was scrupulous about this and would make each potential lover submit to an inspection by her personal Scottish physician before there was even the slightest chance of any hanky-panky. After they had submitted to this, each potential paramour would still have one last test to pass. He would be taken for a personal 'road test' by Catherine's lady-in-waiting and closest confidante, the Countess Anna Praskovya Bruce. The countess was more than aware of what her friend and ruler was looking for in a lover, both in terms of not only endowment but also stamina and vigour. Once they had received a thumbs-up from Countess Bruce, then and only then were they permitted to entertain the empress.

It probably comes as no surprise that the two women would later have a falling out when the empress discovered that her lady-in-waiting had fallen for one of the young men whom she had previously tested for her.

The countess was banished from court and quickly replaced by Anna Protasova (this point is not agreed on by all historians), another lady-in-waiting who would become the next *'madame l'eprouveuse'* – the tester of men's performance. And perform they must. I have written elsewhere that the use of professional foot ticklers was a well-established form of getting an aristocratic Russian woman in the mood for love. Catherine's lovers would have to be comfortable, if not enthusiastically supportive, of this practice . . . along with whatever else took her majesty's pleasure.

If they were not capable of reaching the exacting levels of performance demanded by Catherine, well, there was no shortage of potions available to help them out when nature was waning. It was rumoured that an over-reliance on these aphrodisiacs was the cause of death of one of Catherine's favourite lovers of four years, Alexander Lanskoy. And he was only in his mid-twenties. Apart from his mysterious death, Lanskoy also distinguishes himself by being the only one of Catherine's lovers not to use his sexual prowess to either enrich himself or promote his military or professional career.

A few lovers were little more than overpaid gigolos, such as the whiney young officer Alexander Vasilchikov, who once bemoaned, 'I was nothing more to her than a kind of male cocotte, and I was treated as such. If I made a request for myself or anyone else, she did not reply, but the next day I found a banknote for several thousand roubles in my pocket.'

Now, seeing as a thousand roubles is worth over twenty thousand dollars in today's money, and we don't know what Alexander means precisely by 'several' – let's say he does just mean three – well, that's sixty thousand dollars for a night with the empress. And he was one of her *least* expensive lovers.

Many of her main squeezes were given large estates and very generous pensions.

Stanislaw Poniatowski had been a lover of Catherine's going back to the bad old days when she was still married to 'rat boy', and he was probably the father to one of her children. During this pregnancy, Peter III was heard to wonder, 'God knows where my wife gets her pregnancies. I have no idea whether this child is mine and whether I should take responsibility for it.'

He really should have spent a little less time playing with his toy soldiers!

Actually, Peter was known to hold dinner parties for himself, his mistress (notice the singular) Elizaveta Romanovna

Misbehaving Royally

Voronstova, whom Catherine described as 'broad, puffy, with a pock-marked face and fat, squat, shapeless figure' – she also threw in 'ugly, common and stupid' for good measure – *with* Catherine and Stanislaw. At the conclusion of the meal, both Peter and Catherine would retire with their respective lovers.

This became too much for Stanislaw to bear and he fled the dysfunctional, swinging court.

After Peter's death, Catherine still pined for Stanislaw and did everything to aid her ex-lover's ambitions. In 1762 she wrote to him, saying she intended 'sending Count Keyserling off immediately as ambassador to Poland to make you king'.

She then backed this up with over two and a half million roubles and ordered thousands of troops to the Polish border, just to make sure Stanislaw got his desired job as ruler.

He was crowned in 1764, and it did not end well. Stanislaw would be the last king of Poland.

There was one long-term erotic endeavour at which Catherine had considerably more success: home furnishings. She possessed probably the most notorious and expensive collection of pornographic furniture ever assembled in one room.

It was in a private room just off her chambers in her castle in Gatchina, right outside of Saint Petersburg.

There are some who doubt the veracity of her erotically furnished boudoir, seeing as the only real sources are two photos of a chair and a table taken by a couple of German officers who had stumbled across this 'racy' room during the Second World War.

The chair is intricately carved with depictions of oral sex being performed on both male and female genitals, with some goat-footed fauns getting in on the act. Then there is the table: each of the four legs is an erect penis that grows out of a set of breasts – might I add this is a very well-endowed table. The top is edged by various representations of sex organs, and the dicks look like really handy places to hang a briefcase or bag from at the end of a long day.

I have one argument against the claim that this is another fraudulent accusation meant to dim the 'Great' in Catherine: why would you bother making something as elaborate and expensive as this up? A few years back, a French furniture-maker recreated the supposed table, which can be yours for a mere $500,000.

What we *do* have, though, is quite quaint: Catherine's most prized snuffbox. Once opened, the inside lid contains an enamelled image of a woman giving a reclining gentleman what can only be described as 'hand relief', while another chap pleasures himself as he looks on. There is another similarly pornographic image on the inside of the other lid. Actually, there was a bit of a tradition for naughty snuffboxes that continued well into Victorian times. So we know with some veracity that Catherine was the proud owner of probably more than one of these raunchy trinkets.

Catherine loved spending money, she had lavish tastes and she wasn't afraid of a bit of raunch. So sue her . . . At least in a world where men had followed their bliss for so long, she found her own 'golden age'. And for that reason, I'm happy to believe that the erotic furnishings were, indeed, genuine.

A Naughty Nanny and a Silly Sardine

It was supposedly the great love story of the twentieth century – the playboy king who finally met the one woman he could actually give his heart to. And when the stuffed shirts of the British establishment forbade that love, he would rather abdicate the throne than abandon the one true love of his life.

Well, sort of . . . but not really.

Firstly, let's deal with His Highness, Edward VIII. Sure, as both Prince of Wales and later as King of England, Edward had more than his fair share of lovers, but sometimes quantity does not always equal quality – and in Edward's case, 'quality' in the bedroom was, for want of a better term, just one of his 'shortcomings'. One of his ex-lovers, Lady Thelma Furness, wife of Viscount Furness, described him as a lousy lover who was twice cursed with both premature ejaculation and a somewhat small penis. She and those within her circle, many of whom Edward had been with, called him 'The Little Man' behind his back. And before this can be dismissed as jealous gossip, there are more than a few anecdotes that give veracity to her findings

While attending the Royal Naval College, Osborne, he picked up the insulting nickname 'Sardine'. After one communal shower, one wag had pointed out that Edward should be the 'Prince of Sardines' as opposed to the 'Prince of W(h)ales'. Boys can be so cruel. As could Thelma – she took Edward's dumping badly. It was made even worse by the fact that she had been the one to introduce him to her best friend, Wallis Simpson. Remember, she was the one who made sure that the high-end of London

Town were made aware of his lack of sexual prowess only after he had left her.

Wallis, of course, was no shrinking violet. She had left her first husband, US Navy pilot Lieutenant Earl Winfield Spencer, on the very good grounds that he was a drunken sadist who flaunted his affairs with both men and women in her face. He was a controlling, abusive, mean-spirited bastard, and she was better off without him.

She soon found out just how much better, embarking on affairs with both an Italian ambassador and an Argentine diplomat by the name of Felipe Espil, who incidentally was one of the finest tango dancers of the 1920s. And so it was during this roaring decade that the legend of Wallis's sexual prowess began to take shape.

While journeying through China, she took in not only all the standard tourist sights but also made sure to visit some of the more exclusive and exotic brothels, particularly in decadent Shanghai – places with intriguing names like 'The Fields of Glittering Flowers' and 'The Clubs of Ducks and Mandarins'. It should be pointed out that Wallis went purely as an astute observer of the talented women who worked in such establishments, rather than a participant.

She was also a frequent guest on what were then known as 'flower boats', where you were given a sumptuous Chinese feast followed by erotic shows that catered to pretty much everyone's tastes and peccadilloes. While on these boats, she was taught certain 'perverse practices', as they were known at the time.

She became particularly adept in a technique called Fang Chung, which from what I can gather is a slow, erotic hot oil massage that contains a bit of a nasty surprise. The practitioner spends ages rubbing oil into various parts of a man's body before getting around to the chap's wedding tackle. And just as he is about to climax, they apply a sharp, painful amount of pressure just below the scrotum, which has the desired result of stopping him from achieving orgasm.

I'm not sure if this works, but at least you would have his undivided attention.

It was also considered a useful trick if the man suffered from premature ejaculation. The fact that Edward was crazy for a bit of the ol' Fang Chung also tends to give some credence to Lady Thelma's description of him as a lover. By the time he had fallen under Wallis's spell, though, she was married to her second husband, Ernest Simpson, as well as having an affair with the German ambassador, Joachim von Ribbentrop. Ernest, meanwhile, was seeing a certain Mary Raffray, whom he would later marry. It was all very complicated.

Apart from the whole Fang Chung thing, Wallis satisfied another of Edward's fetishes. He was a long devotee of the female foot. He would literally 'get off' on them, which brings us to the story of the two of them being at a party when, in front of all their friends, Wallis turned to the Prince of Wales and barked, 'Take off my dirty shoes and bring me another pair', at which point, to everyone's amazement, he dropped to his knees and did just that.

This charming anecdote was related by Freda Dudley Ward, another member of the somewhat fast set that they moved in. She would go on to say, 'He made himself the slave of whomsoever he loved and became totally dependent on her: he was like a masochist. He liked being humbled, degraded. He begged for it.'

This probably explains their favourite bedroom ritual, where Wallis would dress up as a nanny and Edward as a small child, and she would berate and humiliate him for hours on end. Which begs the question: just what is it about the British ruling class and their nannies?

We all know how the story ends: Wallis gets a hasty divorce, Edward – now king – declares his love for her, and on 11 December 1936 he abdicates and the two flee to Europe for a brief period. This gives them the perfect opportunity to pose for a few happy snaps with their new friend, Adolf Hitler. Eventually, Edward's fascist tendencies prove too much for the British government, and he and Wallis are discreetly shipped off to the Caribbean where, it was assumed, they could do the least possible harm.

After the war they found themselves in New York and became constant travelling companions with Jimmy Donahue, the heir to the Woolworth chain store fortune. There were rumours flying around that one – maybe both – were having an affair with Mr Donahue. Eventually Jimmy fell out of favour with the couple because of his retinue of much younger men and his habit of eating copious amounts of garlic, the latter being particularly anathema to the duke.

The rest of Edward and Wallis's life seems to be spent consumed with a seething hostility towards the royal family that had disowned them, and an increasingly frosty relationship towards each other. It was said that by the 1950s Wallis had grown tired of his submissive nature.

Well, I guess playing naughty nanny can only be fun for a certain amount of time.

Not So Cool for Cats

Contrary to popular belief, the ancient Egyptians did not worship cats, per se. What they *actually* worshipped was a variety of feline-related deities, of which the most powerful was the cat-headed goddess, Bastet, who oversaw fertility, childbirth, the home, domesticity, women's secrets and, obviously, cats. Bastet seems to have had a lot of work on her paws.

The Egyptians held cats in extremely high esteem and, apart from spiritual connections, there is another more prosaic reason for this devotion. The Egyptian diet was primarily grain based – mice eat grain, cats eat mice.

Cats wore custom-made jewellery, and they were mummified when they died. It was illegal to harm a cat, to the point where, in some eras, the punishment for killing a cat was death. It was also illegal to neglect a cat, and according to some historians, there were periods when it was a capital crime to even deface an *image* of a cat. The Greek historian Herodotus wrote that Egyptians would save a cat from a burning building, even before their own children. He also reports, 'All the inmates of a house where a cat has died a natural death shave their eyebrows.'

All in all, life for puss was pretty good in ancient Egypt, so you know something had to go wrong. And that something happened at the Battle of Pelusium in 525 BC. This was fought between the young pharaoh Psamtik III and the Persian king Cambyses II. The spark for this battle had been some ill blood between Cambyses and Psamtik's father, Amasis, regarding a hostage bride that the old pharaoh had sent to the Persian king. But it was more about an extension of territorial fighting that had been going on for years. So, by the time Cambyses lined up facing Psamtik outside the ancient Egyptian stronghold of Pelusium, it was pretty much business as usual.

Except for one thing: Cambyses was much older and wiser than his combatant . . . and he was also a bit of a bastard.

Cambyses was fully aware of the laws of the land and the esteem that the Egyptians had for their beloved cats, so he came upon a cunning plan to use that knowledge against his enemy. According to some historians, his soldiers advanced on the Egyptians behind a vanguard of, yes, you guessed it, cats. Now, as anyone who owns a cat knows, just trying to wrangle one inside on a cold winter's night is difficult enough, let alone assembling a whole column of them. The phrase 'like herding cats' sums it up best.

The Greek historian Polyaenus goes even further, describing how Cambyses 'ranged before his frontline dogs, sheep, cats, ibises, and whatever the Egyptians held dear'.

What probably happened was even weirder. The first row of Persian shock troops launched themselves on the Egyptians, each waving a cat in front of them, in the same manner as World War I troops would undertake a bayonet charge . . . but much, much more freaky.

Then to further confuse the Egyptians, more cats were released from both the right and left flanks to run, terrified, between the Egyptian soldiers' feet. Remember, these soldiers were told on pain of death from the pharaoh, 'Do nothing to harm the moggies,' or words to that effect. Neither could they strike the Persian shield, which had been painted with images of both cats and Bastet, because this too carried the death penalty. Demoralised and confused, the Egyptians were quickly overwhelmed by the Persians, and the city of Pelusium fell. Then, to make matters worse, after the battle Cambyses had the captured Egyptians parade before him while he hurled insults – and felines – at them.

It Was Wild Before Harry

When we think of sexual misadventure among the kings and queens of England, our minds most often conjure up bawdy images of Henry VIII – woman in one hand, turkey leg in the other. And sure, old Harry has a lot to answer for in the codpiece department, but sexual oddities and dangerous liaisons among the rulers of Britain pre-date his shenanigans by centuries.

Some are lost in the strange shadowland between fact and fiction that produces both the histories of Boudicca, the warrior queen of the Iceni tribe of Celtic Britain, and the legend of King Arthur. Although, the intrigues of the Arthurian legend do give us a heads-up about how things are going to pan out once events,

Reprehensible

for want of a better term, 'get real' in the royal chambers. If you recall, Camelot falls apart once Lancelot can no longer hide his feelings for the king's wife, Guinevere – the knights get cranky and eventually Arthur is tricked into fathering a son with his sister, the enchantress Morgan le Fay, and dispatches him on the battlefield. Throw in a couple of White Walkers and you have a half-decent episode of *Game of Thrones*.

Legends and future Monty Python movies aside, we come to the first recorded mention of sexual misadventure of an English monarch. In the year 746 AD, St Boniface chastised King Ethelbald of Mercia for being 'governed by lust' – a rather prescient warning for the next millennium and a bit. Bed-swapping was so prevalent among the kings that ruled the various regions of early Britain that St Jerome was forced to throw his hands up in surrender and proclaim this rather concerning statement: 'Nothing is more vile than to love a wife like a mistress.' Honestly, keeping track of their various affairs, marriages and trysts is head-spinning, so hang on – this can be a bumpy ride.

It also doesn't help that another Ethelbald – Ethelbald, King of West Sussex – turned up almost eighty years later and married his own stepmother to maintain an alliance with the Franks, or so he said. Ethelred the Unready was an illegitimate ruler, having been born to the concubine Aelgifu, who legend has it also gave birth to two more kings. Although this is hard to clarify because Aelgifu seems almost as popular a name for women as having 'Ethel' in your name was for kings. For example, King Cnut the Great had a mistress called Aelgifu, who may or may not have been a lover to both his father and grandfather – no one's certain on that one. But we can be certain that Cnut's son, Harold Harefoot, had a mistress called Aelgifu, who we know for sure is a totally different Aelgifu. I said it was head-spinning.

As you might imagine, these royal hijinks came to a crashing halt with the reign of Ethelred the Unready's son, Edward the Confessor. What he had to 'confess', I'm not really all that certain. Edward was so chaste that he considered sex, even within marriage, to be a sin. It was a great concept if you are considering potential sainthood, but not so great if you are the queen or a nation desperate for a legitimate heir.

When lustless old Eddie died, Harold of Wessex seized the vacant throne, only to have his dreams of ruling crushed by William the Conqueror at the Battle of Hastings. Let us not forget that, in his pre-conquering days, William was obviously not known as William the Conqueror. Before then, back in Normandy, his nickname was William the Bastard, owing to the fact that he was the fruit of a rather nasty incident between his bisexual father, Robert of Normandy, and a peasant girl, known as Herleva. The story goes that Robert abducted Herleva after seeing her washing clothes in a stream and kept her captive until she bore him a son. So, it looks like William was not the only *bastard* in the family.

Things eventually did get better for poor Herleva; upon her release she hooked up with Baron Herluin, the Vicomte of Conteville.

After the conquest, William would have a son, who was known as William Rufus. Rufus was not-so-secretly gay and apparently

Reprehensible

a brilliant soldier. His sexuality was considered somewhat of a lesser scandal than his flamboyant appearance, particularly once his dress and manner had become all the rage among the young gents at court. One unnamed cleric wrote:

> Then there was the flowing hair and extravagant dress ... and was invented the fashion of shoes with curved points; then the model for young men rival women in the delicacy of person, to mind their gate, to walk with loose gesture, and half-naked. Enverated and effeminate, they unwilling remained what nature had made them, assailers of other's chastity, prodigal of their own. Troops of pathetics and droves of whores followed in Court.

Which begs the question: is this description of an eleventh-century royal or the opening paragraph to a contemporary rock star's biography?

William Rufus would eventually die in a suspicious hunting accident and be succeeded by his younger brother, Henry I. And whereas William Rufus never married or produced an heir, Henry produced over *twenty* children – of which only one was legitimate. Yes, Henry got around. Sadly, his heir William drowned trying to save his half-sister Maude and another half-sister, Matilda, took the throne. Also, sadly, this did not end well for anyone involved, due to the time-honoured pattern of espionage, civil war and murder plots – all the usual stuff.

There soon followed a brief period of relative calm, especially when Henry II married Eleanor of Aquitaine. Although, Henry was not her first husband. Eleanor had been married to Louis VII of France, but that got a bit messy when she learned rumours of the things her husband got up to during the Crusades. Apparently his affection for his knights was somewhat more than just platonic. Then again, in his absence she did keep herself busy, conducting an affair with her uncle, Raymond of Poitou.

It would seem that the rumours about her husband had some substance, as Eleanor had her marriage annulled and swiftly married Henry of Anjou, the future King Henry II. If these two crazy kids couldn't make it last, well, honestly, what hope do any of us have?

Apparently none.

Henry took up with 'Fair Rosamund' of English folklore, as well as her given name, Rosamund Clifford – 'Rose of the World' to her many admirers. An enraged Eleanor urged her sons to rise up in rebellion against their adulterous father, and once again, to no one's great surprise, things didn't end well. Eleanor died alone, imprisoned in 1189 AD. Although, for those keeping score at home, she did outlive Fair Rosamund, who passed away in 1176. Rosamund received a state funeral and a tomb in the choir section of Godstow Abbey, paid for by her family and a grieving Henry. That is, until 1191, when just two years after Henry's death a certain judgemental Bishop of Lincoln, known as Hugh of Lincoln, happened by the abbey. Upon finding that Rosamund's tomb had become something of a shrine surrounded by flowers and candles, he flew into a rage and ordered her body be removed from its resting place and buried outside, as he said, 'with the rest, that the Christian religion may not grow into contempt, and that other women, warned by her example, may abstain from illicit and licentious intercourse'.

If this all seems a bit sad, then let us not forget that we are heading into the great age of chivalry. England's oldest chivalrous order is the long-admired and strangely named 'Order of the Garter'. If, like me, you have often wondered how such a sexy item of female clothing could become the symbol for male virtue, let's move forward to the end of the fourteenth century for an explanation.

Edward III was having a bit of a shindig when the high-stepping Countess of Salisbury is said to have lost a garter. To spare her any embarrassment, he quickly retrieved the garter and announced to the room '*honi soit qui mal y pense*' or 'evil to he who thinks evil'.

Unfortunately for Edward, he didn't take his own advice. Years later he embarked on a doomed affair with a certain Alice Perrers. Alice was a tiler's daughter from Essex, and also one of my favourite characters in medieval history. By the time they hooked up, the ageing and married Edward was showing signs of dementia. Alice was completely open to the opportunities that this presented. Within a short time she had amassed a personal fortune that earned her a place among the wealthiest women in England.

After the death of the queen and due to Edward's advancing ill health, she found herself the most powerful woman in the land at the age of twenty-two. That is, until the court had her banished in around 1377. She was only allowed to return to England so she could attend Edward's funeral where, weeping profusely, she threw herself onto his dead body, clasping his hands in hers.

Misbehaving Royally

However, on closer inspection, it actually turned out that this loving embrace was merely an attempt to prise a ring or two off his fingers while the crowd averted their eyes in embarrassment at her over-the-top display of grief.

Richard II was gay (no biggie) but his extravagant spending did lead to the Peasants' Revolt. He also gave legitimacy to the bastard sons of John of Gaunt, Duke of Lancaster. This split the court, so thank you very much Richard II for kick-starting not only the War of the Roses but for giving us material for one or two of Shakespeare's plays that the world probably could have done without. These tumultuous events led to the crowning of the first Yorkist king Edward IV in 1461, known to us today as Edward the Usurper and to his court as Edward the Lecher. It was said that 'no woman was there anywhere . . . but that he would importunely pursue his appetite and have her'. He had mistresses and bastards all over the country, including three women who would later be described by that goat-hair shirt wearing wowser Thomas More as being 'the merriest, the wiliest, and the holiest harlots in the realm'.

Actually, in the middle of all this royal bed-hopping, I've gotten a bit ahead of myself (don't worry we'll get back to Edward IV), I forgot to mention that Henry V, the Warrior King, was said to have 'fervently followed the services of both Venus and Mars'. But the party had to end sometime, and for that we can thank Henry VI, a man so prudish that when his friends laid on some entertainment in the form of topless dancing maids, he fled the room crying, 'Fy, Fy, for shame!' I can understand why he might not approve, but that does seem like an overreaction, similar to the time when he was told that his wife, Margaret of Anjou, was pregnant and he promptly fainted. It might have been just from general shock, or the fact that he was widely regarded as impotent. Either way, his reaction caused the court to gossip that the child was actually the Duke of Somerset's, and the scandal that followed was a contributing factor in Edward IV (I told you he'd come back) regaining the crown, which gives me a second chance to say that Edward's behaviour had grown worse over time. To be honest, Edward IV was a grade-A cockhead.

As a Guest, Maybe Not So Great

In the year 2000, the good people of Russia gifted a statue of Peter the Great to the British, placing it just near the royal shipyard in London where, in 1698, the tsar had observed the English methods of shipbuilding. Quite frankly, it was the least they could have done, and moreover, I'm surprised the English didn't give it right back. We have to go back to the close of the seventeenth century to get some idea of just how appallingly Peter the Great behaved during his London visit.

As a bright young prince, Peter was well aware of just what a backwater his beloved Russia had become, so as soon as he was able, he embarked on a tour of Europe to ascertain just how far behind his kingdom had fallen. In particular, he wanted to examine the shipbuilding techniques of the world's two leading seafaring nations, which at that time were the Netherlands and Britain.

Misbehaving Royally

According to legend, he would often disguise himself as a humble dock worker to achieve those aims. But considering that he was almost two metres tall (which is tall today, let alone over three centuries ago) and his retinue was known to accommodate 200 or more people, I'm going to pass that off as a bit of Russian spin-doctoring. What we do know is that upon his arrival in London the British monarch William III bent over backwards to make sure that he and his inner circle were well accommodated, and it was arranged that they would stay at Deptford on the Thames, in the mansion of the noted diarist John Evelyn.

Evelyn may have faded from our collective memory, but in his time he was as widely published and read as Samuel Pepys.

The mansion and surrounding estate was said to be one of the finest on the river, and its crowning glory was a decorative garden that had taken over forty years to cultivate into a state of perfection. Evelyn moved out temporarily, considering it a great honour to have the young tsar as a house guest, plus he was doing William III a favour. It would no doubt be a feather in his cap and increase his standing and influence in both the court and the city.

But then he started getting letters from his servants, begging him to return to Deptford, followed by more letters pleading with him to make that return as soon as humanly possible.

To give you some idea of what John Evelyn would discover upon his return, I should point out that Peter had discovered another British industry that he fell in love with almost as much as shipbuilding: brewing. He loved the British beer, and

Reprehensible

constantly requested that his suppliers make each new batch just a bit stronger than the one he and his pals had just polished off.

So the first thing Evelyn noticed upon entering was that many of the expensive paintings in his collection now either sported large bullet holes or tiny little punctures, which he was informed were a result of the tsar's passion for the game of darts. Windows were smashed, often shot through, and let's not forget just how expensive glassmaking was in that era.

There were vomit and urine stains up and down the handwoven rugs. Those areas of flooring not covered in carpet seemed to be damaged by oil and grease. It conjures up images of what might happen if a rebel motorcycle gang booked a chateau on Airbnb for the annual wine tasting and 'ride it like you stole it' initiation weekend.

Then there were the beloved hedgerows in the garden . . .

Apparently Peter and his mates had thought it great sport to get blind drunk and propel each other in wheelbarrows over the flowerbeds and through the hedges – and occasionally through a garden wall.

Needless to say, Peter and his entourage were encouraged to find other suitable lodgings, and eventually Evelyn was compensated – not by the tsar, but by the English state. That compensation covered new floors, all structural damage, repairs to artworks and a considerable amount of new furniture.

God only knows what they did on the original furniture.

So all in all, one statue of Peter the Great three hundred years after the incident sounds like a pretty good deal . . . well, for the Russians at least.

Chapter Three:
Feuds, Fights & Insults

The most legendary beefs usually start with an insult. Although kids today might find it hard to believe, well-known people have been taking verbal (and sometimes literal) shots at each other years before Taylor Swift and Kim Kardashian ever opened their Twitter accounts.

One of the best known and celebrated verbal battles of the twentieth century supposedly occurred at a 1949 London dinner party. The story goes that Winston Churchill, who had probably consumed a bit too much drink, was loudly dominating the evening's conversation. An appalled Lady Nancy Astor commented, 'Winston, if you were my husband, I'd poison your tea.' To which the great orator snapped back, 'Nancy, if I were your husband, I would drink it.' At least that's how it was recorded in the 1952 book *The Glitter and the Gold*, a memoir by Consuelo Vanderbilt Balsan, the beautiful and erudite socialite who is said to be the inspiration for *Downton Abbey*'s Lady Grantham.

And it may have happened that way, but there are recordings of virtually the same exchange occurring years before. It appeared in the gossip sections of both *The New York Tribune* and *The Boston Evening Transcript* at the start of the twentieth century, where it was attributed to a conversation between a drunk man and an angry woman on a New York subway train, overheard by a social tattler who we only know by the pen-name 'The Listener'. Creepy.

Yet others say the exchange has its origins on the vaudeville stage of the late-1800s. So I'm sorry to say that one of the best-known and most oft-repeated insults of all time probably never occurred. Which is a shame, because it's so much funnier than

Reprehensible

the world's oldest recorded insult. This supposed rib-tickler was aimed at the pharaoh Snorfu around 1600 BC, and took the form of a riddle: 'How do you entertain a bored pharaoh? You sail a boatload of young women dressed only in fishing nets down the Nile and urge the pharaoh to go catch a fish.'

However, by Roman times insults had become something of an art form, which is why the poet Martial is featured in this chapter – his epigrams are the standard bearers for having a really good crack at people. More of him later, but suffice to say if he were around today he could make a fortune as the *nasty* judge on one of those talent shows that seem to clog up the airwaves.

But Martial wasn't alone. The Roman playwright Plautus was capable of some really good jibes, such as this from his play *Miles Gloriosus*, where one character, an incessant braggart who boasts of his irresistible allure among women, is brought low: 'Even the prostitutes here pull such faces at him that, as you can see, most of them have ended up with bow-legged lips.'

Or check out the sheer vitriol behind Catullus's 'Poem 33', which contains the classic line of verse, *'Fili, non Potes asse venditare'*, which roughly translates to 'Sonny-boy, you couldn't sell your hairy arse for a penny.' And that's one of Catullus's nicer lines.

Just as the classical world gave us the basis for poetry and theatre, they also gave us the template for bad-mouthing each other. I've included some colourful Roman graffiti in this chapter, just to emphasise that it wasn't only the poets who could turn nasty. The ancient Romans were just as handy at vilification as we are today.

It comes as no shock that Shakespeare elevated the theatrical insult into an art form, particularly in his darkest play, *King Lear*, the most outstanding example of which can be found in the confrontation in Act III between Kent and Oswald.

> KENT: Fellow I know thee.
> OSWALD: What dost thou know me for?
> KENT: A knave, a rascal, an eater of broken meats; a base, proud, shallow, beggarly, three-suited, hundred-pound, filthy, worsted-stocking knave; a lily-livered, action-taking knave; a whoreson, glass-gazing, super-serviceable finical rogue; one-trunk-inheriting slave; one that wouldst be a bawd in way of good service; and art nothing but the composition of a knave, beggar, coward, pander, and the son and heir of a mongrel bitch; one whom I will beat into clamorous whining if thou deniest the least syllable of thy addition.

Mind you, not all geniuses are so eloquent or pithy when it comes to put-downs. In the nineteenth century, the philosopher Kierkegaard was famous for his blistering attacks on what he considered to be the wrongs of the church. For him, the embodiment of these wrongs was lecturer and theologian Hans Lassen Martensen.

Kierkegaard described him with the simple line, 'My opponent is a gob of snot.'

The upside is you couldn't miss his meaning.

Then again, as my grandmother used to tell me, 'Sticks and stones may break your bones, but names will never hurt you.' In the modern era, this is true. Most feuds these days tend to be a series of viperous tweets that escalate quickly until a grownup takes someone's phone away. But this was not always the case.

Reprehensible

For centuries, insults could often lead not to 'sticks and stones' but rather rapiers and pistols. Pig-headed people insisted on settling their differences on the 'field of honour'. And just like most human behaviour, this act became more and more elaborate as the centuries wore on. The etiquette of duelling was so extensive that, in 1837, John Lyde Wilson published a booklet entitled *The Code of Honor*, which gives potential duellers handy tips on the sorts of insults that cannot be ignored and the correct method for the aggrieved party to challenge someone to take up arms.

According to Wilson, the person who sparked the argument should first be sent a note, giving them a chance to reconsider their insult and apologise. If the apology was not forthcoming, Wilson proceeds to advise on the best way to go about choosing your seconds and how to behave on this so-called 'field of honour':

1: The principals are to be respectful in meeting, and neither by look or expression irritate each other. They are to be wholly passive, being entirely under the guidance of their seconds.
2: When once posted, they are not to quit their positions under any circumstances, without leave or direction of their seconds.
3: When the principles are posted, the second giving the word, must tell them to stand firm until he repeats the giving of the word, in the manner it will be given when the parties are at liberty to fire.
4: Each second has a loaded pistol, in order to enforce a fair combat according to the rules agreed on; and if a principal fires before the word or time agreed on, he is at liberty to

Feuds, Fights & Insults

fire at him, and if such second's principals fall, it his duty to do so. [I never realised the second played such a potentially violent role in the actual duel!]

5: If after fire, either party be touched the duel is to end; and no second is excusable who permits a wounded friend to fight; and no second who knows his duty, will permit his friend to fight a man already hit. I am aware there have been many circumstances where a contest has continued, not only after a slight, but severe wounds, had been received. In all such cases, I think the seconds are blamable.

Sure, it's couched in nice language and strict rules for 'gentlemanly behaviour', but at the end of the day it's still the same stupidity as some idiot in a bar shouting, 'Hey, arsehole, you wanna take this out to the car park?!'

Speaking of idiots, the last recorded duel actually took place in France in 1967, by two men who really should have known better: one was the mayor of Marseilles, Gaston Defferre, and the other politician Rene Ribière. The two buffoons chose fencing swords as their weapon of choice. It might have been the much younger Ribière who took the matter more seriously, even to the point where he insisted on sharper swords than the ones originally offered, but it was the mayor who landed two blows, which not only drew blood but also brought the duel to an end.

I mean, I'm talking about a *duel*, in the same era as Batman and the Beatles – for goodness' sake, even I was alive!

And Down He Goes

Around the traps of mid-eleventh-century England there was probably no more powerful, infamous and cunning figure than Earl Godwin, or Godwin of Wessex. He manipulated Edward the Confessor and rose to power under the rule of King Cnut (the Danish king of England whose name you always make sure to spellcheck thoroughly). He was equally adept at using both the sword and marriage to enrich his wealth and influence. He was one of those crafty noblemen who had a good sense of which way the political wind was blowing and just how best to fill his own sails.

One of the crimes he was accused of was the murder of King Edwards' brother, Alfred. Despite the persistent rumours of this crime, he still managed to get his daughter Edith married off to King Edward in 1045, vehemently proclaiming his innocence all the while. Plus, he was a well-known hater of the Normans, which was the fashion at the time.

He died in 1053, and the most believable story of his demise comes from the *Anglo-Saxon Chronicle*, a collection of annals written in Old English detailing the early history of England. It stated: 'On Easter Monday, as he was sitting with the king at a meal, he suddenly sank towards the footstool bereft of speech, and deprived of all his strength.' The account goes on to describe how what we would now consider a stroke kept Earl Godwin in that state for twenty-four hours until he passed away.

But there is another account of the earl's death, written in the next century by the Norman chronicler Aelred of Rievaulx that is far more colourful. It talks of Godwin being at a royal banquet with King Edward when the old rumour about his doing away with Alfred was raised. Godwin stands, furious, and declares for all to hear, 'May this crust which I hold in my hand pass though my throat and leave me unharmed to show that I was guiltless of treason towards you, and that I was innocent of your brother's death!'

Aelred continues, 'He swallowed the crust, but it stuck in his throat and killed him.'

You know you're really disliked by your country's new rulers when they reach back a hundred years to give you a kick in the head.

L'oeil du Tigre

Georges Clemenceau was born in 1841. As a young man he became both a journalist and an ardent anti-monarchist, political rabble-rouser, which resulted in his eventual arrest for, of all things, putting up posters. He even had to flee to America during a crackdown on dissidents. However, upon his return he re-established himself in the political world, eventually rising to become Prime Minister of France from 1906 to 1909, and then again from 1917 to 1920. He is best remembered these days as being one of the principal architects of the Treaty of Versailles.

Also, for reasons about to become obvious, his nickname was *Le Tigre* – The Tiger.

Reprehensible

He was a renowned hothead with a fatalistic approach to life, a fact borne out by his participation in some twenty-two duels. Yes, that is correct – in his youth and not-so-youth, the future prime minister of France took part in *twenty-two* duels. Sort of makes Aaron Burr and Alexander Hamilton look like a pair of duelling amateurs.

He also possessed a rather dark sense of humour.

There was one story that went around Paris regarding Clemenceau purchasing a train ticket on the way to one of these duels. Apparently, he approached the window and asked for a one-way ticket, to which his second exclaimed, 'Isn't that a little pessimistic?'

Georges replied, 'Not at all, I always use my opponent's return ticket for the trip back.'

There are some doubts as to the veracity of that exchange; I would like to believe that it's true – nineteenth-century trash-talk at its finest.

Let's not forget that *Le Tigre* did engage (as if I needed to remind you) in *twenty-two* duels, so maybe he did get a bit cocky and relaxed about the whole procedure. The fact that Clemenceau would revel in its retelling does give some insight into that sense of gallows humour he so enjoyed. For more documented insight into Clemenceau's fatalistic approach towards life, we have only to look at his 'defence' of the man who tried to kill him.

On 19 February 1919, the anarchist Émile Cottin took seven shots at Clemenceau, hitting him once in the chest. To everyone's amazement, Clemenceau did not call for the man's

Feuds, Fights & Insults

execution but jokingly explained his feelings: 'His poor marksmanship must be taken into account. We have just won the most terrible war in history, yet here is a Frenchman who misses his target six out of seven times at point-blank range. Of course this fellow must be punished for the careless use of a dangerous weapon and for poor marksmanship. I suggest he be locked up for eight years with intensive training in a shooting gallery.'

Cottin would avoid the death penalty and spend the next ten years in prison, and then he'd be placed under house arrest. He died in 1936 alongside his fellow anarchists fighting in the Spanish Civil War.

Clemenceau retired from politics at the age of 80, spending his last years travelling, lecturing and writing. He even ventured as far afield as Singapore, where a street was named after him in honour of the visit.

He shuffled off this mortal coil in November 1929 at the age of 88. All we know is that he died of natural causes (which in his case could mean almost anything) and his last wish was to be buried next to his father at Colombier, Switzerland – a place of great beauty – in an unmarked grave, with no funeral procession and no official or religious ceremony. I'm assuming these wishes were followed to the letter; you wouldn't want to upset even *Le Tigre Mort*.

I Wish They'd Put This Bit in the Tapestry

What do you do once you've conquered all of Great Britain? If you are William the Conqueror, you celebrate – and you keep on celebrating, so much so that by 1087 you're enormous. There are many scholars who believe that he was indeed the fattest world leader for many, many centuries, only to be overtaken for this dubious honour by US President Taft, who found himself wedged in the White House bath one cold February morning in 1910. Actually, that was just an insult made up to embarrass Taft. He couldn't have got stuck in the tub – it was custom-made and could 'accommodate four men', which is probably how you measured bathtubs at the time. The story was most likely spread by Teddy Roosevelt's supporters to embarrass Taft.

But don't get me wrong, Taft was enormous.

As was William the Conqueror in the latter stages of his life. So much so that his horse was visibly uncomfortable bearing his weight. You know you're getting more than pleasantly plump when your horse shies away from you. But what was worse for William was that the only person in Europe who could insult him and get away with it did so in front of all his cronies. King Philip I of France enquired loudly, upon seeing William, 'Is your majesty pregnant?'

That was it for William. He was going on a diet. Well, not a *diet* as we would know it. He informed everyone at the palace that he would only consume liquids, by which he meant alcohol, and he would do so while remaining in bed. The 'Stay in Bed and Get Wasted Diet' must have actually had some moderate success. William lost enough weight that he managed to haul himself back into the saddle.

And while seizing the French town of Mantes, he injured himself by bumping hard into the wooden pommel of that saddle and died.

I'm not one for equine conspiracy theories, but I would love to believe that it was the same poor horse who had been forced to drag William's corpulent frame all over England and France, who maybe, just maybe, pulled up a bit short and forced his liege's gut right into that wooden pommel.

Oh, and one last disgusting fact: for a whole multitude of reasons weeks elapsed between William's death and his burial. There had been a half-baked attempt to embalm him, but there was a heat wave. What had started off as a pretty fat corpse started to inflate from the inside, so much so that when the funeral attendants tried to squeeze the body into its way-too-small sarcophagus … the corpse of William the Conqueror burst. Actually, it pretty much exploded. It's one thing to 'make it rain' at your funeral; it's another to make your organs rain on the few mourners who had turned up for the event.

I'm also assuming that none of those few mourners stuck around for the post-service drinks and snacks back at the castle.

Shall We Dance? Maybe Not

Although not exactly the version of the dance we would quickly recognise today, the waltz was incredibly popular in the early

Reprehensible

nineteenth century. One particular devotee to the dance craze was French Admiral de la Susse, considered to be one of the most dashing, handsome men of Europe, and that was at a time when Europe was almost overcrowded with dashing, handsome men.

So of course the admiral was in attendance at an 1816 Paris ball being held in the swish district of Faubourg Saint-Honoré, where he would become embroiled in possibly the silliest of all dancefloor beefs that two men can have. The subject of the admiral's ire was one morbidly obese German, whose name has been lost in the mists of history. Strangely little is known about him, apart from his girth.

There are two differing accounts about what caused all the fuss. The admiral insisted that the obese German had 'waltzed into him'. However, some present observed that it was the admiral, who was somewhat short-sighted, who had been the cause of the collision, much to the anger of the twinkle-toed Teutonic chubster. Either way, what should have been a simple 'excuse me' followed by an equally pleasant 'not to worry' instead escalated into cards being exchanged and a time and place for a duel organised.

The two parties subsequently met at the bucolic Bois de Boulogne (ironically a former royal hunting ground) and duelling pistols were chosen.

Despite his short-sightedness, the admiral got off a cracking shot right at the heart of his adversary, knocking him to the ground. The German lay before the admiral, breathing hard, obviously in pain . . . yet strangely not dying. When the admiral's seconds tore open the German's clothing to look for a bleeding wound, they found instead a dinted metal breastplate.

The admiral was incensed by this cheating, dishonourable behaviour and resorted to what he considered to be the 'chivalrous' solution – kicking the man in the head.

The German apparently survived, although I doubt he ever waltzed as vigorously again.

I have to admit that as a large, uncoordinated man who does enjoy dancing, this story really scares me.

Roman Graffiti

The word graffiti actually comes from the Italian *graffiato*, meaning 'scratched'. And the Italians should know a thing or two about this process – they've been scratching stuff on walls since before Rome was a republic.

Take, for instance, the preserved towns of Pompeii and Herculaneum. Many tourists who have done the day trip to the wonderful heritage locations will talk about the not-so-subtle artwork depicting services on offer in the bars and brothels of the town. However, what is often overlooked is the equally naughty graffiti scratched into the walls of these establishments.

And not just in the bars and brothels . . . Those with a keen eye can spot scandalous graffiti all over the place.

Fortunately for those who may have missed such gems, the always wise and delightful Mary Beard (along with some other historians) have given us the following translations. These are mostly from Pompeii, unless otherwise indicated, and are a

Reprehensible

selection of my personal favourites. I have left out most of the poo stuff – not because I am being censorious, but simply because there was so much poo stuff. Like, a worrying amount of poo stuff, almost bordering on obsessive.

TAVERN OF VERECUNDUS: 'Restituta, take off your tunic, please, and show us your hairy privates.'

BAR/BROTHEL OF INNULUS AND PAPILIO: 'Weep, you girls. My penis has given you up. It now penetrates men's behinds. Goodbye, wondrous femininity.'

ON THE WALL OF A PRIVATE HOUSE: 'Amplicatus, I know that Icarus is buggering you.' And in the next line we have, 'Salvius wrote this.' I'm assuming this addendum was to make sure the reader knows that it is not just idle gossip and slander – Salvius is a man willing to stand by and acknowledge his claim. (Or, alternatively, maybe someone was trying to get Salvius into trouble?)

HOUSE OF CUSPIUS PANSA: 'The finance officer of the emperor Nero says this food is poison.' Think of this as the ancient world's version of the crowd-sourced review forum YELP. And while we are talking bad reviews, there is this comment inscribed into a door at the INN OF THE MULEDRIVERS: 'We have pissed in our beds. Host, I admit that we shouldn't have done this. If you ask: Why? There was no potty.'

Feuds, Fights & Insults

BAR OF ATHICTUS: 'I screwed the barmaid.' I'm going to bet you didn't!

BAR OF NICANOR: 'Lesbianus, you defecate and you write, "Hello, everyone!"' I know I said that I redacted most of the poo references, but that one was just so silly I had to include it.

GLADIATOR BARRACKS: 'Floronius, privileged soldier of the 7th legion, was here. The women did not know of his presence. Only six women came to know, too few for such a stallion.' I have a hunch that Floronius might have written this one himself.

GLADIATOR BARRACKS: 'Celadus the Thracian makes the girls moan!' My feeling here, and it's just wild speculation, is that maybe Celadus and Floronius might have been aware of each other's reputation.

STREET WALL: 'Theophilis, don't perform oral sex on girls against the city wall like a dog.' I find myself wondering what's the main complaint here: technique or location?

THE STREET OF MERCURY: 'Publius Comicius Restitutus stood here with his brother.' I include this to illustrate that not all Roman graffiti was filthy; some of it was equally quite dull.

THE WOOD-WORKING SHOP OF POTITUS, which was located next door to a bar: 'Would that you pay for all your tricks, innkeeper. You sell us water and keep the good wine for yourself.' So complaints about watered down drinks are as old as bars themselves.

VICO DEGLI SCIENZIATI: 'Cruel Lalugus, why do you not love me?' *Ohhh.*

HOUSE OF ORPHEUS: 'I have buggered men.' There's a pretty fair chance you're not on your own in that regard.

ATRIUM AT THE HOUSE OF PINARUS: 'If anyone does not believe in Venus, they should gaze at my girlfriend.' See, they could be romantic!

Then we have the graffiti from an establishment known as THE LUPINARE, which seems to have been either a bar or a brothel, but probably both:

'I screwed a lot of girls here.'

'On 15 June 15, Hermeros screwed here Phileterus *and* Caphisus.' Oh Hermeros, you old braggart, but then again I suppose you can't spell Hermeros without eros.

'Sollemnes, you screw well.' I guess if you found yourself at a loose end in Pompeii, then The Lupinare seemed like a good place to go!

ON A STREET: 'A copper pot went missing from my shop. Anyone who returns it to me will be given 65 sestertii. 20 more will be given for information leading to the capture of the thief.' And while we are talking money . . .

Feuds, Fights & Insults

Above a bench outside THE MARINE GATE: 'If anyone sits here, let him read this first of all: if anyone wants a screw, he should look for Attice – she costs 4 sestertii.' Which only shows just how nice that copper pot must have been.

Much of the graffiti found in the BASILICA – the ancient Roman area for courts, businesses and markets – seems to have been predominantly insults, almost as a way to publicly attack your enemies. Here are a few prime examples:

'Phileros is a eunuch.'

'Epaphra, you are bald.'

Samius to Cornelius: 'Go hang yourself.'

'Epaphra is not good at ball games.' (Epaphra actually gets off relatively lightly, don't you think?)

'The one who buggers a fire burns his penis.' (As true today as it was then.)

And let's not forget this timeless classic: 'Chie, I hope your haemorrhoids rub together so much they hurt worse than they ever have before.'

In fact, there was so much insulting and scandalous graffiti on the walls of the basilica that it takes a lot for this particular gem to stand out: 'Oh walls, you have already held up so much tedious graffiti that I am amazed you have not already collapsed in ruin.'

The following two are from the TOWN OF HERCULANEUM, and, well, they're sort of self-explanatory:

'Appelles the chamberlain with Dexter, a slave of Caesar, ate her most agreeably and had a screw at the same time.'

Obviously the two gentlemen felt that this needed some clarification, because elsewhere in the bar they scribbled, 'Appelles Mus and his brother Dexter each pleasurably had sex with two girls twice.'

But just so you don't think that it's all insults, sex and defecation, there is this last piece of graffiti found scribbled on the wall of a brothel, in Pompeii's VICO D' EUMACHIA: 'Vibius Restitutus slept here alone and missed his darling Urbana.'

The Cardiff Giant

Do you remember that episode of *The Simpsons* where Lisa's school class unearths the skeleton of an angel? Homer quickly decides to make money by displaying it. The town is divided between believers and non-believers, and eventually the whole thing is exposed as a hoax, invented to help market a new shopping mall. That particular episode contained some echoes of an incident that occurred over 150 years ago – an incident that also involved religious sceptics, devout believers, fraudsters and a court case. Even the great huckster P. T. Barnum got involved.

The story begins in 1867. The New York tobacco dealer, cigar manufacturer and virulent atheist George Hull had travelled to Iowa on business and soon found himself locked in an argument with a Methodist preacher. What had sparked the animus was George's incredulity at the revivalist preacher's literal interpretation of an often overlooked passage from Genesis that claimed, 'There were giants in the earth in those days.'

Hours later, George Hull was still reflecting on the heated debate when he concocted the idea to create a stone giant and mock the faithful flock by 'passing it off as a petrified man'. It also occurred to him that by doing this he could make himself a bit of money along the way.

First off, he had to acquire a stone large enough for such a purpose, so while in Iowa he travelled to Fort Dodge and bought himself a five-ton slab of gypsum. He claimed that he was intending to use the rock to create a statue of Abraham Lincoln. The Civil War had only recently ended and statues of the late president were going up all over the North, so this was an extremely plausible cover.

Next, he sent the stone to Chicago, to the studios of two marble sculptors. Over the summer months of 1868, Hull posed naked, reclining, his right arm draped across his belly, as the two artisans chipped away to create a somewhat crude two-and-a-half metre human figure. They then scrubbed the statue with acid in an attempt to give it an aged appearance. Hull even used a large needle to give the impression of pores on the skin of the face. The work was finally done, now all Hull had to do was figure out just how he was going to unleash his 'giant' on an unsuspecting world.

That's when Hull's distant cousin, William 'Stub' Newell, enters the picture. Stub owned a farm in Cardiff, New York. And it just so happens that around that time the valleys in and around the town of Cardiff had gathered a reputation as an excellent

Reprehensible

place to discover fossils. Once the cousins had come to a business arrangement about the division of any future profits, Hull set the wheels in motion.

The giant was placed in an iron box, put on a cargo train under cover of night, and finally unloaded and buried on a section of Stub's farm, behind an old barn.

And then the two men waited . . . almost one full year. Hull had sunk $2000 (over $50,000 in today's money) into the project, so eleven months after burying the giant he must have concluded that it was time to see a return on his investment. He wrote to Stub, telling him the moment had arrived for their giant to be 'discovered', and on 16 October 1869, Stub hired two unsuspecting local farmhands, Gideon Emmons and Henry Nichols, to dig a well just behind his barn, in a place where no well should or would realistically be. Within a few minutes they had uncovered a stone foot, and a few hours later the giant was revealed to the world. All it took was the two farmhands arriving back in town later that same day to get the frenzy started.

The *Syracuse Journal* wrote, 'Men left their work, women caught up their babies and their children in numbers, and all hurried to the scene where the interest of that little community centered.'

In a remarkably short period of time (almost *too* short, one would think), Stub had erected a tent over the giant to keep it safe from the elements. After hearing more than a few doubters questioning his motives, Stub rushed to his own defence, announcing that he would remove the tent and re-bury the giant until there could be further analysis into his fantastic find.

Local scientists had a look, one proclaiming it a statue carved centuries earlier by Jesuit priests. Others believed it to be the petrified remains of one of those giants mentioned in the Book of Genesis. Still others were less than convinced about the whole damn enterprise.

But Stub's decision to attempt to protect the giant had done its trick. Crowds grew and within a few days he had re-erected the small white tent over the dig site and was charging the up to 2500 spectators a week twenty-five cents each for a quick viewing.

I get the feeling that Stub Newell was always going to be the Homer Simpson of this story. However, unlike Homer, Stub knew when to keep his mouth shut. Among the early throng of visitors to Stub's farm were a bevy of investors willing to buy into the giant. He waited until his cousin Hull was on-site (and he was quickly on-site) before the two of them agreed to sell a three-quarter share in the giant to a consortium of business men for the hefty fee of $30,000 ($750,000 today). Not a bad return for Hull when you think about it.

After the deal was done, even more credence was given to the fake statue by no less a figure than the New York State Geologist James Hall, who decreed it to be 'the most remarkable object yet brought to light in our country'.

By this time papers all around the country were writing about the 'Cardiff Giant', a few with guarded skepticism but the majority mostly singing its praises. There was an incredible burst of public interest in archaeology and palaeontology at the time, which had started with ground-breaking finds by British archaeologists in France and then had spread through to the United States. This was one find that managed to combine science with faith – what they call in show business a 'double threat'. So what do you do when you have a property this hot? Well, as any good manager will tell you, you put it out on the road. The Cardiff Giant was completely excavated and embarked on a tour of the American Northwest, which brought it to a larger audience . . . and even more scrutiny.

The noted palaeontologist Othniel Charles Marsh took only the briefest of glances at it and declared the giant to be 'of very recent origin, and a most decided humbug'. The result of this proclamation was swift, and within twenty-four hours the great impresario P. T. Barnum seized on the controversy and offered the shareholders $50,000 for the giant.

His offer was politely declined so, Barnum being Barnum, he answered back as only he knew how. He quickly constructed his *own* giant and displayed it in Manhattan with a very Barnum advertisement: 'What is it? Is it a Statue? Is it a Petrifaction? Is it a Stupendous Fraud? Is it the Remains of a former race?'

We actually had feuding fake giants.

When the Cardiff Giant's tour took it to New York, Hull and the other owners were flabbergasted to see that Barnum's replica was drawing bigger crowds than their exhibit. Incensed, they made the foolhardy decision to take Barnum to court.

The bewildered judge said to the plaintiffs, 'Bring your giant here, and if he swears to his own genuineness as a bona fide petrifaction, you shall have the injunctions you ask for.'

That's as far as the case went.

Feuds, Fights & Insults

But things weren't completely over for fake giants. The sculptor responsible for Barnum's giant took it upon himself to knock out another half a dozen, and within a short period of time there were eight petrified frauds appearing in circuses, fairgrounds and museums up and down the country.

This proved to be giant overexposure, and rather quickly the American public began to lose interest.

The final nail in the plus-sized coffin came in 1870 when the two Chicago sculptors of the original Cardiff Giant gave statements to several newspapers outlining their role in perpetuating the hoax. They also claimed, not unsurprisingly, that they were still owed money by Hull and his partners. Hull had pretty much by this time owned up to the whole scam, pocketed his money and fled.

He would attempt to run a similar scam seven years later in Colorado. It was basically the same fake fossil concept, except this time the giant had a tail. Sadly for Hull, no one bought it, and by this stage he had gone through most of his money. Hull died in 1902.

As for the original Cardiff Giant, you can still see him as a rather curious exhibition in the main barn at the Farmers' Museum in Cooperstown, New York, where he has lived since 1947. Before that, he spent some time as a rather oversized coffee table in the basement rumpus room of Iowan publisher Gardner Cowan.

Reprehensible

The Curious Trial of Formosus

In January 897 AD, one of the strangest events in the long and often bizarre history of the Catholic Church took place in the Basilica of St John Lateran: the trial of Formosus.

There were three things that made this trial particularly odd. Firstly, Formosus wasn't just any old chap. He had once been *Pope* Formosus. Secondly, he had been dead for over six months. And thirdly – and most peculiarly – the star witness at this trial was none other than his recently exhumed body, dressed up in all his papal regalia.

The main accuser at the trial was the newly appointed Pope Stephen VI, a man so duplicitous that he is also known as Pope Stephen VII. It was under his orders that the body of Formosus had been exhumed and was now being charged with a whole raft of crimes, including that old chestnut of heresy as well as perjury and having assumed the papacy illegally.

To find the root of this weirdness, we have to go back just a few years before when Formosus first became Pope and immediately got things off on the wrong papal slipper.

He had some views about the Holy Spirit that were considered heretical to accepted notions of the Trinity. To be fair, figuring out the Holy Spirit conundrum was a real theological can of worms at the time, and would remain so for many centuries to come. Even after a few months of Holy Communion classes as a lad I could never really wrap my head around the whole 'where does Spooky fit in?' question.

On a more terrestrial level, Formosus also argued with the bishops of Rome about the fairest way to divide the income

Feuds, Fights & Insults

the church was receiving from that city's numerous brothels. But what would really bring about his downfall was, in the hotbed of European politics, turning a one-time supporter, the incredibly powerful Count Guy of Spoleto (known as 'Guido' to his mates), into a dangerous enemy. The error would prove fatal.

Pope Formosus was actually in the process of raising an army against Count Guy (this was back in the day when Popes had armies instead of Twitter accounts) when he was paralysed with a mystery illness and promptly and (at least for Guido) conveniently died. He was replaced by Pope Boniface VI, who, after ruling the Church for a mere two weeks, also died, except this time the culprit was a severe attack of gout. It may come as no surprise that quite a few of Count Guy's perceived enemies also seemed to have succumbed to gout at just around this time.

Thus, the path was cleared for Stephen to become Pope. Little is known about Pope Stephen VI's early life except that he had followed his father into the priest business and had steadily risen through the ranks to the level of bishop, ironically appointed to that role by Formosus. It would seem that this rise to power was driven through his prowess at making behind-the-scenes deals and his ability to keep a low profile in times of political crisis. This method of seizing political power is obviously still extremely prevalent in many of today's more dysfunctional political parties.

Which brings us to the trial of Formosus, also known as the Cadaver Synod, which you have to admit is a pretty catchy name for an event – a bit like the headlining band in a ninth-century Catholic Coachella: 'Okay, let's make some noise for Cadaver Synod!'

Lest you think that the trial of a cadaver orchestrated by his successor and at the behest of his enemies would be nothing more than a farce, I would just like to point out that Stephen did appoint a deacon to speak in Formosus's defence. There were times when this deacon would exercise his holy right to remain completely silent. Or, even more ridiculously, he would kneel behind the throne on which Formosus had been dumped and answer for the corpse during cross-examinations.

This resulted in the incredibly ridiculous sight of Pope Stephen wagging his finger in front of the dead pontiff's face and shouting, 'Why did you usurp your papacy?'

To which the deacon hiding behind the throne would answer, 'Because I was evil!'

The only thing that could have made this travesty of a trial even more outrageous would have been if the defence counsel were to have given his answers while drinking a glass of water, just to impress the crowd.

He didn't, sadly.

Not surprisingly, Formosus was found guilty. His decomposing body, stripped of its royal robes, was paraded through the streets of Rome. Three fingers on his right hand – the blessing fingers – were hacked off before he was buried in a pauper's grave. But this wasn't enough for Formosus's enemies. He was exhumed a *second* time (which in itself must be some sort of sin) and was then thrown unceremoniously into the Tiber, thus making him part of the dubious and long-running Roman tradition of throwing dead bodies into the main river that ran through the city. Fortunately, a humble monk, for reasons known only to that monk, rescued Formosus's body and planted him a final time. This turned out to be a rather fortunate act of . . . well, let's call it kindness, because as was often the case in the hectic world of ninth-century Italy, the winds of change were blowing across the stinky old Tiber.

Stephen VI had actually managed to gross out the good people of Rome with the treatment of his predecessor's body and legacy. He lost his papacy and found himself in prison. Then he was strangled to death. His successor, Pope Romanus, quickly set about overturning many of his decrees against those appointed or ordained by Formosus. Sadly for Romanus, he may have moved a little too quickly.

Despite being strangled and discredited, Stephen still had powerful supporters in Rome. So Romanus's time as Pope stretched only from August until the November of 897, when he suddenly died of an unknown cause. Let's just assume it was 'gout'.

So it would seem that we had a situation in early papal politics where even a once-discarded leader somehow had enough factional supporters to be able to rise up and depose his successor and replace them with someone more in line with their own political views.

I leave you free to draw whatever modern political analogies you may from that last paragraph.

The Emancipated Duel

In August 1892, one of the most unusual duels in history took place. There were a few things that set this particular duel apart from others, but the greatest point of difference – one that would give it widespread notoriety – was that the two combatants were women from a particularly rarefied echelon of the social strata. Princess Pauline von Metternich and Countess Anastasia Kielmannsegg were both bitter rivals in the hothouse of Viennese high society, and there had been hostility simmering between the two for years.

In the months leading up to the duel, Princess Pauline was made the Honorary President of the Vienna Musical and Theatrical Exhibition, a position of great prestige. Countess Anastasia also had an official position at the same exhibition. She was the President of the Ladies' Committee of the Exhibition. And it did not take long for the pre-existing animosity between the two women to surface. According to sources at the time, the princess and the countess had a heated exchange over several items at the exhibition that culminated in insults being traded over one particular floral display. It escalated to the point where the two women decided it could only be honourably resolved with a duel.

So that's the second strange thing about this incident – it would seem that these two educated, powerful, intelligent women were willing to meet on the field of honour over a flower arrangement.

In his book *The Duel: A History of Duelling*, Robert Baldick writes about how a movement was emerging at the time that encouraged the 'new woman' to fight her own duels, as opposed to getting a man to represent her in the quarrel. He talks about

Séverine, a French journalist who passed off her duelling duties to a male colleague. For this act, the Paris League openly rebuked her for her failure to advance the emancipation of women. One of her fellow Parisians, Gisèle d'Estoc, who had once duelled with an actress, said that a woman who resorts to using a male champion had committed a 'deed of inferiority'.

To our modern sensibilities, this seems like a confusing mixture of forward-thinking early feminism combined with barbaric, medieval concepts of honour and personal justice. Which brings me to a third unusual aspect of this 'emancipated duel' – the seconds assisting the duellists and the individual overseeing the whole event to make sure everyone stuck to the rules, the Baroness Lubinska, were also all women.

Now the baroness also possessed a medical degree, which was also unusual for a woman at the time, even a baroness. This led to a fourth strange wrinkle of this duel – it would be conducted topless.

Both the Princess Pauline and Countess Anastasia had agreed that the weapon of choice would be a rapier, and that the duel would not be to the death. Rather, the victor would be decided by who drew first blood. Baroness Lubinska was concerned that a stray piece of dirty clothing could find its way into a wound, and this could cause an infection resulting in death. I guess this is something you would want to avoid in a duel that had been organised specifically *not* to be fatal.

Oddly enough, there is an actual precedent for this thinking. In 1806, the British Parliamentarian Humphrey Howarth got into a quarrel with the Earl of Buckingham while out boozing after the Brighton Races. The result of this argument was the

Reprehensible

age-old challenge of 'pistols at dawn'. Much to everyone's surprise, Howarth turned up the next morning stark bollock naked, declaring, 'If any part of the clothing is carried into the body by a gunshot wound, festering ensues; and therefore I meet you thus.'

The Earl of Buckingham refused to draw a gun against a naked man and the whole thing was called off.

On the occasion of the emancipated duel, the two women were stripped to the waist to begin combat, while all male servants were told to remove themselves to a safe distance and turn the other way.

It would seem that Princess Pauline was declared the winner. The duel was stopped during the third round, and although Pauline had a cut on her nose, it was decided that the wound she had inflicted on the countess's arm was considerably more significant.

According to the British social magazine of the time, *The Pall Mall Gazette*, the seconds then interceded and 'advised them to embrace, kiss and make friends'.

News of the duel even made it as far away as the United States, where *The Los Angeles Times* patronisingly reported, 'It was a real fight, and both were wounded – no hair pulling or plain scratching but a duel with rapiers.'

Speaking of regressive male attitudes, it probably comes as no surprise that the notoriety of the story of two women duelling topless soon spawned an unforseen business opportunity. Drawings and photographic recreations of the duel were in hot demand for gentlemen to add to their private collections.

You See, That's How Rumours Get Started

Gerald of Wales lived from 1146 to 1223 AD. He achieved the status of royal cleric, travelled widely and wrote extensively. He was a great defender and promoter of Norman authority and ideals. He was also a devoted anti-Irish and anti-Gaelic propagandist. What else could explain this incredibly bizarre description of an Irish coronation ceremony?

> There is in the northern and farther part of Ulster, namely Kenelcunill, a certain people which is accustomed to appoint its king with a rite altogether outlandish and abominable.
>
> When the whole people of that land has been gathered together in one place, a white mare is brought forward into the middle of the assembly.
>
> He who is to be inaugurated, not as a chief but as a beast; not as a king but as an outlaw, has bestial intercourse with her before all, professing to be a beast also.
>
> The mare is then killed immediately, cut up in pieces and boiled in water. A bath is prepared for the man afterwards in the same water. He sits in the bath surrounded by all his people and all, he and they, eat the meat of the mare which is brought to them. He quaffs and drinks of the broth in which he is bathed, not in any cup, nor using his hand, but just dipping his mouth into it round about him. When this unrighteous rite has been carried out, his kingship and dominion have been conferred.

Reprehensible

Gerald of Wales sounds quite authoritative in his description of this extremely bizarre coronation ceremony, and for many years the Norman nobility were more than happy to take his historical accounts as truth. In hindsight, though, Gerald of Wales was not the first creator of fake stories to harm the reputation of his master's enemies, and sadly he wouldn't be the last.

The Bone Wars

If you were to ask the average person in the last twenty years, 'Who is the world's pre-eminent palaeontologist?' they'd probably give you a shrug of the shoulders before answering, 'I don't know. Ross from *Friends*, I guess.'

If, however, you asked someone the same question in the latter part of the nineteenth century, they would have immediately answered either Othniel C. Marsh or Edward Drinker Cope. Or probably both, seeing as those two men had achieved fame or, moreover, *infamy* as the central figures in a feud that lasted from the 1870s to the 1890s, a feud that would become known as the Bone Wars. It was also often referred to as the Great Dinosaur Rush but, come on, the Bone Wars sounds so much cooler.

Like most great feuds, it started with two men from incredibly different backgrounds who move from a mutual – if somewhat begrudging – respect into conflict and outright hatred. Cope was the respectable son of wealthy Quakers. Marsh came from the wrong side of the tracks in Upstate New York. He had made his name as a palaeontologist through hard work and determination, and as such, he regarded Cope as something of a rich man 'dabbling' in dinosaurs. (Palaeontology was actually a fashionable hobby of the times.) Cope regarded Marsh as uncouth and ungentlemanly.

The fact that Cope worked with the esteemed Academy of Natural Sciences in Philadelphia and Marsh held a position at the equally worthy Yale Peabody Museum of Natural History did not defuse their mutual scepticism about the other's genuine calling. These were two dogs ready to carp over the same pile of bones. All it needed was the right pile of bones to turn a passing dislike into a full-blown feud.

And in 1868, the right pile of bones just happened to turn up.

In that year, Cope had been sent a very strange fossil from Kansas. After examining the bones for a while, he named the specimen *Elasmosaurus* and then, rather unfortunately for him, placed the skull on the end of what had been the creature's tail. In his defence, up until that point no one had figured out that the rather unusually long section of bones was actually the dinosaur's neck – not its tail. In scientific terms, Cope had assembled the fossil arse about.

Marsh immediately seized on this mistake, launching a series of lectures proclaiming his rival's stupidity. Cope responded, as you would, by using his wealth to attempt to buy all the copies of the scientific journal in which he had displayed his findings, including the dramatically arse-about illustrations.

This was the first public shot in the Bone Wars.

Reprehensible

Trouble had certainly been brewing a few years before when Cope discovered a bountiful fossil site in New Jersey. Marsh, on hearing this news, had gone in and quietly bribed the excavators to send the most exciting finds to him rather than his rival. The pattern of subterfuge and skulduggery would go on to explode in the years to come as the Bone Wars headed west towards the Rockies. That's when things really started to get out of hand.

In 1877, Arthur Lakes, a Colorado geologist, writer and schoolteacher, had come across some 'saurian' bones while hiking. He informed the two best known palaeontologists of the time. Marsh was informed first and immediately sent Lakes a hundred dollars to keep the find a secret. On realising that Cope was already aware of the find, Marsh dispatched an agent to secure the land. Not one to be left out, Cope secured another site in Colorado.

By this stage, two unscrupulous fossil finders who worked for Union Pacific railway, hoping to get themselves into the middle of a bidding war, leaked news that they had found large quantities of fossils in the Como Bluff region of Wyoming.

An agent acting on behalf of Cope actually stole fossils from the Como Bluff site owned by Marsh. Just after this, one of the fossil finders, who was sick of Marsh's less-than-forthcoming ways with monies owed, switched allegiance to Cope. So by the time that both Cope and Marsh had relocated themselves physically to Colorado, the area of Como Bluff had become the epicentre of the Bone Wars.

There was spying, bribery and outright theft between the two camps. At one point, work was interrupted so that the feuding archaeological workforces could engage in an all-out rock-throwing battle from one dig site to the other. I can't help but think that the producers from *Time Team* could take a leaf out of the story of the Bone Wars, just to ramp up the action a little.

Perhaps even more disturbing than that was the fact that both Marsh and Cope would destroy undisturbed portions of dig sites – often with dynamite – so that their competitor couldn't find anything left to plunder among the detritus when they left.

I use the word 'plunder' intentionally. Sure, both men were motivated by scientific glory and academic acclaim, but fossils were and still are big business. Museums, universities and private collectors would pay huge amounts of money for these incredibly fashionable fossils.

That's not to say that no scientific good came from the digs. Dinosaurs as well known as *Stegosaurus*, *Allosaurus* and *Diplodocus* were first unearthed during the Bone Wars. In fact, between the two of them, Cope and Marsh discovered and named about 130 new species of dinosaur, as well as many others, some of which were later dismissed as possibly judicious (or accidental) rearrangements. Both palaeontologists knew the value of keeping up with publicity.

After a while, more and more archaeological teams flooded into the area, including one from Harvard. Cope and Marsh would spend their final years in bitter acrimony, either in front of Congressional hearings or in the pages of the *New York Herald*. Marsh lost his prestigious and well-paid position at the Geological Society.

Both men had amassed considerable fortunes and had wasted them fighting each other in the courts. Another unfortunate result was the black mark against American palaeontology and scientific endeavour on the world stage, which would take decades to overcome.

Perhaps the strangest moment of their feud would actually involve their own bones. Just before he died in 1897, Cope made it known that he wanted his skull preserved, for one purpose and one purpose only – that upon Marsh's death their two skulls could be examined side by side. Then the world would know that Cope was the smarter of the two of them.

Marsh probably proved him wrong by declining this challenge outright, choosing to be buried intact. (Cope's skull, to this day, sits in a storage facility at the University of Pennsylvania.)

Over a century later, the story of these two obsessed and bitter enemies was still so compelling that HBO considered making a television series about them, starring James Gandolfini and Steve Carell. Unfortunately, Gandolfini died before the project eventuated, which is why 'Ross' is still probably the best known palaeontologist of our time.

John Wilkes and the Georgian Mic Drop

John Wilkes is probably one of the most confounding characters of eighteenth-century British politics. At one point he championed freedom of the press and was a provocateur of the establishment, which had almost unchallengeable powers at the time. A wit, a duellist, a bankrupt, a journalist, a politician and a scoundrel,

Wilkes is considered to be both one of the founders of English Radicalism and a self-serving bigot.

Out of all the contradictions of his long life (1725–1797), his one constant was an absolute loathing towards John Montagu, better known as the Fourth Earl of Sandwich (yes, that guy – the one who named but didn't invent the sandwich). And the feeling was certainly mutual.

They were both members of that hotbed of sexual misbehaviour that had sprung up in the middle part of the eighteenth century known as the Hellfire Club, which regarded itself as a congenial society of 'Medmenham Monks', who sought knowledge by exploring extreme forms of pagan and Christian rituals. Basically, they were a bunch of upper-class toffs having orgies in abandoned abbeys and cellars, or anywhere else they could organise to gather for a bit of pseudo-black-mass robes-off hijinks.

It was rumoured that the falling out between Wilkes and Montagu had its origins in their completely opposed political beliefs. Montagu was a staunch believer in the status quo as opposed to Wilkes's youthful radicalism. Then there is another story that, apparently just for a bit of fun, Wilkes attended a night of debauchery at the Hellfire Club in the company of a rather strange guest. He had brought along a baboon dressed up in a cape and robes.

Montagu thought that this completely lowered the whole tone of the orgy and was furious at Wilkes for spoiling the night's fun.

Okay, it's just a rumour, but it's a *good* rumour.

Wilkes, despite being married to Mary Meade, to whom he owed both his wealth and status, was an appalling pants man who was always going to end up buck naked with other like-minded gentlemen of that notoriously over-sexed part of England known as Buckinghamshire.

The fact that Wilkes was encouraged to enter politics by his fellow members of this secret society was probably something of a harbinger of his later crash or crash-through political career.

Actually, it was mostly crash.

His first attempt to gain a seat in parliament in 1754 came to nothing, despite the fact he committed one of the greatest acts of voter fraud imaginable. The story goes that Wilkes caught wind that a shipload of his opponents' supporters were making their way up from London to vote against him. This flood of ring-ins was certainly dubious, but not as dubious as Wilkes's response: he bribed the ship's captain to sail these interlopers, not to their intended destination of Berwick, but rather to far-off Norway.

Three years later, he knew better and pursued a more conventional pathway to office, sinking the not inconsiderable sum of 7000 pounds (over a million dollars in today's money), mostly in bribes, into his campaign. He soon found himself the Right Honourable Member for Aylesbury, a place where he could escalate the battle with his lifelong foe, the Fourth Earl of Sandwich.

Even though both men were card-carrying members of the Medmenham Monks, they were at opposite ends of the political spectrum. But even better than having political dirt, these two were more than aware of each other's 'extracurricular activities'.

Which brings us to one of the greatest put-downs in political history.

Sandwich once loudly proclaimed that Wilkes would die either by hanging or the pox. To which Wilkes shot back, 'That depends, my lord, whether I embrace your principles or your mistress!'

That's one serious burn! It would be at this point in today's world that Wilkes would have dropped his mic and walked off stage.

Bad to the Bone

Obviously, we are not the first generation to be concerned with and somewhat obsessed by the undead. The whole rising-from-the-grave and feasting-on-the-living caper has been a bog-standard part of human folklore for centuries. What we didn't realise until recently was just how serious our medieval forebears took their zombie-proofing tactics. If newly discovered gravesites in North Yorkshire are any indication, it would appear that villagers from the lost hamlet of Wharram Percy were exceedingly concerned with making sure that the dead stayed beneath the soil.

Archaeologists came across the buried remains of many folk dating back to the eleventh and fourteenth centuries. Among these remains they also discovered around ten individuals whose bodies had been mutilated in a peculiar way and, in some cases, burned. Stranger still, evidence suggested that these violent acts had occurred *post-mortem*, and probably after burial.

Reprehensible

Some scholars leaped to a conclusion of cannibalism. While cannibalism was not unheard of in that part of England, especially during times of medieval famine, their reasoning was based more on the observation that the cuts made into the skeletons were mostly found around the head and neck area. But this wouldn't have been the carving method of your average starving cannibal serf, who would have sliced away at the more delicious joints and large muscle groups.

So the archaeologists proposed a different theory, as reported in the April 2017 edition of *New Scientist:* 'The idea that the Wharram Percy bones are the remains of corpses burnt and dismembered to stop them walking from their graves seems to fit the evidence best,' says Simon Mays, skeletal biologist at Historic England. 'If we are right then this is the first good archaeological evidence we have for this practice. It shows us a dark side of medieval beliefs and provides a graphic reminder of how different the medieval view of the world was from our own.'

You just keep believing that Simon.

Digging deeper into the folklore of the British Isles, we find the undead described in somewhat different terms to how they were envisaged throughout the rest of Europe. On the Continent, the undead were often considered to be the wandering corpses of those who had been wronged – say, *murdered* – and were now seeking revenge on the culprits who had treated them poorly. In Romania and parts of Eastern Europe, a zombie could be someone who had died while suffering from the heartbreak of unrequited love or who had simply just died unmarried, despite being of a marrying age.

It was also a common belief that if a cat, a guaranteed spreader of disease, came too close to a corpse it was pretty certain you'd soon have a zombie on your hands. Then again, this was pretty much good sense when death from war, famine and in particular *pestilence* were so prevalent, and cats even less fussy than they are these days. So many corpses, so many cats . . .

In Britain, however, the undead were often characterised as people who had been pretty awful when they were alive and continued to be pretty awful after death. William of Newburgh talks about these malevolent walking dead in his twelfth-century work *The History of English Affairs* where, among other stories, he relates the tale of one particularly nasty (and dead) fat bastard. At night, he would visit his poor wife, who wasn't exactly grieving, and continue to make the same nuisance of himself as he had when he was above ground: 'Not only did he terrify her when he woke her up, but he also nearly crushed her under the immense weight of his body!'

William's writings from the period would also strengthen the argument that these mutilated skeletons in North Yorkshire were actually the result of villagers trying to keep the not-so-dear departed where they belonged.

He tells the story of the village of Berwick in Scotland, where the parishioners were beset by the wandering corpse of a man who had been a 'scoundrel' in life and was terrifying them in death. William writes about how the corpse would nightly rise from the grave and be 'followed by a pack of loud barking dogs'. The dogs, he assumed, were actual living dogs disturbed by this supernatural visitation.

The villagers believed 'the very air would become infected and corrupted by the repeated wandering of this foul corpse, causing disease and the deaths of many people'. A remedy was devised: 'They enlisted ten young men to dig up the abominable corpse. Once they had chopped it limb from limb, they set it alight and made it food for the fire. When this was done, the affliction ceased.'

This remedy, according to William, came from the rotten mouth of the zombie himself: 'For this monster, while it was being animated – as it is said – by Satan, is said to have told certain people who it encountered by chance that they would not have any peace so long as he was unburned.'

Then William goes on to tell the story of the wicked priest who had the notorious nickname of *'Hunderpriest'* meaning 'Houndpriest', which he had gained from his extravagant obsession with hunting. After his death, his corpse pursued his still-living mistress (yes, he was a naughty priest) until a monk came to the woman's aid. One night he came upon the zombie *Hunderpriest* and went at it with a battleaxe before following it back to its resting place, where he dug it up and burned it.

William's final tale is of a husband who fell to his death from the rafters of his home while spying on his wife committing adultery. He was buried but soon rose from the dead and, like the previous dead Scotsman, would roam at night accompanied by a pack of baying hounds, spreading disease.

Two brothers who had lost their father to the zombie's curse took it upon themselves to dig the body up, cut out the heart, dismember and burn it. Or, as William describes it, 'When that infernal monster was thus completely destroyed, the pestilence that had prowled among the people ceased, as though the air, which had been corrupted by his loathsome activity was cleansed by the fire that had consumed that wretched cadaver.'

It would seem that we have always had a morbid fear of the walking dead, but the idea of being bitten by a zombie and then *becoming* a zombie is a pretty modern concept – and probably just a good way of making sure you can make sequels to the original series.

Hans Christian Bore

In 1857, Charles Dickens scribbled a short note and posted it on the mirror in the guest room of his house. It simply read: 'Hans Christian Andersen slept in this room for five weeks – which seemed to the family AGES!' The note, in effect, marked the end of a friendship that had started a decade before as a mutual admiration society.

In July of 1847, Dickens was already a literary star with classics such as *Oliver Twist* and *A Christmas Carol* established bestsellers. Andersen was starting to gain a reputation outside of his native Denmark. By 1837, his first collection of fairy tales had been published, which, although slow to sell at first, contained such classic stories as 'Thumbelina', 'The Emperor's New Clothes' and 'The Little Mermaid'. It was an 1845 translation of that last story that brought him the first burst of international fame from which his popularity exploded.

Reprehensible

Upon meeting, Andersen described Dickens with these words: 'He quite answers to the best ideas I had formed on him.' Dickens, who was never averse to a bit of flattery, was somewhat taken by the younger man, and the next day he presented Andersen with a copy of his new book, *The Chimes*, with the inscription, 'Hans Christian Andersen, from his friend and admirer, Charles Dickens. London, July 1847'.

I think I need to point out that, as gifted a writer as Hans Christian Andersen was, his personal life was somewhat complicated. One of his (fortunately) unpublished works was his personal diary. He would often (actually, *very* often) just make the symbol '+' on the page. It would seem that that symbol meant he had masturbated. He would write about visitors both male and female arriving at his house to pay their respects. After he had described the visit, a '+' (or even multiple '+'s) would appear on the diary's page.

Or he would head off into Copenhagen to visit with prostitutes – not to engage in sex but rather to have as long a conversation as his money would allow. He would recall these conversations in his diary, and then the crosses would appear . . .

He was, dare I say, prolific in both his professional and personal callings.

For the next nine years there was a steady stream of correspondence between the two great men of letters. Well, actually, that stream pretty much just flowed from Denmark to England. Andersen was a bit smitten, platonically speaking, with Dickens, and his letters would include long, gushing passages extolling Dickens's brilliance. He would also send new work for his friend

Feuds, Fights & Insults

to evaluate, and brag to his peers about his close relationship to the great English writer. Sometimes Dickens would reply, sometimes not, for as much as he loved being reminded of his greatness, there was a needy tone to Andersen's letters.

It is for this reason that historians are divided about the nature of Dickens's letter to Andersen, sent in July 1856: 'In these nine years you have not faded out of the hearts of the English people but have become even better known and more beloved.' Some people believe that Dickens's gushing prose was motivated by guilt, others that he wrote it with genuine affection. Some cynics think he was actually taking the piss. There's little guessing which camp Hans Christian Andersen fell into, but instead of answering that letter personally, he announced to the Danish press that he would be visiting England with the express purpose of seeing his esteemed fellow author. Dickens would only find out about the intended visit when it was later reported in the London press.

To avoid further embarrassment, Andersen quickly wrote and informed him, 'My visit is for you alone. Above all, always leave me a small corner in your heart.'

Dickens acquiesced, and after being promised by Andersen that he would be staying no more than two weeks – and probably somewhat less than that – the reunion of the two men was underway and Andersen boarded a steamer to London.

And that's when the duckling gets ugly.

Dickens let slip his concerns about his upcoming house guest when he warned another friend, who was thinking of visiting, 'Hans Christian Andersen may perhaps be with us, but you won't

Reprehensible

mind – especially as he speaks no language but his own Danish and is suspected of not even knowing that.'

Within a few days Dickens would be forced to amend his opinion: 'He speaks French like Peter the Wild Boy and English like the Deaf and Dumb School. He could not pronounce the name of his own book *The Improvisatore* in Italian; and his translatress appears to make out that he can't speak Danish!'

But, sadly, it took even less than a few days for the unfortunate visit to turn sour. Upon waking on his first morning in the Dickens household, Andersen let it be known how disappointed he was that his host had not provided him with a servant to perform the task of giving him a morning shave. He then went on at great lengths to explain to Dickens that if a servant was not available to perform such a task, it was considered – according to ancient Danish custom – that a guest's morning shave was the responsibility of the eldest son.

I'm here to report that there is and never has been any such Danish custom regarding the shaving of house guests. They do have some rather wacky customs about bats, but that's for another story.

Dickens was then forced to engage the local barber and a hansom cab to make sure that Andersen received his morning shave, at his. This enraged the great author – Andersen, that is, not Dickens. Andersen would regularly complain that Dickens was shirking his shaving duties, according to Danish custom, which I feel I need to reiterate *never existed*!

Speaking of hansom cabs, Dickens would later relate to his friend, William Jerdan, 'Whenever [Andersen] got to London,

Feuds, Fights & Insults

he got into a wild engagement of Cabs and Sherry, and never seemed to get out of them again until he came back here, and cut paper into all sorts of patterns, and gathered the strangest little nosegays in the woods.'

I originally thought that 'Cabs and Sherry' must have been some sort of company in the city that Andersen was at odds with, until I came across this other paragraph by Dickens:

> One day he came to Tavistock Square, apparently suffering from corns that had ripened in two hours. It turned out that a cab driver had brought him from the City, by the way of the new unfinished thoroughfare through Clerkenwell. Satisfied that the cabman was bent on robbery and murder, he put his watch and money into his boots – together with his Bradshaw [railway timetable], a pocketbook, a pair of scissors, a penknife, a book or two, a few letters of introduction and some other miscellaneous property.

This raises a couple of questions. How bloody big were those boots? What sort of person recovers from an uncomfortable altercation by cutting paper into patterns? (The collecting of 'nosegays' – small bouquets of flowers – I *almost* get.) It turns out Andersen was the sort of disagreeable, drunk passenger that ride-share schemes put on the 'don't pick up' list.

Then there was the time Andersen received a bad review and spent the afternoon loudly weeping on Dickens's front lawn. Or the night he attended a play in which Dickens starred in the lead role. Andersen left in a huff because Dickens got more attention than he did at the after-show soirée. And let's not forget, he said he'd stay – at most – two weeks! He ended up freeloading for more than five weeks.

Suffice to say, after one rather innocuous letter where Dickens recalls the weather during Andersen's visit, Charles never contacted Andersen again. Perhaps the last words should go to Dickens's daughter Kate, who would later recall Andersen as 'a bony bore' who 'stayed on and on'.

I Didn't Learn That in High School Latin

All I can really recall from high school Latin is that 'there is a dog in the street' (*canis est in via* seemed to cover it) and apparently some bloke called Grumio was a slave cook. I *may* have heard of the poet Martial (born Marcus Valerius Martialis) and how he followed in the footsteps of the great Roman poets Virgil and Horace.

But that's about it.

It was only later in life that I came to appreciate the works of Martial and discovered that he wrote in something called epigrams – short poems usually written to comment on the foibles and intrigue of Roman life, particularly among the rich and powerful. These epigrams would range from the most noble of satiric musings through to the downright filthy and bitchy.

Let's examine some of those that you definitely wouldn't find in a Year Nine Latin exam, starting with this all-time classic putdown:

You're an informer, and a lying witness, a defrauder and a middle-man, a cocksucker and a provocateur. Vacerra, I can't understand why you're not rich.
(11.6, trans. Nisbet)

Or this smackdown, directed towards one of Martial's casual acquaintances, warning him of the dangers of deploying, to use a modern phrase, 'too much information':

You often tell me you've been sodomised,
Callistratus, as if you know me well.
You're not as candid as you wish to seem.
Who tells such things has more he *doesn't* tell.
(12.35, trans. McLean)

And while on the subject, there is this somewhat bizarre insult from another epigram:

Want to know how bony your arse is, Sabellus? It's so bony you could bone other people with it.
(3.98, trans. Nisbet)

I get the feeling that you really had to know Sabellus and his bony backside to understand this physically impossible jibe. Or maybe something got lost in the translation?

One epigram that definitely does not risk misinterpretation is the 1608 translation by Francis Davison, which captures all the filth and venom of Martial's original words and relates them in a way that is still wonderfully disgusting, not only to those

Reprehensible

of the early seventeenth century but to us, reading it over four centuries later:

> I muse not that your Dog turds oft doth eat;
> To a tongue that licks your lips, a turd's sweet meat.
> (Epigrams 1, 83)

Then there are times when you get the feeling that Martial is serving as Rome's gossip columnist, albeit one who would happily write and publish in the sort of language that not even the raunchiest of newspapers would ever consider using today. Not only does he chide the powerful and wealthy Aeschylus for visiting a well-known prostitute, he also claims that he always gives her extra money just so she won't tell anyone of his visits.

Seriously powerful Romans must have viewed hearing the news that Martial was composing some verse about them as the ancient equivalent of 'Ronan Farrow is thinking of doing a profile piece on you; is there anything we should be worried about?'

There was, however, one person whom Martial would often write about in the most glowing of terms imaginable, and that was, well . . . Martial himself! This is actually the first poem from his first book of epigrams (talk about a sense of self-promotion):

> Here is the one you read and ask for:
> Martial known the world around
> For witty books of epigrams, whom you devoted reader crowned
> With fame, while he has life and breath;
> Such as few poets get in death.
> (1.1, trans. Mclean)

I feel I need to reiterate that this is the opening to his *first-ever* volume of epigrams. As Brooke Clark points out in her article '10 Reasons You Should Be Reading Martial', 'The tone he strikes is more Kanye West than small press poet.'

By the time he gets to his second-last book, his sense of self-worth shows no sign of waning. He is by then an international hit, and he wants everyone to share in his glory:

> My recondite Muse does not beguile just Rome's spare time,
> nor do these poems reach only the ears of the leisured;
> No, my book is reread by the tough centurion beside the battle standard amid Getic frosts. Even Britain is said to have our poems by heart.
> (11.3 II. 1-5, trans. Nisbet)

To be totally honest, not all of Martial's work is bitchy, braggadocios or filthy. He is, at times, capable of great beauty in his writing. There is heartfelt sorrow and exalted words of love beautifully crafted into his work.

That aside, I can't help but feel that if I'd had a bit more of the potty-mouthed, scurrilous Martial in my studies and a bit less of the endless verb conjugations, I might have actually passed my high school Latin.

Chapter Four:
Wayward Geniuses

There is a wonderful book by science writer Florian Freistetter titled *Isaac Newton: The Asshole Who Reinvented the Universe*, which includes the sage words of David K. Love, who, apart from being an authority on the work of Newton's forerunner Johannes Kepler, is also a Fellow of the Royal Astronomical Society. He encapsulates the waywardness of not just Newton but many other geniuses when he says, 'Sir Isaac Newton is something of a paradoxical figure. On one hand, he was an undeniable genius. On the other hand, he was a thoroughly unpleasant individual, who unnecessarily made enemies and who also devoted huge amounts of time to researching what would be now seen as absurd ideas on alchemy and the contents of the Bible.'

One of Newton's more fanciful Biblical equations led him to pronounce that the world would end in 2060. His calculations are based on a passage from the Book of Daniel in the Old Testament, and are as follows:

> So then the time times & half a time are 42 months or 1260 days or three years & an half, reckoning twelve months to a year & 30 days to a month as was done in the Calendar of the primitive year. And the days of short-lived Beasts being put for the years of [long-]lived kingdoms the period of 1260 days, if dated from the complete conquest of the three kings A.C. 800, will end 2060. It may end later, but I see no reason for its ending sooner.

Well, that's a relief.

He was also an alchemist, always on the hunt for what was called 'the philosopher's stone', a mystical element that could

Reprehensible

turn base metals into silver or gold. And he was an appalling misogynist who most probably died a virgin. As you will see in this chapter, he was also a dark and somewhat scary teenager and young man. Quite the résumé for someone considered to be the embodiment of the Age of Enlightenment.

That's the problem with finding out the quirks of geniuses; they also tend to be many of our personal heroes.

Which brings me to the can of worms known as C.S. Lewis. Before I start wading into that quagmire, might I first state that as a child I *loved* the Narnia books. From the age of eight to eleven I always had one by my bedside. I'm not saying that I actually ventured into my grandparents' wardrobe in search of a portal into a mystical realm, but the thought did cross my mind on more than one occasion.

However, these days Lewis deeply divides the literary world. To some, particularly those of an evangelical persuasion, a virtual cult has grown up around C.S. Lewis and his fantastical and theological writings. One place of worship in California actually created a stained-glass window made in his image. Then there are those who deride him as a racist, imperialist Christian apologist.

As for me, I remember *The Chronicles of Narnia* as a great collection of stories that I just sort of grew out of – stories right up there with his friend and rival J.R.R. Tolkien.

Lewis first met Tolkien in 1926 at a Merton College English faculty meeting at Oxford. Lewis would record this meeting in his diary, using these words to describe the man who would go on to be his life-long pal: 'smooth, pale, fluent little chap ... no harm in him; only needs a smack or so.'

Wayward Geniuses

Ah, the smack.

This brings up one point of contention not widely discussed in seminary classrooms about C.S. Lewis: was he or was he not a kinky sadist?

One of Lewis's greatest friends was the poet Arthur Greeves. Their friendship lasted decades, and when they could not be together in person, they were enthusiastic letter writers. Even as young men, they would pour out their thoughts to each other on matters of religion, literature, love and . . . I'll just let this extract from a 1917 letter from a nineteen-year-old Lewis speak for itself (bearing in mind that he could be talking about Greeve's sister, Lily): '"Across my knee" of course makes one think of positions for Whipping: or rather not for whipping (you couldn't get any swing) but for that torture with hairbrushes. This position with its childish nursery associations would have something beautifully intimate, and also very humiliating for the victim.'

This does not seem like a letter written by a young man who was just 'BDSM curious'. The creator of Aslan seems fairly well educated in the nature of handing out corporal punishment. Another interesting detail: he signed the letter as 'Philomastix', which is Greek for 'lover of the whip'.

Then there was the time when, as a student, he was thrown out of an Oxford party for the simple reason that he was offering his fellow students a shilling each if he could take them into a bedroom and give them a spanking.

Talk about your *Fifty Shades of Narnia*.

However, not all literary geniuses were students of the Marquis de Sade. Some, like Victor Hugo and Johann Wolfgang von Goethe, had simple, run-of-the-mill foot fetishes.

Reprehensible

Just look at the great Russian poet Alexander Pushkin, who in his outstanding verse novel *Eugene Onegin* slips in this foot-related stanza:

> Alas, on every stray amusement
> I've wasted far too many hours,
> Yet were they wholly innocent
> I'd still wander those bright bowers.
> I love youth's frantic energy,
> The crush, the lights, the gaiety,
> The girls in fashionable dress,
> I love their little feet, confess
> That, search all Russia though,
> You'll not find three lovely pair.
> Ah, they made me long despair.
> Two slender feet . . . Now sad and cold
> I still remember, and it seems
> They yet can thrill me in my dreams

Published in serial form between 1825 and 1832, the complete *Eugene Onegin* did not see the light of day until 1833, and Pushkin regarded it as his favourite work. And that's a poet with a pretty amazing back catalogue.

As far as poems go, it's rather lovely – it's just about a part of the anatomy that normally doesn't get a lot of attention. But hey, what's normal?

That's what sets them apart from the rest of us. Sure, some of their behaviour can be dismissed as eccentric, like Victor Hugo

Wayward Geniuses

writing in just a large grey shawl in an empty room (not nude, as is often reported), deprived of all comforts, to aid his concentration.

Or chess genius Bobby Fischer, who reportedly had some of the fillings in his teeth removed to stop the Russians from transmitting radio waves into his head. (Now that I read it back, his behaviour goes way off the eccentric chart and ventures deep into 'that's a bit of a worry' territory.) But back to eccentric . . .

No one batted an eye when Salvador Dali opened up his jewel-encrusted cigarette box to offer them a moustache, all waxed and fashioned to resemble his own. (They were probably too busy keeping an eye on the great painter's barely trained ocelot.)

Then there was that master of opera, Richard Wagner, who would carry on lengthy conversations with his King Charles spaniel, Pep. It's sort of fun to think that when he was writing the opera *Tannhäuser* he would actually play passages to Pep and ask for his opinion. Sort of like a Wagnerian version of Ron Burgundy and Baxter.

But there is a line where the 'creative eccentric' blurs into the 'wayward genius', and that's what this chapter explores. As philosopher Immanuel Kant once said, 'Genius is the ability to independently arrive at and understand concepts that would normally have to be taught to another person.'

He, like Newton, died a virgin.

Your Move, Elon

Nikola Tesla (1856–1943), among others of his era but greatly more so, helped create much of what we regard as the modern world. A polymath, we can see his theories and inventions at work every day in the areas of electricity, wireless communications, X-rays and radio – there is even a theory that he invented a 'death ray', a concept that would later be popularised by science fiction writers in the 20s and 30s. Although never fully proved, I add it for dramatic effect.

He did, however, create over three hundred patents, developed the first motor to run on AC power, along with pioneering radio control devices, the plasma lamp, and much of what we would consider to be the modern torpedo – and that's just the tip of the invention iceberg. And just for fun he fluently spoke eight different languages.

What could possibly drive one single individual to have the intellect and purpose to create so many amazing inventions – inventions that seemed to come directly from his singularly fervent imagination?

In a word: celibacy.

This was driven by several factors. He was a life-long germophobe, was obsessed with personal hygiene, and had more than a few personal quirks, one of which was oystersaritis-phobia, or an irrational fear of pearls. They disgusted him to the point where he once sent a secretary home from work because she had arrived with a string of the 'offensive', softly glowing orbs around her neck. It was well known that he could not even engage in a conversation with a woman who was wearing any sort of pearl adornment. And seeing as pearls were the height of nineteenth-century fashion among the ladies in whose circles he travelled, it must have made life interesting, to say the least.

But what probably kept him out of the sack more than anything was his long-held belief that, in his own words, 'I do not think that you can name many great inventions that have been made by married men.' Apparently even a great mind can be selective when it comes to rearranging historical facts.

It would seem that he channelled all of his pent-up romantic and sexual energy into his work and speculations on future inventions. At the start of the twentieth century he wrote an essay predicting what we would now call a 'smart phone'. Many of his inventions and theories are still classified to this day. (I did mention 'death ray'.)

That is not to say he never found love or companionship; it just came rather late in his life and it was, well, more than just a bit odd. Rather than attempt to encapsulate this unique relationship myself, I think it only right that Nikola Tesla be allowed to speak for himself:

> I have been feeding pigeons, thousands of them for years. But there was one, a beautiful bird with light grey tips on its wings – that one was different, it was a female. I had only to wish and call her and she would come flying to me.
>
> I loved that pigeon as man loves a woman, and she loved me. As long as I had her, there was purpose to my life.

It's amazing how that statement can be sweet, odd and scary at the same time. I think it's best not to ponder too long on, firstly, just how Tesla knew that the pigeon was female and, secondly and more worryingly, how this could be equated to male–female human love. However, like all great love stories, it comes with a tragic conclusion. Tesla was by this late stage of his life living in the Hotel New Yorker when one day the pigeon flew into his room and he had a shuddering premonition of her imminent demise.

She passed away very soon after, he would later write in his journal. 'When that pigeon died, something went out of my life. Up to that time I knew with certainty that I would complete my work, no matter how ambitious my program, but when that something went out of my life, I knew my life's work was finished.'

He, too, died soon after writing those words, some say from a broken heart.

It would be a century later before the name 'Tesla' would once again be linked with both visionary engineering and erratic behaviour. So on one side you have a genius pigeon fancier who never made any money, and on the other side a genius billionaire whose sex life we know way too much about.

I guess that's some form of progress.

Jean-Paul Sartre's Crabs (It's Not What You Think – It's Weirder)

John-Paul Sartre was the archetypal manifestation of the twentieth-century intellectual – a writer, philosopher, fearless breaker of political and social taboos . . . and a man deeply frightened of shellfish. Yes, that's right. The great thinker had an irrational fear of most sea creatures, but had a particular dread of crustaceans.

This was a man who was stalwart enough in his convictions that he actually hid from the Nobel Prize Committee rather than compromise his ethics and accept its award, yet he probably could not have sat through Disney's *The Little Mermaid* without running from the cinema terrified out of his mind halfway through the first verse of 'Under the Sea'.

Sartre traced his fear back to a painting he had seen as a child. The work depicted a giant crab claw rising from the ocean about to drag some poor human down to a watery grave. This fear was so strong that it often kept him out of the ocean.

There is a story that he suffered from a panic attack in the water off the Riviera while swimming with his great love Simone de Beauvoir. He became convinced that a giant octopus was pursuing him, intent on drowning him in the depths of the sea. He had to be rescued, and afterwards sat on the shore shaking in terror at his perceived predicament.

Simone was also present when one of the strangest crab-related incidents of Sartre's life would take place. The year was 1929. Both were exceptionally gifted students at the École normale supérieure. Sartre was seeking inspiration for some writing he was working on, so he decided to inject himself with a dose of mescaline, just so he could record the effect that it would have on his mind.

I think we should also note that Sartre's experimentation with the psychedelic drug occurred almost forty years before it would catch on with the rest of the Western world. I'm not saying that that's a *good* thing, but at least he didn't put out a double album with half-hour-long guitar solos. However, he did have what hippies would later refer to as a 'bummer trip'. As his biographer Gary Cox would later write, 'Sartre does not appear to have had a bad trip in the classic sense of suffering a major panic attack . . . But it was not a good trip and he did not enjoy it.'

Jean-Paul had taken way too high a dosage and, from the dark recesses of his repressed childhood terrors, he began imagining menacing crabs and lobsters, along with octopi and jellyfish. Even after the initial trip had worn off he still suffered from hallucinations – hallucinations of a rather specific and somewhat curious nature.

Jean-Paul would later relate the tale in a 1971 *New York Times* interview with Professor John Gerassi: 'Yeah, after I took mescaline I started seeing crabs around me all the time. They followed me in the street, into class. I got used to them. I would wake up in the morning and say, "Good morning, my little ones, how did you sleep?" I would talk to them all the time. I would say, "Okay, guys, we're going to class now, so we have to be still and quiet," and they would be there around my desk, absolutely still, until the bell rang.'

Gerassi then asked, 'A lot of them?' To which Sartre almost nonchalantly replied, 'Actually, no, just three or four.'

Fortunately, after an entire year of hanging out with the crabs, Sartre sought help from a young psychiatrist named Jacques Lacan. Lacan would go on to be one of the twentieth century's leading thinkers in the field. Through psychoanalysis, Lacan came to the conclusion that the crabs were a manifestation of Sartre's childhood grab bag of fears; firstly, of being alone and alienated. And then, more literally, his morbid fear of crabs.

Sartre would return to his crab obsession years later in the play *The Condemned of Altona*, where one of the play's protagonists, Franz, has a horrific vision of the future, where crabs from the thirtieth century are judging humanity and Franz is the defendant for our species.

He never touched mescaline again (that we know of) and spent most of his adult life, according to another biographer, Annie Cohen-Solal, getting by on a daily regime of 'two packs of cigarettes, several tobacco pipes, over a quart of alcohol (wine, beer, vodka, whisky etc.), two hundred milligrams of amphetamines, fifteen grams of aspirin, a boatload of barbiturates, some coffee, tea and a few "heavy" meals'. Amazingly, Sartre actually made it to the age of seventy-four.

We Need to Talk About Isaac

There is no doubting that Sir Isaac Newton was one of the towering figures of his day. He is still seen as the greatest scientist, the living embodiment of the English Enlightenment, and a man who rose to great power and respect through the force of his deeds and intellect.

He was also a misanthrope, a religious zealot, a wacky alchemist and a misogynist with weird attitudes to not only women but also pretty much all of his fellow human beings. And he had a very nasty and petty vindictive streak.

This is why it's going to take more than just one passage to unload his somewhat considerable personal baggage, but I'm guessing a pretty good place to start is with his own words. Just before his nineteenth birthday, a young Newton wrote down an extensive list of sins, which he considered himself guilty of during the previous year. It is a great insight into not only a devout but also somewhat troubled soul. His confessions contain some trivial (activities undertaken on the Sabbath) and some which are, quite frankly, terrifying.

He divides them into two groups, the first being 'Before Whitsunday, 1662':

1: Using the word (God) openly. *Okay, blasphemy was a little bit stricter in its definition back in the day.*
2: Eating an apple in Thy House. *I get it, you shouldn't snack during mass. The role of that particular fruit in his later work is actually up for debate. The first mention of Newton, a falling apple and its relation to his theory of gravity comes in a biography written by his younger contemporary and acolyte, William Stuckley. There is, however, evidence that an aged Newton, who had read the biography, would relate the apple story (minus the blow to his head) to the point of boring the breeches off most of his colleagues.*
3: Making a feather on Thy day. *I'm assuming this has something to do with either fishing or farting.*
4: Denying that I made it. *I'm going to go with farting. Actually, it's probably a physics experiment involving a vacuum and a*

feather that has its origin with the work of Galileo but wasn't finally proven until Newton perfected the vacuum. This is my theory anyway.

5: Making a mouse trap on Thy day. *Probably just a mouse trap.*
6: Contriving of the chimes on Thy day. *This is just playing on some chimes, as you do.*
7: Squirting water on Thy day. *No idea what this refers to. I'm guessing it means washing or cleaning something on Sunday, because I can't remember any scripture saying you can't take a pee on the Sabbath.*
8: Making pies on Thy day. *Come on, this can't be a sin. I know it's toiling but it's toiling to make a pie.*
9: Swimming in a kimnel on Thy day. *A kimnel was most usually a large wooden tub, often used for salting meat. So, yuck, Isaac, yuck!*
10: Putting a pin in John Keys hat on Thy day to pick [prick] him. *That's just childish.*
11: Carelessly hearing and committing many sermons. *Look, we've all dozed off at church – don't be too hard on yourself, young man.*
12: Refusing to go to the close at my mother's command. *Probably just a stage he was going through.*
13: Threatening my father and mother Smith to burne them and the house over them. *Talk about burying the lead! We have to wade through all that 'on Thy day' crap before we find out young Isaac threatened to burn down the house of his mother and his stepfather with them both in it. You sort of get the feeling that someone may have a great sense of mathematics but a pretty lousy sense of prioritising sins.*

14: Wishing death and hoping it to some. *I think I made my feeling clear in the above sin.*
15: Striking many. *Um, any chance of defining 'many'? Apparently not, but I think you might be getting a better picture of why we need to keep an eye on Sir Isaac, and why one of the best titled works about the great man comes from the Austrian astronomer Florian Freistetter:* Isaac Newton: The Asshole Who Reinvented the Universe.
16: Having unclean thoughts, words, actions and dreams. *Almost worryingly normal.*
17: Stealing cherry cobs from Eduard Storer. *In light of recent information, I think Eduard got off lightly.*
18: Denying that I did so. *Trust me, Mr Storer, don't push it. This kid is dangerous.*
19: Denying a crossbow to my mother and grandmother though I knew of it. *Oh great – the kid's somehow got his hands on a bloody crossbow, and he's denying its existence. As they say on the Crime Channel, 'This is a serious red flag!'*
20: Setting my heart on money, learning pleasure more than Thee. *I can't help but feel that we're glossing over the whole burning, punching, death-wishing, crossbow thing!*
21: A relapse.
22: A relapse. *Not exactly sure what these two relapses are referring to. I just hope that it doesn't involve either fire or that crossbow.*
23: Breaking again of my covenant renewed in the Lord's Supper.
24: Punching my sister. *Oh, he's a charmer.*
25: Robbing my mother's box of plums and sugar.

26: Calling Dorothy Rose a jade. *A 'jade' means a 'disreputable woman' – I mentioned earlier that he has serious issues with women . . .*
27: Gluttony is my illness. *Quite frankly, young man, gluttony is the least of your problems.*
28: Peevishness with my mother.
29: Peevishness with my sister. *You really want to peeve them, tell them about the crossbow.*
30: Falling out with the servants. *I'm just going to assume that he was not a joy to work for.*
31: Divers commissions of all my duties. *Well, I guess it's hard to stay focused when you are splitting your time between changing the face of science and plotting the murders of those around you, plus all that crossbow practice. (I mean, seriously, am I the only person who's worried that this guy has a deadly weapon?)*
32: Idle discourse on Thy day and at other times.
33: Not turning nearer to Thee for my affections.
34: Not living according to my belief.
35: Not loving Thee for Thy self.
36: Not loving Thee for Thy goodness to us.
37: Not desiring Thy ordinances.
38: Not longing for Thee in [illegible].
39: Fearing man above Thee.
So 32 through 39 is just your regular laundry list of God-bothering sins – the usual, 'I'm not worthy' stuff. Then . . .
40: Using unlawful means to bring us out of distress. *And that's all he says on 'unlawful' behaviour before ducking back into the pious young man routine.*

41: Caring for worldly things more than God.
42: Not craving a blessing from God on our honest endeavours.
43: Missing chapel.
44: Beating Arthur Storer. *Arthur was the son of Eduard Storer, from whom Newton had stolen the cherry cobs. Newton was also said to have a rather clumsy crush on Arthur's sister, Katherine. The three children were virtually raised together. Arthur, like his friend and sometimes bully Isaac, would go on to a distinguished scientific career of his own, and after emigrating was considered to be the first astronomer of the American colonies. Newton would actually often cite Storer in his later work. Arthur even discovered a comet that was named Storer's Comet in his honour, so at least he got some recognition. That is, until some guy later predicted the comet's return . . . and that guy's name was Halley.*
Still, Arthur ended up with a planetarium named after him in Prince Frederick, Maryland. So it wasn't all bad for the Storers.
45: Peevishness at Master Clarke for a piece of bread and butter. *So, he roughly equates not sharing bread and butter with handing out a beating to poor young Arthur.*
46: Striving to cheat with a brass halfe crown. *Once again, see sin 40 – it would seem his crimes were not just violent but cunning.*
47: Twisting a cord on Sunday morning. *Whatever!*
48: Reading the history of the Christian champions on Sunday. *Oh, you self-serving little suck-up.*

Then there came a shorter list of sins he had committed after Whitsunday, 1662. These start with the usual suspects.

49: Gluttony
50: Gluttony

Then . . .
51: Using Wilford's towel to spare my own. *There is no embellishing of this story other than the somewhat creepy fact that Newton used another man's towel rather than dampening his own.*
52: Negligence at the chapel.
53: Sermons at St Marge. *I'm assuming more negligence.*
54: Lying about a louse. *The dirty bugger.*
55: Denying my chamber fellow of the knowledge of him that took him for a sot. *That's more than just a bit uppity.*
56: Neglecting to pray.
57: Helping Petit to make his water watch at 12 of the clock on Saturday night. *Once again, he engaged in science on the Sabbath.*

So, there we are – these 'confessions' paint a somewhat unusual portrait of a man of undeniable genius but somewhat troubling personal traits. As I mentioned at the start, it's going to take more than a few segments to trawl through all of Newton's tales of misbehaviour, like the time he stuck a needle in his own face . . . or his worrying prediction for the end of the world. I'll put it like this: don't make any firm plans for 2062.

And They All Lived Happily Ever After, Really

In my own humble opinion, *King Lear* is not only the greatest of Shakespeare's tragedies, but it is also one of the most moving plays ever performed in any language, on any stage. Whose heart doesn't melt in the final scene as (spoiler alert) Lear cradles the body of his daughter Cordelia in his arms, his world crashing in around him?

Well, if you were a theatregoer from the late-seventeenth up until the mid-nineteenth century, your heart would be uplifted and actually filled with joy! You wouldn't have been watching the dark, brooding tragedy we know and love. You would have been at a performance of Nahum Tate's bastardisation, *A History of King Lear* – the tragicomic romp with the happy ending! The one where Lear regains his throne, where Cordelia lives and goes on to marry Edgar, who at one point declares, 'Truth and virtue shall at last succeed.' The one where the pivotal character of the Fool has been completely removed!

Written in 1681, Tate describes how he came up with the idea to fiddle about with Shakespeare's masterpiece. Reflecting on the original play, written nearly eighty years earlier, he told how he had discovered, 'A Heap of Jewels, unstrung and unpolisht, yet so dazzling in their Disorder that I soon perceived I had seized a treasure.' Tate felt compelled to 'rectify what was wanting in the Regularity and Probability of the Tale'. I guess these days it would be like hearing that Maroon 5 were about to release a more toe-tapping version of Pink Floyd's *Dark Side of the Moon*.

And, to add insult to injury, Tate's play was an instant hit. In his words, he was 'rakt with no small Fear' on its debut, however he 'found it well receiv'd by the Audience'. So much so that for the next century and a half it would be pretty much the only version of *Lear* to be performed on the English-speaking stage.

Although derided by scholars, paying audiences flocked to see this '*King Lear* Lite'. The author, critic and moralist Samuel Johnson preferred the happy ending, saying that he had always found the death of Cordelia unbearable. He wrote, 'In the present case the public has decided. Cordelia, from the time of Tate, has always retired with victory and felicity.'

Even the great eighteenth and nineteenth-century Shakespearean actors, such as David Garrick and Edmund Kean, performed Tate's *Lear*, not Shakespeare's. While Garrick was known to adapt Tate's text and often reinstated some of the original, he never varied from that travesty of having a happy ending. This prompted Garrick's contemporary, playwright and poet Frances Brooke, to marvel why Garrick should 'prefer the adulterated cup of Tate to the pure genuine draught offered him by the master he avows to serve with such fervency and devotion'.

Shakespeare's original play lived on only in printed form and was considered far too dark to be commercially viable on the stage.

The theatrical world was spared Tate's travesty for a few years in the early part of the nineteenth century but not, sadly, for its reprehensible crimes against drama. It was actually banned because it was thought that – even with the happy ending – the actions of an ailing and possibly insane king could be interpreted as an insult towards the erratic behaviour of the monarch, King George III.

After the ban was lifted in 1823, Edmund Kean decided that, although he had previously performed Tate's *Lear*, he would respond to the growing chorus of critical demands and give the London audience Shakespeare's original – in all its tragic glory.

The show folded after only a few performances.

However, by the late 1830s, more and more productions upped the Shakespeare content and slowly audiences were weaned off Tate's sanitised version. By 1845, Samuel Phelps, also working in that great English tradition as both theatre manager and actor, had restored *Lear* to its original Shakespearean glory. After a 150-year run, Tate's play was relegated to history, apart from the very occasional academically curious revival.

In the United States, however, Tate's version would continue to be performed for another thirty years. The first notable performance of the original was in 1875, when Edwin Booth took up the role of the tragic king. And if that surname sounds familiar, Edwin was the brother of John Wilkes Booth – fellow actor, and the man who assassinated Abraham Lincoln at Ford's Theatre.

Bake and Shake

The Ancient Greeks were incredibly comfortable with dildos. (Now there's a sentence I never thought I'd write.) Dildo jokes abound in the plays of Herondas and Aristophanes. In fact, Aristophanes' *Lysistrata*, first staged in 411 BC, is one long string of dildo gags.

Dildos appear in Greek art and pottery, and were particularly popular on drinking vessels used by both sexes – depictions of people engaging in erotic acts with these toys, some of which were double-ended or were attached to either a man or a woman by use of a cloth or leather strap. So it would seem that both the double-dildo and the strap-on dildo have been around since ancient times. (I sort of always assumed that anyway.)

Actually, the oldest carved phallus hails from a region we now know as Germany. It is 28,000 years old and archaeologists believe that, due to its impressive proportions – 20 centimetres long and 3 centimetres wide – its primary use was not just ceremonial, if you get my drift. The ancient Egyptians were said to use unripe bananas, carved stone or wood. There's even one particularly unpleasant sounding sex toy made out of camel dung, shaped by hand and left to harden in the sun before being covered with resin.

So by the Golden Age of Hellenic culture, the Greeks would have been well aware that the dildo had been around for centuries. They even had cute slang names for their sex toys that roughly translate as either 'sliders' or 'strikers', the reasons for which I will leave up to your reprehensible imagination.

Now just like any other treasured household item, not all dildos were created equal. The best ones came from a small town called Miletus (in modern-day Turkey) and were finely carved from ivory, rare woods or even marble.

Another popular alternative was a firmly padded leather phallus, which, once oiled up, seemed to be popular with both the men and the ladies.

But what if your budget did not run to such hand-crafted luxury items?

Well, you'd still be in luck. Around the fifth century BC a new word came into common use among sex-toy-loving Greeks: *olisbo-kollix*. This word quite simply translates to 'bread-stick dildo'. And this is one of those occasions where the translation explains exactly what the object was and what it was used for.

There are some historians who disagree, believing that this was just a crude name made up to mock phallus-shaped bread. But there are more than a few remnants of pottery that depict *olisbo-kollix* being put into genuine sexual practice. Either way, just try and keep a straight face the next time you see someone walking past with a baguette proudly poking out of their grocery bag.

Jingle Them Bells

When I was a child my grandmother would get very upset when we substituted the original lyrics of 'Jingle Bells' with the eternally amusing 'Jingle Bells, Batman Smells' rendition. She complained that we were profaning a beloved and joyous Christmas carol.

Well, Mumma (as we used to call her), 'Jingle Bells' is not actually a Christmas carol – it was written to celebrate the American holiday Thanksgiving. But more than that, it was originally a drinking song, extolling the virtues of drunken street racing, written in a tavern by a man who most historians regard as being a bit of a jerk.

The jerk in question was James Lord Pierpont, who came from some seriously noble family stock. James Pierpont (J. P.) Morgan, the uber-wealthy financier, was his uncle, and his father was a well-respected man of the cloth and something of a minor poet.

James Lord, however, ran away from home at an early age to become an unsuccessful whaler. He abandoned his first wife with his father, had a failed attempt at gold prospecting, and by 1850 was living in the town of Medford, Massachusetts.

According to Kyna Hamill, a professor of literature at Boston University and vice-president of the Medford Historical Society, a certain pastime popular in that town was the genesis for the song. In a 2014 interview on CBS's *Daybreak* program, she explained, 'Medford was home to a series of sleigh races that used to occur on a street called Salem Street, and because of this event, which pretty much happened in the middle of the nineteenth century, these sleigh races – which you could pretty much call drag races – down this street was one of the most popular events. Because of that, the influence and inspiration of the song, we believe, came from those races.'

Hamill goes on to talk about how Medford was a town famous for rum-making and high spirits. 'Some of the words [in "Jingle Bells"] are actually associated with the idea that this is a song you sing while you're drunk, talking about an event that happened while you were drunk.'

Reprehensible

For example, all you have to do is look at the lyrics of the now rarely (if ever) sung second and fourth verses:

> A day or two ago
> I thought I'd take a ride
> And soon Miss Fanny Bright
> Was seated by my side,
> The horse was lean and lank
> Misfortune seemed his lot
> He got into a drifted bank
> And then we got upsot.

And the fourth verse gets even more rowdy.

> Now the ground is white
> Go it while you're young,
> Take the girls tonight
> And sing this sleighing song:
> Just get a bobtailed bay
> Two forty as his speed
> Hitch him to an open sleigh
> And crack you'll take the lead.

Apparently the custom of the time was to jiggle the ice cubes in your drink in time with the 'jingle bells' in the chorus of the song.

So how did the song become a beloved Christmas carol?

Well, James Lord barely waited for his first abandoned wife to die (he didn't even attend the funeral) before marrying the daughter of the mayor of Savannah, Georgia. Once in town he became musical director of the local Unitarian church. During a Thanksgiving service he performed the song (probably censoring out the latter verses) and it was an instant hit. It was performed again at Christmas, and the song we know today (sort of) grew in popularity and was officially published, with Savannah laying claim to being the home of 'Jingle Bells'.

And so does Medford, Massachusetts.

And they both have plaques that say as much.

Either way, I'm still with,

Jingle bells, Batman smells
Robin laid an egg.
The Batmobile
Lost a wheel
And the Joker got away.

This version came into popular usage within a year of the television show *Batman*, starring Adam West and Burt Ward, going to air in 1966. There is one theory that the Batman version was spread globally through the children of US military personnel scattered around the globe during this time of Cold War tension, after originating on a Californian military base.

Could be . . . or it could also be that 'smells' rhymes with 'bells', and kids liked Batman.

Descartes & the Cross-Eyed Women

I am fully aware that 'Descartes & the Cross-Eyed Women' sounds like the name of an appalling hipster folk band, but the fact is that for much of his life the great philosopher René Descartes had a thing for cross-eyed women. Actually, it was more than just a 'thing' – it bordered on a fetish.

He explained as much in a letter to Queen Catherine of Sweden, just one of the many powerful women of Europe with whom he regularly corresponded.

He was talking about himself as a boy when he wrote these words: 'I loved a girl of my own age . . . who was slightly cross-eyed; by which means, the impression made in my brain when I looked at her wandering eye was joined so much to that which also occurred when the passion of love moved me, that for a long time afterward, in seeing cross-eyed women, I felt more inclined to love them than others, simply because they had that defect: and I didn't know that was the reason.'

I'd love to think that her reply was, 'New phone, who dis?'

But obviously that's impossible. Her actual reply is unknown, but also not needed. Descartes was using one of the most powerful women in the world as a sounding board, someone in front of whom he could unravel his thoughts, even if only on paper.

Descartes would then go on to state that once he had recognised the cause for his attraction to such women, he was able, by free will and deduction, to 'cure' himself of this fascination.

Descartes' fetish for cross-eyed women seems quite mild when compared to the masochistic urges of fellow philosopher

Jean-Jacques Rousseau, who would confess, over a century after Descartes' death: 'To be at the knees of an imperious mistress, to obey her orders, to have to beg her pardon, have been for me the sweetest delights.'

And this was something that Rousseau had long been aware of. He once only half-joked that when he was a child he suspected that his governess stopped spanking him because she realised that he was enjoying it just a bit too much.

Ah, philosophers – such a fun crowd.

Man Your Pumps

The ancient Roman medical practitioner Galen (Claudius Galenus) had some pretty unusual musings when it came to human sexuality – one being that procreation was only possible when both the male and the female achieved orgasm. Galen believed that the 'vital heat' created by a sexual frisson was essential for conception to occur.

Well, it was worth a try.

Somewhat even more unusual was his recommended remedy for men who were having difficulty achieving an erection. Galen seemed to think that the body needed a certain amount of internal 'wind' to inflate the male organ. He also adhered to the belief that spices, dried peas and mustards (all thought to create excessive flatulence) could also play a vital role in helping to inflate a man's jumping castle. To be fair, he did seem to assume that blood also played a part in getting the job done – Galen was a bit of a pioneer in that field. He was the one, after all, who in the second century AD gave us the first schematic layout for the circulatory system.

Galen was pretty concerned with all matters sexual. He considered it essential to a man's health that his seed be released on a regular timetable.

Thanks, Galen – where were you when my mother discovered my adolescent stash of porn magazines? You could have given her a wonderful dissertation on why I was keeping myself free of pneumonia and all the other diseases you warned against.

Maybe you could have used this explanation, from your essay *On the Affected Parts*?

> Diogenes the Cynic, it is related, was mighty of all people in regard to everything from self-control to endurance. He indulged with sexual lusts, not associating it with pleasure, an attractive good thing to some, but because of the harm that retention of semen would cause if he avoided the habit of releasing it. When a prostitute who promised to visit him was delayed for some time, he rubbed his genitals with his hand, ejecting semen. After the whore [sorry, I don't like that word, but it's the translation I'm going off of] arrived he sent her away, saying, "My hand celebrated the wedding-hymn first". But it is clearly correct that likewise the disciplined man does not on account of pleasure indulge in lusts, but in order to relieve hindrance acting as if this was not associated with pleasure.

Probably wouldn't have worked on my mother . . .

She would have pointed out that the above was a rather narrow reading that had obviously been chosen for a self-serving purpose. And I would have giggled at the unintentional pun.

Well, If You Gotta Go . . .

Chrysippus was one of the great minds of the ancient world – if you doubted that, all you had to do was ask him. Apparently an Athenian man once did just that. When he inquired of Chrysippus which teacher of philosophy he should send his son to study under, the great Stoic thinker replied, 'To me, for if I thought there was anyone better than myself, I would have gone to him to teach *me* philosophy.'

Chrysippus actually did study under two great philosophers of the time after moving to Athens from Soli, in Asia Minor, around 250 BC. He had read and expanded on the original writings of the founding father of Stoicism, a philosophy centred on discipline over the emotions and the repression of pleasure and pain, Zeno of Citium, and had been such a brilliant student of the other great Stoic thinker, Cleanthes, that when Cleanthes passed away around 230 BC, Chrysippus found himself as the third head of the Stoics.

Stoicism flourished in both the ancient Greek and Roman world, and this philosophy of personal ethics informed by logic over passion and emotion has long been a constant thread through

Reprehensible

Western culture, enjoying revivals in both the Renaissance and then again in more recent times. (Stoicsm is not to be confused with Modern Stoicism, which is its own movement that first gained international attention in 2012 with the launch of the first-annual Stoic Week, a festival of philosophy that draws crowds in the thousands.) Chrysippus was such a dominant figure within this school of thought that for centuries the motto of the Stoics was, 'If Chrysippus had not existed, neither would Stoa [the founder of the philosophy].'

He wrote over 700 works on philosophy, and an old woman who lived with him maintained that Chrysippus would pump out some five hundred lines of wisdom a day. In short, he was a philosophical heavyweight.

Sadly, none of his work has survived, and what we know about him today is mostly through quotes used by later philosophers . . . and the weird-arse story about how he died. For this, we are fortunate to have the writings of Diogenes Laërtius, who gives us two varying accounts of the death of the great thinker, written some three hundred years after the reported fateful incident.

They both start at the same point: Chrysippus had spent the day at the 143rd Olympiad and then attended a feast at which he consumed more than his fair share of wine. While walking home, he saw an old woman feeding figs to a donkey and, in his inebriated state, found this to be hysterically funny. He then drunkenly suggested, 'Now give the donkey pure wine to wash down the figs,' pure wine being a potable that had not been diluted, or sweetened or flavoured with herbs.

Well, that did it.

Wayward Geniuses

The donkey started guzzling down the wine and Chrysippus absolutely lost it, breaking into fits of hysterical laughter. We do know that Chrysippus had a rather unusual laugh, particularly when he'd had a few drinks. Diogenes Laërtius noted that the philosopher would keep his upper body completely motionless but enthusiastically wiggle his legs in time with his chortling.

On this day, however, the sight of the fig- and wine-consuming donkey made his body quiver all over. The seventy-three-year-old foamed at the mouth, still chortling hysterically, and promptly died, as onlookers tried to help to no avail.

One of the founding fathers of a philosophy that sought to extinguish emotions had died of excessive laughter. For those of you who like your irony served dry with a twist, this does seem a fitting end.

Even though Laërtius tells this version of events, he then digresses and comments that it is his personal belief that Chrysippus had probably died of alcohol poisoning after a hard day's drinking. He found it just too hard to believe that someone could actually die from inebriated donkey related chortling despite being well aware of the story of the Greek artist Zeuxis, who in the 5th century BC had mockingly painted Aphrodite as an old woman, as opposed to her usual representation as the young goddess of love and beauty. Zeuxis found this caricature so amusing that he also laughed himself to death. The Greeks said that this was a form of divine retribution. (I guess you probably had to be there.)

Then there are other figures in history who have supposedly died from having a laugh, like King Martin of Aragon, who in 1410 met his maker after his court jester apparently told him a fatal joke that coincided with a bout of indigestion. I wonder if that jester ever had trouble getting gigs after that, particularly ones involving feasts. The Italian poet, satirist, playwright and inventor of modern literate pornography, Pietro Aretino, was said to have suffocated from laughing too much, as did Thomas Urquhart, the Scottish writer and aristocrat who found the news that Charles II had been made king too hilarious to handle.

In modern times, laughing deaths have been linked to the 'Ecky Thump' routine performed by the Goodies (a personal favourite), the movie *A Fish Called Wanda*, and one chap in a New York hospital in the 1990s who didn't make it to the end of one particularly funny episode of Seinfeld.

Mozart: Two Pianos, One Cup

There is no denying that Wolfgang Amadeus Mozart was one of the greatest composers in Western music, if not *the* greatest. And like all geniuses, 'Wolfie' had his fair share of personality tics. The one that is most often cited is his juvenile love of toilet humour. Tom Hulce, portraying Mozart in the movie *Amadeus*, has the maestro finish off a piano concerto by standing up from his stool and loudly farting at the audience. The good folk of Vienna roar with laughter and burst into rapturous applause. It's a cute scene, but it only tells part of the story.

I like a good fart joke just as much as the next person, but Mozart's taste in scatology moves beyond the simply humorous and ends up in the realms of something decidedly more fetishist. Among his over six hundred compositions was a choral piece written for six people that bore the title 'Lick My Arse'. Sadly, the lyrics to this song have been lost over the centuries.

We do, however, have the lyrics to his follow-up hit 'Lick My Arse Nice and Clean'.

Imagine, if you will, a Viennese parlour in the second half of the eighteenth century. There have been witty conversation, drinks are flowing, and a silence falls over the room as six choristers take their place to sing the latest offering from the great Mozart. And it goes a little something like this:

Lick my arse nicely,
Lick it nice and clean,
Nice and clean, lick my arse.
That's a greasy desire,
Nicely buttered, like the licking of roast meat, my daily activity.
Three will lick more than two,
Come on, just try it.
And lick, lick, lick.
Everybody lick his own arse himself.

That's exactly how it went, and I really think it loses nothing in translation.

You would have to agree that one song on the topic of anallingus can be dismissed as bawdy humour, but two songs – and with that amount of detail – it's starting to look like the great composer had a bit of a felching fixation.

This is borne out even more in Mozart's personal correspondence.

There was the letter to an attractive cousin that speaks of his desire to 'shit on her nose' and then watch it 'drip down her chin'. But it is the letters to his own mother where things get fruity. He tells her, 'Yesterday, though, we heard the king of farts. It smelled as sweet as honey tarts. While it wasn't in the strongest of voice, it still came on as a powerful noise.'

Okay, probably inappropriate but certainly not as bad as what he wrote to his cousin, but wait, there's more! In another letter to his mother he signs off, 'I now wish you goodnight, shit in your bed with all your might, sleep with peace on your mind and try to kiss your own behind.' He continues: 'Oh my arse burns like fire! What on earth is the meaning of this . . . maybe muck wants to come out? Yes, yes muck.'

I did mention that these were letters to his *mother*, didn't I?

From all this, I think we can safely state that, yes, Mozart was a genius and, yes, he had a few faecal preoccupations. And this is just a guess, but I'm also assuming he had pretty awful breath.

Some Fine Farters

In her wonderfully titled 2007 book *On Farting: Language and Laughter in the Middle Ages*, Valerie Allen explains to us that, 'There was a lot of moralisation about farts and shit, that they are the living daily reminder that we are going to die and that's all we are, we are mortal, and sinful as well.' This is, of course, not just true for the Middle Ages but for all time. Then there are those of us who don't live on lofty old Mount Pious (and I'm definitely not saying Valerie Allen does). We love nothing more than a good ol' trouser cough.

St Augustine wrote in the fifth century of famous performers who would 'produce at will such musical sounds from their behind (without any stink) that they seem to be singing from that region'. The plays of Aristophanes are littered with fart jokes, and even back before then, farts gave us what many historians regard as the first-ever recorded joke. This particular rib tickler comes from the ancient Sumerians around the year 1900 BC. It translates as, 'Something which has never occurred since time immemorial: a young woman did not fart in her husband's lap.' I guess you had to be there.

One of the most celebrated of all flatulists (yes, that's the word for a professional farter) was a beloved performer from the twelfth-century English court of Henry II. Although known under many names – Roland le Sarcare, Roland le Fartere, Roland le Petour – he is remembered today simply as Roland the Farter. And Roland was famous for one simple act: every Christmas he would perform for the court his show-stopping routine, 'One Jump, One Whistle and One Fart'.

So enamoured was Henry II of Roland's act that he gave him a manor house in Hemingstone, Suffolk, and a thousand acres of land – not bad for turning up once a year and performing your little flatulence jig. Unfortunately for Roland, Henry III was something of a prude and considered Roland's act to be 'indecent'.

Reprehensible

As a result, he confiscated both his manor and all his lands. But hey, that's show business.

Although high-performance farting never fully disappeared from the entertainment arena, it would take many centuries for a flatulist to emerge with an entrepreneurial talent to rival Roland's. By 1892, a young entertainer was becoming the talk of Paris. He was born Joseph Pujol, but he performed under the name Le Pétomane – 'The Manic Farter'.

According to Pujol, he had discovered his amazing ability as a boy while swimming near his childhood home on the Côte d'Azur. As he dived beneath the waves, he felt a shot of cold water up his backside. He would later claim that the process of holding his breath had also given him the ability to 'inhale' water up his rectum.

For a while, this was the basis of his act: he would draw up and then shoot jets of water out of his bum. By the time he was an adult, these jets could be up to five metres long. As time went by, he also came to the realisation that he could apparently 'inhale' air into his backside. After a short stint in the army, he toured France using this new-found talent to perform renditions of 'La Marseillaise' and 'Au Clair de la Lune', as well as a whole range of comic noises and 'impressions'.

By 1892, his act had expanded and he was hired to perform an hour-and-a-half show at no less an establishment than the Moulin Rouge.

Music journalist and fart historian Jim Dawson describes how Pujol would appear on stage: 'He dressed in a tuxedo and announced each sound as if he were presenting a music solo.

Of course, the incongruence of a dignified gentleman letting farts only added to the humour.'

But in a ninety-minute set you have to be able to do more than a few tunes with your bum to keep the fickle Parisian audience entertained. Pujol could apparently smoke a cigarette with his sphincter; he could also blow out candles on a cake. One of the highlights of his act relied on his long-held knack for shooting water out of his bum and across the stage. This culminated in his knocking out a few of the theatre's footlights.

When reports got around that some women had fainted during his performance, the Moulin Rouge was said to have stationed nurses throughout the theatre in case the Manic Farter's performance proved too much for audience members to handle. (This clever piece of marketing would be used by horror movie promoters years later.)

Pujol became one of the highest paid performers in Europe, and to supplement his income he would put on private shows for wealthy gentlemen. To satisfy their medical curiosity, he would ditch the tuxedo and perform his routine completely naked. Such was the interest in him that there was even a medical thesis written in 1904 about his anatomical gift, wonderfully titled *An Extraordinary Case of Rectal Breathing and of Musical Anus.*

After a three-year gig at the Moulin Rouge, Pujol had a falling out with management. Bizarrely enough, they sued him for 'breach of contract' after he was caught giving a quick demonstration out the front of a local gingerbread stand. Go figure.

Pujol won a settlement and opened his own nightclub, where he spent the next few years happily farting away, much to the amusement of his considerable fan base. The club closed down in World War I, and little was heard of him until he passed away peacefully in 1945 at the ripe old age of 88. Which proves the enduring adage: 'Better out than in.'

These days the most acclaimed farter is Paul Oldfield, who is better known by his stage name, Mr Methane. Methane has been touring regularly in his green tights and superhero cape since the 1990s and has appeared in television commercials, many comedy festivals and, due to his musical bum, has even put out a Christmas album. Although, Methane does complain that video sharing on the internet has caused much of his live work to dry up.

But, as Roland the Farter would say, 'That's show business.'

H.G. Well, Well, Wells

There are some hardcore science fiction fans who suffer from the dreadful prejudice that they flock to alternative worlds to make up for the gaping hole left by their inability to form intense physical relationships with other human beings. Indulging in marathon gaming sessions, elaborate dress-ups and cosplay doesn't exactly help this perception.

Maybe these cultural snobs would change their minds and stop looking down their snooty noses if they knew just what a relentless mattress artist the universally acknowledged father of that unfairly maligned genre actually was. I am, of course, talking about H.G. Wells, who in his later years would reflect back on his life with these words: 'I have done what I pleased, so that every bit of sexual impulse in me has expressed itself. I am a very immoral person. I have preyed on people who love me.'

Actually, he was so enthusiastically 'on the job' that it's amazing he ever found time to write over a hundred books of essays, history and futurology. His four main novels, from *The Time Machine* through to *The Island of Doctor Moreau*, *The Invisible Man* and, of course, *The War of the Worlds* were all written in a frantic four-year period between 1895 and 1898.

He was, it would seem, a man who was unafraid to apply maximum effort and force of will into any endeavour he undertook. He would later brag that during his affair with the novelist Elizabeth von Arnim he had broken her hotel bed on two separate occasions. Although, in the words of another great Englishman, George Michael, Wells preferred his sexual exploits 'Outside'.

He described two al fresco episodes during his affair with the feminist scholar and writer Amber Reeves, where they would make love 'among windy bushes in a windy twilight near Hythe'. On another occasion, he convinced a church sexton that he and Amber wanted to inspect the belfry for purely architectural reasons, and once alone had made sweet love in that belfry. Over twenty-five years later, Wells would recall his 1908 affair with Amber as 'unregretted exhilaration and happiness'. He fails to mention that Amber's father, Pember (now there's a name you don't hear much these days), was said to have lain in wait for Wells out the front of his London club, brandishing a loaded revolver.

Considering the failed marriages, affairs with well-known women and his siring of at least one illegitimate child, it's amazing that Wells managed to keep himself out of the scandal sheets of the London papers. He even nurtured a long-term affair with his beloved Moura, the Baroness Budberg, who apart from being Maxim Gorky's English translator was also considered to be a Russian spy, and just for good measure she was also the lover of British spy Robert Bruce Lockhart, who many consider to be the real-life inspiration for James Bond. Moura seems to have been an expert in what we now know as 'multi-tasking'.

Then there was his affair with the socialist writer Odette Keun. Wells would later write about their initial meeting, where he was summoned up to a hotel room to meet a 'dark and slender young woman in a flimsy wrap and an aroma of jasmine [who] flung herself upon me with protests of adoration'. Odette, it turns out, was more than a handful. She once threatened to publish a book on their affair, complete with extracts from the hundreds of pornographic letters H.G. had sent her. Wells dismissed this, saying he would either sue the publisher or, if that proved unfruitful, he would revel in the reputation that the book would bestow upon him.

On another occasion, Odette turned up at Amber's house with a pistol and proposed that both women hunt down the man who had caused them such heartache. Fortunately, Amber declined.

And let's not forget that Wells was by no means a handsome man. He was short, more than a bit pudgy, and also possessed a rather unpleasant, high-pitched, whiny speaking voice. Despite these conventional limitations, one lover described him as smelling of walnuts, and another of smelling like honey. So I guess if you're the sort of woman who gets aroused by muesli bars, H.G. Wells would have been exactly your sort of man. Yet another paramour described him as a lover who 'frisked like a nice animal'. Make of that what you will. Wells described himself as the 'Don Juan of the intelligentsia', so I guess in the end it was that mind of his they were after as much as his bed-breaking abilities.

His second wife, Jane, a former student of his (you could sort of see that coming), often turned a blind eye to his shenanigans. Wells, who seems to have had an excuse for everything, simply said of Jane: '[She] had always regarded my sexual imaginativeness as a sort of constitutional disease.'

One of his other great quotes regarding his sex life was, 'Sex is as necessary as fresh air', which, although romantic, is not, according to my high school science, biologically true. And there is this classic line: 'Moral indignation is jealousy with a halo.' Even if you don't respect the sentiment, you have to enjoy the wit.

But of all his statements rationalising his randy behaviour, there is this classic, almost proto-feminist, example that he would use when casting his mind over his years of bed-hopping. He said that as early as his teenage years he had fantasised about 'free, ambitious, self-reliant women who would mate with me and go their way'.

Sure, he may have been an early proponent of what would later come to be called free love. And, yes, he predicted many of the technological and social changes that would come to embody the last hundred years of human achievement. But he is still the source – and must carry the blame – for one of the greatest over-indulgences of 1970s bloated rock-and-roll. I am referring, of course, to Jeff Wayne's dreadful *War of the Worlds* concept album, which was cherished by rock nerds like myself. That's right, science fiction nerds, you're not the only dateless losers with a connection to H.G. Wells.

And before I am done with the randy ol' Mr Wells, I feel I have to relate one last story that, though probably apocryphal, is still too good not to mention.

According to rumours, Wells kept all of his book reviews, the good and the bad. One afternoon, he and his lover at the time gathered together a pile of the bad ones and made frantic love on top of them before then setting them alight.

Anyone who has ever had to cop a bad review, I include this anecdote just for you.

'Wherever You Be, Let Your Wind Fly Free . . .'

This line by Molly Bloom from James Joyce's iconic doorstopper of a novel *Ulysses* is just one of the myriad examples that illustrate the importance given to bodily functions – and flatulence, in particular – in the writings of the great Irish genius. His characters are constantly defecating, belching, urinating and masturbating – it's a joyous mixture of poetic language and end-of-season footy trip. The role played by farting in his *personal* life is a bit more specific and probably not something that would appeal to most people. To understand this, it is essential to read the 1909 love letters written by Joyce to his wife, Nora Barnacle.

First off, I have to say that I love the fact that Joyce's wife had a name that could have been lifted straight off the page of one of his novels. And second, I should say that these letters can be interpreted as tender, erotic, pornographic or just plain gross, depending on both the reader's moral standpoint and the nature of the particular passage that is being read. Also keep in mind that these are the writings of a lonely 27-year-old, longing for his wife at home.

Some are quite poetic: 'You are always my beautiful wild flower of the hedges, my dark-blue rain drenched flower'. The fact that this is preceded by a reference to Nora as 'my little frigging mistress! My little fucking whore' should not diminish its sweetness. I'm not one to pass judgement on what pet names other couples use to arouse each other, but suffice to say that in modern times this is one sext that probably would warrant deleting.

Joyce then goes on and gets more than a bit raunchy, letting Nora know just how much he enjoys her distinctive pillow talk: 'little whore tells me she wants me to roger her arseways'.

The only comment I can pass on this phraseology is that I sort of regret the fact that 'roger' has virtually slipped out of our sexual lexicon. It is, however, the inclusion of the word 'arseways' that gives something of a whiff of what is about to come.

Reading further, you soon realise that the author of *The Dubliners* and *Finnegans Wake*, among other great masterpieces, was more than just an observer of the levelling nature of farting, grounding as it does all humans in their most base, vulnerable and silly states. No, he was actually turned on by the act. I think this becomes more than evident in the letter that includes these immortal lines, where he is reminiscing on a night of passion with Nora:

> Fat dirty farts came spluttering out of your backside. You had an arse full of farts that night ... big fat fellows, long windy ones, quick little naughty farties [gotta love that phrase] ending in a long gush ... I think I would know Nora's farts anywhere.
>
> I think I could pick hers out in a room of farting women. It is a rather girlish noise not like the wet windy fart which I imagine fat wives have. It is sudden and dry and dirty like what a bold girl would let off in fun in a dormitory at night. I hope Nora will let off no end of her farts so that I may know their smell also.

The other parts of these letters oscillate wildly between the profane and the profound, sometimes sweetly endearing and sometimes troubling and weird. But, personally, I find the contents of the letters off-putting and soul-touching at the same time, much like the first time I attempted to read *Ulysses*.

The Original Booze Cruise

I've been on a few holiday cruises in my time and have found them by and large quite fun, if a little overindulgent. Let's be honest; even for a modest drinker (which I am not) something happens once land disappears over the horizon and life becomes a twenty-four-hour happy hour. There are many historical precedents for this.

Seafaring and booze have been constant companions since Roman and Greek sailors complained of the algae that would accumulate in the water barrels they would take on campaigns. For years, the British navy virtually floated on a daily ration of rum and sometimes madeira. The French, unsurprisingly, kept their sailors well supplied with wine while the Dutch, as one might expect, handed out gin on a daily basis once their navy ships had left shore. During the American Revolutionary War, the Continental Navy made sure that each sailor received half a pint of rum each day, with more rum to be distributed to help soothe combat nerves.

Sailors have for centuries been used as an emblem for excess drinking, and for quite some time this was probably a fair analysis. But most likely no expedition was more booze-fueled than the great second voyage of discovery undertaken by the Portuguese explorer Ferdinand Magellan, who we all learned at school was the first person to circumnavigate the globe.

In 1517, with backing from King Charles I of Spain – and not the Portuguese, which would become something of a sore point later – he set sail with five ships, all laden to capacity with some 417 wineskins, to be used for the simple purpose of keeping his crew happy. We don't know exactly just how much wine each skin contained, but we do know for certain that the cost of this huge amount of wine was considerably more than the price of Magellan's flagship, the *San Antonio*.

Reprehensible

Then there were the 253 kegs of sherry, which, just like the wine, proved to be one of the greatest expenses of the trip. In fact, Magellan spent more money on providing his crew with just sherry than he did on fitting out his whole little fleet with weapons, which were crucial to have on such a long and dangerous voyage. Obviously alcohol was an important part of any voyage's budget, but the extent of this lopsided provisioning had little precedent.

There is one theory about why so much grog was needed on this particular journey. Unlike the passengers on a modern-day holiday cruise, Magellan's crew was a pretty rough lot (okay, stop snickering). They came from all over Europe and many were ex-prisoners, while some were actual prisoners 'seconded' for the journey. Alcohol was considered one way of holding off mutiny plots.

This didn't work, by the way. Some of the crews mutinied anyway, and Magellan had the ringleaders hung, drawn and quartered. (Look, he might have been liberal with the drinks, but that didn't make him a nice guy.) And it's no wonder they mutinied – conditions on board were especially harsh, and it actually managed to get even worse.

Once they were out on the Pacific Ocean they quickly ran out of food and potable water. One sailor who kept a journal of the voyage describes how the men would catch rats to either eat themselves or sell for exorbitant prices to their fellow sailors. In his defence, Magellan really had no idea how big the Pacific actually was, so it's understandable that he under-catered, and it also emphasises just how much he over-catered on the wine and sherry.

By the time the fleet stumbled across Guam in the Western Pacific, they were at the point of complete starvation, but they still had enough booze to keep themselves well inebriated. Having replenished their supplies on the island, they continued on to the Philippines, where things took a determined turn for the worse.

Apart from being a cruel disciplinarian and a rabid colonialist, Magellan was also a zealous evangelical Christian – in his first few weeks in the Philippines it is said that he converted over two thousand of its local inhabitants. To impress his new Christian friends, he got involved in a tribal skirmish with local leader Lapu-Lapu and 1500 of his warrior mates on the island of Mactan on 27 April 1521. Tribal skirmishes rarely end well for the colonialist, and Magellan was brought down by a spear.

A year later, when the one remaining ship, the *Victoria*, limped back to port with only eighteen survivors, the bad press against Magellan really started to escalate. The Portuguese already regarded him as something of a traitor, and some early deserters had arrived back in Spain, where they bad-mouthed him relentlessly. *Victoria*'s captain, Juan Sebastián Elcano, who some say was actually the first person to circumnavigate the globe because, well, he made it home, did not hold back on running his former leader's reputation into the dirt either.

It would take several years and the publishing of the diary of Antonio Pigafetta, another survivor of the journey, before Magellan was seen in a more favorable light. However, he is still remembered to this day in the Philippines on Lapu-Lapu Day. It's a day honouring the leader who repelled Magellan and his

Reprehensible

boozy mates, and involves excessive partying and heavy drinking, which does seem a bit ironic.

As for comparing Magellan's voyage with a holiday cruise, of course this sixteenth-century voyage was far more harrowing. There were bloody mutinies, savage battles, starvation and disease – but at least no one knocked over the champagne fountain, locked themselves naked outside their cabin or urinated at the swim-up bar.

Chapter Five:
Vanity Not–So–Fair

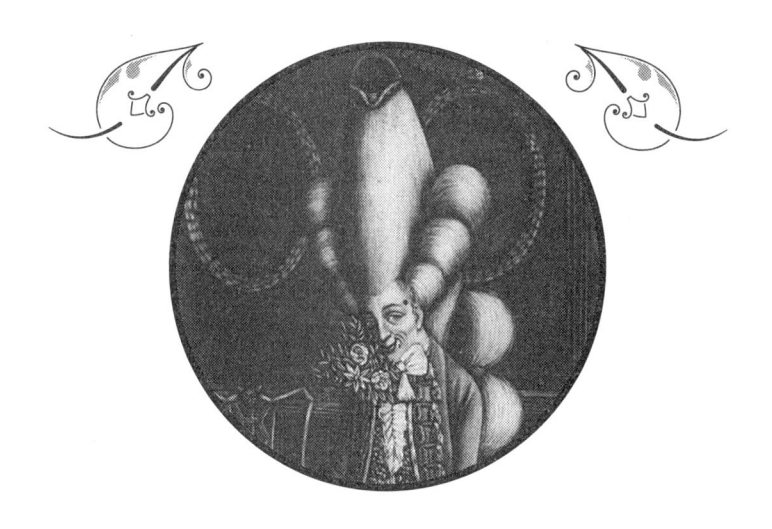

'Vanity plagues us all. From lowly selfie-takers pouting at their phones and zapping their images into the cold infinity of cyberspace, all the way to those occupying the highest offices in the land. It's unseemly, this desperate campaign to control how we are seen by the world. But it's also deeply human, something that unifies us all, this lonely pettiness, this struggling against our forever-thwarted egos.'

Richard Lawson, 'Donald Trump's Official Photographer Obliges This Vain Request', *Vanity Fair,* 4 April 2017

In light of that brilliant quote, I would like to dedicate this next chapter to the memory of Robert Cornelius – lamp manufacturer, chemistry buff and amateur photographer, who in 1839 took the world's first selfie.

Not only was it the world's first selfie, but it was also the first portrait of a human being photographed in the United States of America. Yes, America, your first photo of a human being was a bloody selfie!

To be precise, it was daguerreotype, which instead of film used a highly polished silver-plated sheet of copper. After being chemically treated, the sheet became 'light sensitive', which is the key phrase here. Some daguerreotypes could take up to fifteen minutes to create an image, which is way beyond the attention span of even the most devoted Instagram influencer.

Cornelius had actually made some improvements on the chemical process, and on the day he took the shot it was bright and sunny out in front of his families' lamp and chandelier shop, which meant he had three to fifteen minutes to release the lens, run around to the front of the camera, pose, and then pop the lens cap back on. Loads of time, although he did have to keep incredibly still.

But why a selfie? Well, he was experimenting and maybe didn't want to risk embarrassing himself in front of his family and friends. And anyway, he was also a bit of spunk! With his tousled hair, open-necked shirt and intense, inquisitive gaze . . . oh yeah, he'd get a 'swipe right' any day. He looks less like a lamp-making nerd and more like the lead singer of a mid-nineties indie rock group.

Vanity Not-So-Fair

Obviously human vanity pre-dates the invention of the daguerreotype or the painter's palette or the sculptor's block of stone. We've been checking ourselves out since we first discovered ponds, and by that I mean the small bodies of water, not the moisturiser. We all remember the Greek myth of Narcissus, and no matter which version you read, it ends one of two ways: the handsome but vain young hunter either drowns or is turned into a flower.

The problem with ponds is that they are so damn unreliable and weather dependent, which is why archaeologists have concluded that highly polished slabs of obsidian found in modern-day Turkey, dating back to 6000 years ago, are probably the first mirrors. That's a thousand years after humans started applying pigments to their face for decoration or ceremonial purposes, which only goes to show just how trusting pre-historic societies must have been. 'Oh, I told him it looks fantastic. I just can't believe he's actually leaving the cave looking like that!'

Soon we were polishing up all sorts of metals just so we could get a decent look at ourselves. The ancient Egyptians, Greeks and Romans were particularly adept at shining up copper and bronze for use as mirrors. It was the Romans in the first century AD who came up with the brilliant idea of coating such a mirror with a thin layer of glass, and something we would recognise today as a mirror was born.

While we are on the subject of mirrors, I recently discovered that the 30th president of the United States, Calvin Coolidge, used to shave while wearing his hat. I'm not sure if this is an act of vanity or just good ol' eccentric behaviour. It did have at least one fan – his future wife, Grace. When the *New Yorker* magazine inquired how they met, they reported, 'Calvin heard

Grace laughing through a window; she'd just noticed the bachelor lawyer shaving with his hat.'

What Grace was doing looking through the window of the 'bachelor lawyer' was never actually explained.

For those of us who don't like having a beard, the morning shave is just a daily reminder of the ageing process. That, however, is not the reason Lincoln grew the style of beard that he has become so linked with. It was grown in response to a young girl informing the great man that 'all the ladies like whiskers', which must have made Honest Abe think, *Yeah, but what about a beard without a moustache*? And a century later all the bass players in the world had a facial-hair role model.

There's also always been the tradition of enshrining the rich and powerful through portraiture – and not just to record themselves for vanity and posterity. Sometimes the portrait could serve a more *romantic* purpose. Eligible princes and princesses would have their portrait painted as a way of introducing themselves to other single monarchs.

One of my favourite stories in this vein is of Henry VIII commissioning his favorite portrait artist, Hans Holbein the Younger, to travel to Düren to paint Anne of Cleves and bring the portrait back to London so that Henry could check her out before he proposed.

He adored the painting. A formal proposal of marriage was sent.

Unfortunately, on the wedding day Henry decided that Anne's actual face did not match her 'profile pic', and the marriage lasted only six months.

Speaking of royals and images, one of the most poignant photographs ever taken was actually another selfie.

Vanity Not-So-Fair

It was in 1913, and the young Grand Duchess Anastasia posed motionless in front a mirror, photographing herself on the new wondrous toy of technology: the Kodak Brownie. Knowing as we do that the Russian Revolution is just three years away, and that Anastasia and the rest of the Romanov royal family are doomed, there is something incredibly haunting about this image. It is almost impossible to tear your eyes away from her pensive gaze.

But let's not assume that vanity is a sin of just the rich, the powerful and the beautiful. I am a vain bugger, even though I have no right to be. I can get caught up in my own reflection just as much as any budgerigar. I'm simply saying this to make you feel that if you recognise any of your own vain quirks in the next chapter, you are not alone. To paraphrase Carly Simon, 'You probably thought that song was about you, didn't you?'

Caca Dauphin

It would be something of an understatement to say that throughout history – and up to this very day – royalty has been the original and strongest of all fashion 'influencers'. Take, for example, the ridiculously long pointy shoes worn by Polish nobles in the fourteenth century called 'crakows', a reference to the city of Krakow. These became so ridiculously long that eventually fashionable men were reduced to attaching the tips of their crakows to their knees with a small chain to stop from tripping over them.

Then there was the surge in wearing pearls brought on by Queen Elizabeth I's love for these signifiers of chastity. Less frequently mentioned is the bizarre dental fashion that occurred late in Elizabeth's reign ... The Virgin Queen had something of a sweet tooth, and sugar was becoming more and more available if still extremely expensive. What her majesty did not have, however, was any comprehension of dental hygiene, so after years of tucking into sweeties and not brushing, her teeth had become blackened with decay.

This led to the short-lived but incredibly odd practice of the fine ladies at court artificially blackening their teeth both in tribute, and also to give the impression that they too could afford copious amounts of tooth-rotting sugar.

Princess Alexandra, the wife of Edward VII, was a major fashion influencer and caused a whole generation of European women back pain with ridiculously tight corsets.

But before we look down our modern noses at the hot fashions of the past, just observe the way sales surge for any

Vanity Not-So-Fair

designer item of clothing or accessory worn by the Duchesses of Sussex and Cambridge (or Meghan and Kate to their friends and family).

Royal families all over the world have often set the hot trends, particularly among the sycophant set, who had both the means and the desire to be seen supporting their royal betters. But even that can barely explain what became the height of fashion in France during the early 1780s.

Marie Antoinette and Louis XVI had just produced their second child, a son and heir by the name of Louis Joseph Xavier François. And the court went berserk. People lined up to adore the new prince, who was said to be a beautiful child. And it wasn't just his angelic face that made a good impression.

Apparently the contents of his diapers were a rather fetching yellowish-green. The royal baby pooped out a shade so pleasing to the French aristocrats that all the fashionable women of Paris were soon emulating it, handing over huge sums of money to dressmakers, milliners and ribbon makers – anyone who could satisfy their desire to dress and display the newest shade craze sweeping through the upper classes, a shade that was simply known as 'caca dauphin'.

Thankfully this was nothing more than a passing fashion, and France would soon have greater problems than aristocrats cravenly dressing in the colour of a prince's soiled nappy. It's exactly this kind of shit that brought on the Revolution in 1789.

Over thirty years later a writer for the British women's magazine *Belle Assemblée* would write with understandable incredulity, 'Finally, have we not seen, and this undoubtedly is the height of ignominy, have we not seen the fair sex seeking the colour of their ribbons in the very excrement of the royal infant? The colour caca dauphin adorned every dress, and this word, which I cannot now write without repugnance, was then in the mouths of all the best-bred women! What a ridiculous taste, that would attempt to dress beauty in disgusting images.'

Disgusting? I couldn't agree more, but maybe – just maybe – the next time I'm getting some painting done around the house I'm going to ask the designer, 'Do you have anything, say, a tad more . . . *caca dauphin?*'

Chester A. Arthur, Pants Man

Chester A. Arthur is one of those US presidents whose main function these days is as a name to have up your sleeve when playing pub trivia. He was America's twenty-first President and came to power after the assassination of James Garfield.

Strangely enough, becoming vice-president was the first time Arthur had actually ever held a publicly elected position. Before that he was an attorney and civil servant. His last job on the public payroll was Collector of the Port of New York, a job title that just seems open to graft and corruption, which he was accused of and fired for by the then recently elected President Rutherford B. Hayes in 1878. For most people, this would have meant the end of their political career. But Arthur was such a powerbroker in the north-east section of the Republican Party that in 1880 he found himself as Garfield's running mate, and eventually a most unlikely vice-president.

It would seem that, apart from money and power, Arthur had one other obsession: clothes. He was an out-and-out dandy; the press of the day dubbed him 'Elegant Arthur', the 'Gentleman Boss' and even 'Dude of all the White House Residents'.

To celebrate his rise to the vice-presidency, Arthur took himself off on a shopping spree at the venerable tailors Brooks Brothers. (Yes, the same clothier you know today – they've actually been around since 1818.) Elegant Arthur proceeded to spend over $700 (around $18,000 today) on clothes in one afternoon.

What he actually bought that day is not known, although he did have a penchant for high hats, silk scarves, frock coats and tailored trousers.

To say that he had a thing for tailored trousers is actually an understatement. During his time in the White House it was recorded that Chester A. Arthur owned over eighty pairs of high-end, bespoke trousers.

Now that's a lot of pants.

And it wasn't as if he bought his trousers in bulk. He was incredibly fastidious about his clothing. One story involves him testing his poor tailor's patience as he spent a whole afternoon trying on over twenty pairs of trousers (all of which had been made to his somewhat bulky measurements) before finally settling on just the one pair that he actually liked.

At least he wasn't merely a shopaholic – he did actually get around to wearing all eighty pairs of those pants. Arthur was known to change outfits several times a day, sort of like a Beyoncé show, but in the Oval Office, and with a lot less dancing. The only quick-change president that came anywhere close to Arthur's routine was twentieth-century style icon and fellow Brooks Brothers aficionado, John F. Kennedy.

None less than presidential authority and fellow man about town Gore Vidal described Chester A. Arthur as 'the most fastidious and fashionable president'. And let's not forget that Gore was no slouch in either the fastidious or fashionable departments. Vidal once claimed that by the age of twenty-five he had enjoyed over one hundred sexual partners, both male and female. I include this for no other reason than that Gore Vidal is one of my favourite writers. But back to our pants man.

To get the full measure of the man, you have to remember that Arthur, upon ascending to the most powerful position in America, thought it unnecessary to hire a bodyguard, but did employ a full-time valet.

He could also play the banjo, which reminds me of the age-old saying, 'The true definition of a gentleman is one who can play the banjo but chooses not to.' Which is completely unfair to the Dude and totally superfluous, but it does make me giggle.

Wigging Out

The source of Europe's passion for elaborately coiffed wigs in the 1600s was probably the French court of Henry IV, and in particular Henry's son Louis XIII, who was so embarrassed by his

Vanity Not-So-Fair

baldness that he thought the best way to hide his shiny pate was by wearing more and more outlandish wigs.

It's amazing that a political leader would imagine that they could hide their baldness by adopting an outlandish method of hair display . . .

One of the other reasons to disguise baldness during that time was that it was seen as a symptom of syphilis, which was seeping through Europe, as it was prone to do. The great diarist Samuel Pepys wrote of his syphilitic brother: 'If he lives, he will not be able to show his head – which will be a very great shame to me.'

Baldness was associated with illness and death, and it was in this environment that wigs flourished. Louis XIV had no less than forty-eight wig makers on staff, as did his cousin Charles II of England; it was also suspected that both men had the clap. This also being one of the stinkier times in human history, the wig was often drenched with pomade, a heavily scented oil.

While most of the men in high society wore wigs, women mostly wore what we would call extensions – elaborate headpieces woven into their already existing hair. What they did have in common, however, was that they were all heavily powdered, and this powder could be extremely expensive, seeing as it was scented with rare and expensive spices. Then there was the whole rigmarole of applying the powder, which went everywhere. There were capes, conical masks to cover the face and, if your budget could stretch that far, a whole room set aside for the messy powdering process. It's where we get the phrase 'powder room' from.

Although eighty per cent of the population were wigless, for the upper twenty per cent wigs – and heavily powdered wigs at that – were a sign of wealth, status and taste. This is shown in the 1778 novel *The Sylph* by the Duchess of Devonshire, Georgiana Cavendish, which contains this wonderful passage:

> Monsieur bowed and shrugged, just like an overgrown monkey. In a moment I was overwhelmed with a cloud of powder. 'What are you doing? I do not mean to be powdered,' I said.
>
> 'Not powdered!' repeated Sir William. 'Why you would not be so barbarous as to appear without – it positively is not decent.'

A basic wig would set a gentleman back around a week's wages, while a top-shelf example could cost a small fortune. This is no wonder, considering that it would take up to six artisans toiling for more than a week to fashion such a wig out of the best and most costly of human hair. This is from where we get the expression 'big wig'.

Wigs were also greatly valued on the black market. In fact, after money and jewellery, wigs were among the most commonly stolen items by the highwaymen that plagued Europe, and particularly Britain, in the eighteenth century. There were tales of robbers slicing through the backs of carriages to steal wigs directly off gentlemen's heads. The notorious thief and prison escapee Jack Sheppard, when he was eventually arrested for the fourth and final time, was found to have several wigs among the booty he was trying to fence.

But perhaps my favourite description of wig thievery comes from the writings of British social historian William Andrews, in his 1904 book *At The Sign of the Barber's Pole: Studies in Hirsute*

History. He talks about how over a century before it was not an uncommon sight on a city street to see a butcher making a delivery with a tray on his shoulder, on which would rest a large joint of beef or a suckling pig covered in cloth to keep the flies away.

He goes on to explain that instead of a suckling pig under that cloth, some enterprising thieves would place a small boy, and then if the 'butcher' was of a sufficient height to make him a good head and shoulders taller than the average man in the street, you would have a cunning plan for wig thievery. By these means the boy would be able to reach out and, with all the stealth of a pickpocket, snap up the wig of an unsuspecting passerby. There was usually a third accomplice, someone who would run to the victim's 'aid' but would actually hold them up while the butcher, the boy and the purloined wig would make their escape through the crowded back alleys.

One particular eighteenth century periodical, *The Gentleman's Magazine*, wrote several articles about robberies where 'the hair raising was literally executed', which shows that lousy puns and journalism have a long and awful tradition.

By the early nineteenth century the fashion for wigs was slowly abating. One of the final nails in the coffin for wigs was the 1795 Hair Powder Tax. This was introduced by Pitt the Younger in an attempt to alleviate the enormous debt being accrued through the Napoleonic wars. It was among a vast array of taxes brought in to fund those wars along with taxes on playing cards, perfume, watches, hats, medicines and gloves, before the government finally relinquished them and introduced an income tax in 1799.

Reprehensible

What made the Hair Powder Tax different was that it wasn't a tax levied at the point of purchase. Rather, it was a certificate that was obtained for the cost of one guinea (around two hundred and fifty dollars) that gave the bearer permission to wear hair powder for the period of twelve months.

There were exceptions – the royal family and their servants, clergymen who earned less than a hundred pounds per year and certain members of the armed forces. A father with more than one unmarried daughter could purchase two certificates, which would cover all his daughters, and in some cases a single certificate would cover all the servants in a house.

This tax became a useful way of charting the demise of the wig in Britain. In 1812, 46,664 certificates were issued, but by 1855 this figure had dropped to only 997 folk who couldn't give up their powdered hair. And a century after its creation the Hair Powder Tax barely raked in a thousand pounds of revenue. Which begs the question, who the hell was still using hair powder in 1895?

Strike a Pose

Imagine you are playing a game of historical charades. Your topic is dictators, and your first challenge is Hitler. Easy: you comb your hair over your forehead at a silly angle then use the end of a comb under your nose for the moustache.

Next, Mussolini: hands on hips, chin out, nodding at a non-existent, adoring crowd.

Vanity Not-So-Fair

Then it's time for Napoleon: stick half your hand into a gap in your shirt.

Everyone knows the 'Napoleon pose' from portraits, movie portrayals, and even afternoon cartoons when the animators wanted to illustrate that one of the characters might be an egomaniac with an inferiority complex.

Why was Bonaparte so willing to have himself portrayed in that particular pose?

Apparently he was desperate to appear aristocratic and, bizarrely enough, going about with your hand stuck in your waistcoat or jacket was considered to be a sign of impeccable breeding. In 1737, François Nivelon wrote a guide to etiquette called *The Rudiments of Genteel Behaviour* that described such a pose as demonstrating 'manly boldness tempered with modesty'. By Napoleon's time the practice had somewhat died out, but then one painting changed all that.

Napoleon didn't actually sit for the most famous 'hand-in-waistcoat' portrait, *Napoleon in His Study* (1812) by Jacques-Louis David, but when the Emperor saw it, he exclaimed, 'You have understood me, my dear David!'

From then on Bonaparte walked around with one hand stuck firmly in his jacket or waistcoat, and many subsequent portraits have depicted him in this manner.

There may, however, be another reason why Bonaparte was so fond of striking this outlandish pose – he was incredibly vain about his hands and would go out of his way to protect them. When not wearing gloves, he would keep one hand tucked into his vest and the other in a pocket, just to keep them out of the

Reprehensible

sun and wind. According to one of his inner circle, a certain Betsy Balcombe, 'His hand was the fattest and the prettiest in the world; his knuckles dimpled like those of a baby, his fingers tapered and perfectly formed, and his nails perfect.'

It's sort of fun imagining the man dubbed by his foes as 'The Nightmare of Europe' going around being as overprotective of his paws as a modern-day hand model.

We also have Madame Balcombe to thank for another unusual insight into Bonaparte's behaviour: he was completely tone deaf.

Nothing wrong with that – so am I. Can't carry a tune to save my life, and as such, I don't ever inflict my singing voice on anyone outside of my home bathroom. Napoleon, however, had no such qualms about who had to endure his atonal serenading. His need to inflict aural torture would increase whenever he found himself a bit stressed, which I can safely assume was a fair amount of the time.

Betsy wrote, 'He began to hum, became abstracted, and, leaving his seat, marched around the room, keeping time to the song he was singing ... Napoleon's voice was most unmusical, nor do I think he had any ear for music; for neither on this occasion, nor in any of his subsequent attempts at singing could I ever discover what tune it was he was executing.' Fortunately Napoleon died a full century before the invention of karaoke, otherwise he probably would have been 'that guy' – you know the one, usually from sales, who can't sing yet confidently bangs out an appalling version of 'Stairway to Heaven' at the Christmas party, all eight minutes and two seconds of it!

Another account regarding Bonaparte's singing comes from Louis-Joseph Marchand, who as his valet from 1814 to 1821 heard Napoleon break into song on many painful occasions. 'The Emperor, should he start to sing, which he did sometimes while thinking of something else . . . was rarely in tune and would repeat the same words for fifteen minutes.'

Then there was the Little Corporal's whole issue with cards, where his behaviour was almost worryingly predictable.

Laure Junot, the Duchess of Abrantès, recalled in one of her memoirs, 'It was the most laughable thing in the world to see him play at any game: he, whose quick perception and prompt judgement immediately seized on and mastered everything else which came his way, was, curiously enough, never able to understand the maneuvers of any game, however simple. Thus his only resource was to cheat.'

Napoleon's favourite card game was a version of what we recognise as blackjack, because it was easy to grasp and as the diplomat Louis Antoine Fauvelet de Bourrienne would later write, 'In general he was not fond of playing cards; but if he did play, vingt-et-un was his favourite game, because it is more rapid than many others. In short, it afforded him an opportunity of cheating. For example, he would ask for a card; if it proved a bad one he would say nothing, but lay it down on the table and wait till the dealer had drawn his. If the dealer produced a good card, then Bonaparte would throw away his hand without showing it, and give up his stake. If, on the contrary, the dealer's card made him exceed twenty-one, Bonaparte also threw his cards aside without showing them and asked for the payment of his stake.

Reprehensible

He was much diverted by these little tricks, especially when they were played off undetected; and I confess that even we were courteous enough to humour him, and wink at his cheating.'

Now doesn't that sound like a fun night – sitting around while the most powerful person in the room is brazenly cheating you out of your money and then probably having to cop a spray from him about his imagined gambling prowess?

There was one person who could actually call Bonaparte out on this pathetic behaviour and, not surprisingly, it was his own mother.

Playing cards was one way of filling out the long nights during Bonaparte's exile at the island of Elba. One guest described how things went when Napoleon's mother caught on to his ruse: 'When Napoleon was losing at cards he cheated without scruple, and all submitted with such grace as they could muster, except the stern Corsican lady, who in her tone would say, "Napoleon, you are cheating." To this he would reply, "Madame, you are rich, you can afford to lose, but I am poor and must win."'

On one occasion when his mother rebuked him for cheating it was said that Napoleon simply bundled up all the money on the table and ran off to his room.

Although, the next day he did send his valet around to return the other players' money.

Whether this was done under his mother's instructions was sadly never recorded.

My Lord, I Am Not Vain . . . Just Well Groomed

Although the word 'manscaping' only entered the *Oxford English Dictionary* in the last twenty years, the conundrum of why aging men have little hair where they want it and a surplus of hair where they don't is as old as reflections and insecurity.

It is somewhat odd that one of the best-preserved guides to manscaping actually comes from the 1654 edition of a much earlier work. I say odd because this edition was published – and sold well – in England at a time when Oliver Cromwell and his joyless mates were ruling the land, and preening and male vanity were considered the sort of foolishness that you would associate with the 'cavaliers' – those courtly, royalist gentlemen with flair. I'm no monarchist, but you have to admit that if you were organising an end-of-year office party you'd seek out the cavaliers from the sales department to help with the planning as opposed to wowser puritans from accounts payable.

Be that as it may, in the late sixteenth century Peter Levens, a chap with no acknowledged medical training, published *The Pathway to Health*, which proved to be a bestseller for over a century and was a sort of precursor to that section of the newsagents where magazines with covers of handsome chaps with ridiculous abs smile out at us and tell us about 'thirty days to buffed triceps' and 'how to wear a blazer for both the office and the weekend'. (On the second one, I'm assuming on the top part of your body and over your shirt usually does the job.) All of these modern 'lad mags' have endless pages on male grooming, which products are best for our hair, what Peruvian mud extract

Reprehensible

can give us a tingling scalp and the endless debates about whether you should go grey and what to do about hair loss.

And it would seem that a seventeenth-century gentleman was just as concerned about hair loss as today's preening manscapers – maybe even more so. Instead of laser treatments and other modern remedies, he was willing to follow Mr Levens's advice: 'Take the ashes of Culver-dung in Lye, and wash the head therewith. Also Walnut leaves beaten with Beares suet restoreth the haire that is plucked away.'

Sound intriguing? Well, 'Culver-dung' is chicken manure. Suet is the hard fat that grows around an animal's liver and kidneys and was probably a regular ingredient in your great-grandmother's cooking, but unfortunately in this case the 'Beare' is actually a bear.

Things are just as 'wrong town' when the journal describes how a man might go about removing hair from those areas of his body that he wanted to be smooth and hairless: 'Take the shells of two Eggs, beat them small, and stil them with a good fire. And with that water anoint that place.'

So it's basically a recipe for a crushed-eggshell tea that you rub into any overly hirsute part of your anatomy. However, if you wanted to take things up a notch you could always . . . 'Take hard Cats dung, dry it and beat it to powder, and temper it with strong Vinegar, then wash the place with the same where you would have no hair to grow.'

There are several problems with this theory. Obviously, it never actually worked, but then there is the more frightening predicament. Do you know how your cat walks around the house with that superior attitude? Well, imagine how puss is going to look down her nose at you once you've dried out her poop and rubbed it all over your privates.

If, however, this procedure ever did work, and the science certainly isn't in its favour, the journal then offers this handy hint on how to maintain your freshly manscaped bits: 'Take the bloud [blood] of a Snaile without a shel, [so I'm assuming any large garden-variety grub would suffice], and it hindereth greatly the growing up of haire.'

And at a time when everyone was always just a bit on the nose, there is this wince-inducing cure for those who suffer from a 'stench' in the armpits: 'First, pluck away the haires of the arm holes, and wash them with white Wine and rosewater that cassia ligna [a form of cinnamon] has been sodden in, and use it three or four times.'

For those of you who are keen, the 1654 edition has been recently augmented and can now be bought online. (Just run it by your cat first.)

I Came, I Saw, I Combed Over

You can almost understand why Julius Caesar may have been self-conscious of his receding hairline. Imagine this scenario: it's 49 BC; you are the most powerful general in the Roman Empire, and you're about to make yourself the most powerful man in the Western World. You have crossed the Rubicon River, high

Reprehensible

in the saddle, leading your soldiers towards Rome, towards your destiny.

These men worship you, and together they chant in full voice, 'Home we bring our bald whoremonger, Romans. Lock your wives away!'

Whoremonger? You can live with that. Adulterer? Well, you have been a busy boy. But *bald?* Really, guys, come on – give your future dictator a break.

Caesar was probably not the inventor of the comb-over, but he is the first great figure in history that we know for certain sported this sad hairstyle.

There were contemporary accounts of Caesar combing his hair forward. Plus, a few years ago in a river in France, a bust was discovered. It is considered to be one of the few known representations of Caesar created during his lifetime. It's a shame to think that it may just be the *only* contemporary statue of him that has survived to this day.

It depicts a handsome, middle-aged man with craggy, stern features and thinning hair, the middle section of which appears to be combed forward so that it touches the top of his forehead.

Plus, we also have all those coins. Caesar was the first Roman to put his likeness on the currency, and what they depict is a man with a somewhat broken hairline crowned with a wreath of leaves – either bay leaves or gold fashioned in the shape of bay leaves. It is thought that Caesar would use the head gear to fasten the forward part of his comb-over into place.

An article published a few years back in a journal by the American Anthropological Association concluded that by the time of his death Caesar may have been completely bald. They also claim that he did, however, have worrying amounts of hair sprouting out of his ears.

As outlandish as this may sound, there are accounts of Caesar going to great lengths to rid himself of excess hair from places where he didn't want it to grow. Not content with merely shaving, he would have others tweeze out any offending follicles.

Look, I've got to come clean on this. As I've reached my fifties I'm not immune to reaching for the tweezers from time to time in an attempt to tame my unruly, at times fecund, eyebrows.

But having a slave going up and down your body and into your orifices to pluck out hairs? That shows a certain dedication to male vanity. Then again, you have to remember that we are talking about Julius Caesar here. Many years before becoming dictator, pirates kidnapped him on his way to Rhodes. He berated his captors – not for imprisoning him, but for the fact that their ransom was on the low side.

He Did What With a What?

Gouverneur Morris was one of the Founding Fathers of the United States and is often referred to as the 'Penman of the Constitution', for it was he who, in 1787, gave us the final draft of the seminal document, making its language less verbose, tightening its message and finally coming up with the immortal opening words, 'We the People of the United States . . .'

He was also well known for having a wooden leg, which can still be seen today in pride of place at the New York Historical Society. This loss of a leg was put down to a carriage accident that he had suffered in 1780, resulting in a hasty amputation by a doctor who was not Morris's regular physician. In a cruel twist of fate, when Morris's doctor arrived back in town he promptly told his patient that the amputation was completely unnecessary.

This, however, was not the biggest scandal surrounding Morris and his newly attached wooden appendage. Rumours abounded for years that the carriage accident had merely been a cover story, and that the real cause of his leg injury was jumping from a balcony to escape an early-returning husband whose wife Morris had been in the business of pleasuring.

Even among that randy old bunch known as the Founding Fathers (well, certainly more than a couple of them) Morris stood out as being more randy than the rest and, even after losing his leg, he did not show any signs that he was going to slow down his behaviour.

As Richard Brookhiser wrote in his book *Gentleman Revolutionary: Gouverneur Morris, the Rake Who Wrote the Constitution*, the statesman continued to ride horses, climb church steeples, shoot river rapids and shake his wooden leg dancing. Nor did it diminish his trysts, so much so that friend and fellow patriot John Jay wrote that he wished Morris 'had lost something else'.

He did have a particular thing for the married ladies. While living in Paris he undertook a three-year love affair with the novelist Comtesse Adelaide de Flahaut, who was apparently having problems with her husband, probably because that husband was thirty-five years her senior. The affair was conducted right under the husband's nose, in and around his apartment at the Louvre, before it was converted into an art gallery. Mind you, I don't think that a bustling gallery would have slowed Morris down – he also had a bit of a thing for sex in public places and was apparently quite turned on by the prospect of being caught.

The following is an excerpt from Morris's personal diary, where he regularly uses the words 'celebrate' and 'celebrating' as euphemisms for intercourse: 'Go to the Louvre . . . We take the Chance of Interruption and celebrate in the Passage while [Mademoiselle] is at the Harpsichord in the Drawing Room. The husband is below. Visitors are hourly expected. The Doors are all open.'

I don't know if it added to his sense of excitement, but Morris carried on with this and other affairs while serving as an American minister to France during that tumultuous period that would become known as the Reign of Terror. Despite his own revolutionary background, Morris staunchly supported the monarchy, even devising a plan to rescue Louis XVI and Marie Antoinette from the guillotine, which came to naught. He did, however, manage to snap up all of Marie Antoinette's Versailles furniture at a bargain price and have it shipped home to the Bronx.

He was nothing if not a pragmatist.

This fact is borne out in another story from his days on the dangerous revolutionary streets of Paris. Apparently one day he was riding through town in a carriage with yet another of his

Reprehensible

lady friends. An angry mob soon blocked their way, convinced that aristocrats must be inside such an ornate mode of transport.

Quickly summing up the situation, Morris snapped off his wooden leg and waved it out the carriage window, shouting, '*Vive la Révolution!*', then quickly speeding off in the carriage before the bemused crowd had a chance to regain their composure.

After his return from Paris, Morris continued his busy schedule, both publicly and privately. He eventually settled down at the age of 57, marrying his housekeeper and suspected long-time lover, Anne Cary Randolph, who herself was no stranger to scandal. In 1792, at the age of seventeen, she had had an affair with her brother-in-law, which had produced one stillborn child – that is, according to Anne. She was charged with the murder of the infant but was later acquitted. On their wedding day in 1809, Morris wrote in his diary, 'I marry this day Anne Cary Randolph. No small surprise to my guests.'

Morris would then go on to one of his crowning achievements. Since 1807, he had been part of a commission into laying out a master development plan for Manhattan. In 1811 the grid pattern that we know today was established, and Morris was at the centre of shaping one of the greatest cities the world has ever seen.

The next noteworthy moment in Morris's life comes from his painful and preposterous death. In the autumn of 1816 he was having considerable trouble passing urine. Modern-day doctors think that he may have had prostate cancer. Morris, however, did not feel the need to consult a physician and simply believed that he must have had some sort of blockage along his urinary tract. So being a pragmatist and man of action, he decided to

Vanity Not-So-Fair

remedy the matter himself. He fashioned a probe out a piece of whalebone and stuck it up his urethra.

What could possibly go wrong?

Quite a bit actually.

Morris caused no end of internal damage, which then quickly got infected, and he passed away soon after. It is somewhat ironic that the organ that would dictate so much of his behaviour while alive would be the same organ that would lead to his demise.

This also caused a bit of a problem for the obituary writers of the day. How do you describe the unfortunate circumstances surrounding the passing of such a public figure?

One Boston newspaper probably expressed it best, writing that Morris had passed away from 'a short but distressing illness'.

Oddly enough, Morris wasn't the only framer of the American Constitution who met an untimely and unnatural death. Most famously there was the death of former Secretary of the Treasury Alexander Hamilton, who was killed by Vice President Aaron Burr in that infamous 1804 duel.

These two however were a couple of years behind the duelling death of Richard Spaight, who had been the North Carolina delegate to the Constitutional Convention. By 1802 former Governor Spaight found himself embroiled in conflict with state legislator John Stanly over political loyalties and perceived backstabbing. This had started as an exchange of letters but soon escalated into more insulting correspondence, which was published for all and sundry in the local *Newbern Gazette*. Eventually the two men met behind the nearby Masonic lodge and pistols were chosen.

However, it soon became apparent that neither man happened to be a particularly skilled marksman. The first round of shots failed to find their marks, as did the second and the third. By this stage surely honour would have been satisfied and both men could have just gone home to bed, but sadly a fourth shot was insisted upon and Spaight fell to the ground, clutching his side in agony. He died the next day.

The next victim of the 'Curse of the Constitution' fell into place on 5 June 1806, when fellow framer and signer of the Constitution George Wythe died from a violent illness after a breakfast he had eaten ten days earlier. Another man at that breakfast, Michael Brown, had also become ill and died just after eating that fatal meal. As he lay dying, Wythe was convinced that the cause of the sickness was poison, and that the culprit was his wastrel of a great-nephew, George Wythe Sweeney Jr.

Now George Jr did have a mountain of gambling debts and probably didn't help his cause by trying to cash a cheque forged in his great uncle's name while the great man was lying in agony on his deathbed. After Wythe's death, George Junior was arrested, but they could only ever make the forgery charge stick.

After this incident the Curse of the Constitution takes a bit of a break, before striking again in New York in 1829.

John Lansing had been the representative from New York at the Constitutional Convention, and although he didn't really contribute much and actually left the convention after disagreeing with some of its directions, he was there long enough for the Curse to get him!

How else can you explain the bizarre events that transpired that cold December? Lansing was a very prominent man about town; he had been Mayor of Albany, Chancellor of New York and was still Regent of the University of the State of New York. However, accolades notwithstanding, on 12 December he left his hotel room in New York, saying he was off to post a letter. He was never seen again . . .

Even so, we can safely say that no matter what befell John Lansing, I seriously doubt that it could have been worse than the results of DIY penis surgery involving whalebone.

The Dandy's Dandy

Before he died alone, suffering from syphilis and destitute from gambling and other debts, George Bryan 'Beau' Brummell was one of the most popular and sartorially influential men in Regency Britain. This is best illustrated by the following, if somewhat disturbing, passage from an 1826 periodical published for the smart urban sophisticate known as *The English Spy*, which describes how much power Brummell had over the other fashion-conscious men of London: 'When he first appeared in this stiffened cravat, its sensation was prodigious; dandies were struck dumb with envy, and washer women miscarried.'

Catherine Gore, a bestselling novelist of the period, often populated her works with satirical representations of this new breed of urban lad about town, a breed we would now refer to as the young metrosexual man. While never actually naming Brummell, he was clearly an object of her ridicule, as was his ever-growing group of followers. She described a character based on Brummell as 'a nobody, who made himself somebody, and gave the law to everybody'.

Brummell was actually far from a 'nobody' – his father was the former secretary to the Prime Minister, Lord North, and he had spent his childhood in the rarefied luxury of a Hampton Court Palace apartment.

Following his education at Eton and Oxford, Brummell joined the elite cavalry regiment the 10th Royal Hussars, under the direct leadership of the Prince of Wales. It was during this period that Brummell not only cultivated his extensive list of powerful contacts – the prince in particular took a shine to him – but it also formed the basis of his own unique sense of masculine style.

And this is where we need to understand something about Brummell and his fellow dandies. Their mode of dressing was initially a reaction to the over-the-top, wigged and flouncy excesses of the century of male dressing that had preceded them. Brummell disdained this mode of dress and referred to its adherents as 'macaronis', implying that they had merely aped the dress and manners of those men they had met while on the 'Grand Tour' – the obligatory trip through Italy and France that most well-to-do young men took at least once in their lives.

Brummell and his ilk were rebelling against the lace, the ornate silk, the powder and cloaks of their forefathers. They took their lead from well-tailored clothing that echoed the uniforms that they had worn both at Eton and in the military.

In her 1960 book *The Dandy: Brummell to Beerbohm*, American academic Ellen Moers wrote, 'The dandy's independence is expressed in his rejection of any visible distinction but elegance... His independence, assurance, originality, self-control and refinement should all be visible in the cut of his clothes.'

Fortunately for everyone else around them, dandies also rebelled against their ancestors' habit of masking body odour with scented talcum powder and perfumes. Instead, they placed an emphasis on personal hygiene centred on the rare practice of taking regular baths.

Moers is richly quoted in an article written by William A. Phillips and Jeffrey A. Nigro for the Jane Austen Society of North America, 'A Revolution in Masculine Style: How Beau Brummell Changed Jane Austen's World', to give us some wonderful insight into Brummell's attitude towards personal hygiene, and the debt that we all owe him, through his 'four rules':

1: Bathe daily. In the early nineteenth century, daily bathing, even for the most genteel of English people, meant simply washing face, hands and arms. 'It was Brummell's insistence on washing his entire body each day that made his contemporaries... view him as eccentric.' (My grandfather used to call cursory washing of the face and other bits a 'bird's bath', which was cute but still stinky.)

2: Bathing beats 'sweating'. Contrary to the belief of medical 'experts' of his day that chafing and perspiring could rid the body of toxins and ensure optimal health, 'Brummell maintained that soaking rather than sweating rid the body of germs and grime.' (And I wish everyone who takes the same bus up to the shops that I do would please follow Beau's excellent example.)

3: Bathe in hot water. Brummell's contemporaries believed that hot water was unhealthy while cool or cold water did more good for the body. (I think we've all had a sports coach who thought along the same lines.)

4: Eschew creams, lotions, powders and scents. Brummell applied the same rules of simplicity to his toilet that he did to the design, cut and colour of his garments, refusing to douse himself with the stifling scents and lotions prized by the young men and women of the day. (Wise words indeed.)

So, for those rules at least, Brummell had started to make London a slightly less whiffy city.

Maybe I'm just showing my age here, but to me Brummell and his dandies appear to be reacting to the fussiness and turpitude of previous generations just as the heroes of my youth – the punks and new-wavers – were reacting to the excess and pomposity of what had become known as progressive rock. The endless drum solos, the preposterous concept albums, guitars with more than one bloody neck – my heroes pared rock back to its basics, and in that they restored its vitality. But then there's the eternal problem. What was elegant and restrained quickly morphs into pirate blouses and puffy pants, and before you know it you have A Flock of Seagulls scoring a top-ten hit.

And despite the fact that this analogy definitely dates both my record collection and me, I'm going to stand by it.

Vanity Not-So-Fair

What began as a rebellion against ostentation soon morphed into its own heavily regulated movement for sartorial excesses. There are stories of Brummell spending five hours a day just to choose what he considered to be the perfect outfit. Often with the Prince Regent, the future King George VI, as a bemused spectator, Brummell would fill the floor of his dressing room with cravats, rejecting some for not being perfectly tied or others for looking too perfectly tied. Then there were the stories of him insisting that the best cleansing liquid for his boots was French champagne.

Brummell revelled in the scandal his behaviour created. He would sit in the window of his club, casting caustic judgements and commentary on the outfits of fellow Londoners walking by. And his withering wit wasn't just for those poor sods in the passing parade. He once refused to pay the Duke of Bedford the respect that the duke would normally have expected from such a non-titled upstart. He grabbed the duke's coat by the lapel, rubbing it between his thumb and forefinger, and patronisingly exclaimed, 'Bedford, do you call this thing a *coat*?'

Then there were the trousers.

Brummell was particularly fond of his legs, and he wasn't the only dandy about town to express this opinion. One stated that Brummell could gain employment just by being paid to walk, so rare and perfect were his legs. When a statue of Apollo went on display in London, more than one observer compared its calf muscles to Brummell's. And when a friend wondered if Brummell had injured his leg, Beau complained, 'Yes, and it's my favourite.'

Reprehensible

As such, he liked his trousers tight – the tighter the better – so much so that Brummell was rumoured to have invented the 'Prince Albert', and not the Prince himself. The idea was that Brummell would have a small piercing in his penis that he could then attach a length of ribbon to and tuck his member between his legs so as to maintain the perfect cut of his extremely tight pants. He didn't want anything showing that might draw attention away from his shapely legs.

But it wasn't his tight trousers that would prove to be Beau Brummell's downfall – it was his spending and the loss of his royal BFF.

When asked what he considered to be an acceptable amount of money to spend on clothing, Brummell replied, 'Why, with tolerable economy, I think it may be done with 800 pounds.' This was at a time when a well-respected craftsman was making barely 50 pounds a year. You also have to remember that Brummell ran with a crowd who were considerably wealthier than he was, and just keeping up with them was breaking his financial back.

Compounding his misfortunes, after years of decrying the pastime, he had developed a serious gambling habit. Because of his lofty status he had been able to seek out quite a lot of credit, which only added fuel to this fire. Being a 'man of honour', he would strive to repay these debts, until in 1816 he found himself no longer able to meet his financial obligations.

Then there was his falling out with the Prince Regent, which had started a few years before when the prince began to distance himself from some of Brummell's more outrageous, politically troubling friendships.

Vanity Not-So-Fair

In 1813, Brummell, along with Henry Mildmay, Henry Pierrepoint and Lord Alvanley, hosted a ball at their private club, known as Waiter's, which Byron had dubbed 'the Dandy Club'. The three other men appear to be best known for being part of Brummell's 'dandy rat pack'. All seem to have come from families of varying wealth and influence, to which they contributed not particularly much at all.

During the night's festivities, the Prince Regent had come over to say hello to Alvanley and Pierrepoint, but then snubbed both Brummell and Mildmay, at which point Brummell loudly asked, 'Alvanley, who's your fat friend?' Not what you would call a good move. Even though some in London society applauded his outrageousness, the loose comment would mark the beginning of the end for Beau.

He fled from London to Paris to escape his debt and was given a smattering of financial assistance from his old friends Lord Alvanley and the Marquess of Worcester. His life became more and more desperate, to the point where he was forced to spend time in a Calais debtors' prison, and he suffered a slow descent into syphilitic madness. He died, alone, broke and dishevelled, in the Le Bon Sauveur Asylum in 1840.

But don't worry – Brummell would not soon be forgotten. His legacy would live on in the lyrics to Billy Joel's 'Still Rock and Roll To Me': 'How about a pair of pink sidewinders and bright orange pair of pants. You could really be a Beau Brummell, baby, if you just give it half a chance.' (Not one of Mr Joel's greater moments, in my opinion.) There is also a statue of the man who was once at the centre of London society, erected in 2002, in

Jermyn Street, a part of the city known for its high-end gentlemen's fashion boutiques – a part of the city Brummell knew only too well.

They've Always Been Around

Out of all the subcultures of male vanity none has been more cockroach-like in its resistance to fading discreetly away than that of the damned hipster. This is maybe because the last person to call himself a 'hipster' would actually be a hipster. It's more a term of ridicule, much like being a 'trendy' in the eighties, or like being a 'yuppie' in the eighties – or simply *being* in the eighties. (Let's be honest, it was a pretty awful decade.)

The derivation of the word hipster predates ironic tattoos, over-priced coffee and pop-up shops (that sell fittings for pop-up restaurants) by more than a century.

There are those who believe the word 'hipster' is related to the practice of smoking opium. 'Hop' was an early-twentieth-century term for the drug, and the smoking of an opium pipe was usually done lying on one's side, thus placing weight on one's 'hip'.

There is another somewhat cooler theory about the derivation of the words 'hip' and 'hipster'. Some historians believe it is derived from the West African word *'hipi'*, which means to 'open one's eyes'. As far back as 1902, the word 'hip' was common in African American communities to indicate someone who was 'aware' or 'in the know' or, as the kids would say today, 'woke'. (Actually, the

Vanity Not-So-Fair

kids don't say that anymore, based on the simple fact that if I know the word 'woke', then the kids stopped using it ages ago.)

By the 1930s, 'hipster' had been appropriated into white culture to describe a young person who was into jazz culture and music. Then in the 1940s it became more of a term associated with the intellectual world of Kerouac's beatniks, reaching its zenith in Allen Ginsberg's poem 'Howl', where he talks about 'angelheaded hipsters burning for the ancient heavenly connection to the starry dynamo in the machinery of night'.

And then it just fell out of fashion.

My only recollection of the word 'hipster' in later years was when it was resurrected by the quintessentially nineties show *Seinfeld*, where it is used as an insult for Kramer. Several times he is dismissed as a 'hipster doofus', the humour coming from not only the combination of the two words, but also from the fact that 'hipster' had by then acquired a somewhat arcane, *un*-cool meaning.

Then in the early 2000s *The New York Times* and *Time Out New York* wrote about the new subculture of the recently ultra-hip suburb of Williamsburg. However, they used the word 'bohemians' to describe the folk who dwelled there. Other terms were 'new fogies', 'modern dandies' and 'wankers' – the last one usually used by older men who couldn't fit into their new skinny jeans, looked bad with a beard and now regretted seeing the old discarded vinyl albums from their youth going for ridiculous prices at weekend community markets.

As I said, hipsters refuse to be identified as hipsters, so how can we definitively spot one?

Can I offer this observation from the humour writer and performer Sol Smith? (Oh, and by the way, it was written over one hundred and twenty years ago):

> There lived in Macon [Georgia] a dandified individual, whom we shall call Jenks. This individual had a tolerably favourable opinion of his personal appearance. His fingers were hooped with rings, and his shirt-bosom was decked with a magnificent breast-pin; coat, hat, vest and boots were made exactly to fit.
> He wore kid gloves of remarkable whiteness; his hair was oiled and dressed in the latest and best style. And to complete his killing appearance, he sported an enormous pair of Real Whiskers!
> Of these whiskers, Jenks was as proud as a young cat is of her tail when she first discovers she has one.

I'm pretty certain he's describing the guy who owns the antique clothes store down the street from me, and the fact that Jenks goes on to shave and sell his whiskers to an envious stockbroker for fifty bucks makes me even more sure.

Eyebrows Moved the Cheese

As one who possesses a pair of unwieldly, free-range eyebrows that require some dedicated maintenance, my heart goes out to the ladies of the eighteenth century. Their quest for the perfect brow had them plucking and sculpting, and using dangerous black lead-based make-up to darken them. In some cases, they even went to the unthinkable lengths of using mouse pelts to replace them – a sort of eyebrow merkin.

Actually, there is some debate on this topic. Some dismiss it as pure hyperbole, while others point out that there is enough evidence (mostly in the form of satirical poetry and comic plays) to suggest that it was an actual thing, but maybe just not common practice.

Take, for instance, this popular 1798 poem by Matthew Price:

Helen was just dipt into bed
Her eye-brows on the toilet lay
Away the kitten with them fled
As fees belonging to her prey

For this misfortune careless Jane,
Assure yourself was loudly rated
And madam, getting up again
With her own hand the mouse-trap baited.

On little things as sages write,
Depends our human joys or sorrows
If we don't catch a mouse tonight
Alas, no eyebrows for tomorrow.

A few years later, in 1734, Jonathan Swift joins in with his poem, 'A Beautiful Nymph Going to Bed':

Reprehensible

> Her eyebrows from a mouse's hide
> Stuck on with art on either side,
> Pulls off with care and first displays 'em
> Then in play-books smoothly lays 'em.

The nymph in question is a young actress named Corinna, hence the reference to 'play-books'. This has given some credence to the theory that maybe some women did use mouse-pelt eyebrows, but perhaps just on stage as part of their arsenal of theatrical make-up.

Either way, there does seem to be enough evidence that for a part of the eighteenth century some women used mouse-pelts as one part of their extensive brow regimes. It was a cruel irony that the lead-based make-up they were using as another part of that regime was actually the culprit causing their brows to thin or even disappear.

And, despite the poetry, it was not the done thing to set traps to capture mice so their pelts could be skinned and shaped into fine, thick eyebrows. According to a cartoon from the era, women would buy their mouse eyebrows from the same high-end establishments that sold wigs and cosmetics.

Chapter Six:
SCOUNDRELS, BOTH DIRTY & ROTTEN

I was born in 1961 and raised in a deeply Catholic household. Given those two facts, it is quite obvious that I would have one over-riding spiritual hero: Maxwell Smart aka Agent 86 from the hit spy parody *Get Smart*. Smart, who was played by Don Adams, was famous for his catchphrases, such as 'missed it by *that* much' when one of his shots in a gunbattle went wide, and, when told he was about to be inserted into a dangerous situation, would reply, 'And loving it'.

But the one catchphrase that sticks out in my mind would often occur at the end of an episode after Max, with the help of Agent 99, played by Barbara Feldon (my first crush), had overpowered and captured that episode's supervillain. He would take a moment to reflect, and then almost wistfully say, 'If only he'd used his powers for *good* instead of evil.' (The supervillains were mostly male, but every now and then a female supervillain would come along.) Despite the context in which it was used, depending on the episode, it spoke volumes to my young sense of right and wrong.

'If only he'd used his powers for good instead of evil' is in some ways how we judge scoundrels. There is an almost begrudging admiration for their guile and intellect to go along with the sheer effrontery. The condemnation for the crimes they have perpetrated is often followed by a sense of sadness at the waste of their talents.

These days, when we think about scoundrels the first name that probably pops into our mind is Bernie Madoff, who, upon his arrest in December 2008, was responsible for the largest Ponzi scheme of all time, having defrauded almost 65 *billion* dollars from his unsuspecting clients.

Reprehensible

The Ponzi scheme, in its simplest form, is a fraud that lures in investors with rates of return that far outstrip any other investment scheme available on the market. The incoming capital is not wholly (or in some cases, not at all) being invested in products, the markets or property, and the outlandish profits are the result of the influx of money being provided by fresh investors.

The scam gets its name from Charles Ponzi, an investor in Boston during the 1920s. You would think that meant he was the original scoundrel who had discovered this ruse to part people from their hard-earned cash, but the first account of what we would consider to be a Ponzi scheme took place in Germany between 1869 and 1872, perpetrated by Adele Spitzeder. (A 'Spitzeder scheme' doesn't quite have the same ring to it.)

Adele had morphed from being a promising young actor and folk singer into a shady banker after her theatrical career had begun to fade. She was so successful at scamming people that, before she was caught, she was considered to be the wealthiest woman in Bavaria. When things finally went pear-shaped for Adele, almost 400 million euros in today's money had been lost to her 38,000 investors.

Since there were no actual laws on the books that adequately covered her crimes, she only spent three years in prison for 'bad accounting' and 'mishandling other people's money'.

After her release, she tried a few more schemes and was once again arrested in 1880 for attempting to establish a bank without the proper papers and permits. In between swindles, she still found time to write her memoirs and occasionally perform as a folk singer under the name 'Adele Vio'.

Speaking of scoundrels with an artistic bent, one person who did eventually use his talents for an incredible amount of good was not, occasionally, above getting involved in a bit of forgery. I'm talking about the great Renaissance genius Michelangelo. There were times in his career when he would copy or do his own version of classical statues in a Roman or Greek style. He would then bury these statues and give them some judicious rubbing before exhuming them again to enhance what would be seen as an appropriate patina of antiquity. This practice of passing off statues as coming from another era was actually common.

In 1496, Michelangelo crafted a statue of a sleeping cupid, which, after the usual ageing process of being buried in acidic soil, was then sold by art dealer Baldassare del Milanese to the wealthy cardinal Riario of San Giorgio. The cardinal soon figured out what was going on and confronted the dealer. Strangely enough, the cardinal allowed Michelangelo to keep his portion of the money from the forged statue. Moreover, the incident actually helped increase the reputation of the young artist.

Most scoundrels' plans would never flourish if they didn't have a clear idea of their target market. Where there are people hoping for an investment that is too good to believe, there you will find a scoundrel with a scheme. Where there are people with a desperate desire for a miracle cure for their illness, there you will find a scoundrel with a bogus elixir.

And when people are distraught with grief, oh, you better believe there is a scoundrel ready to prey on that grief.

People have been claiming to communicate with the dead since we first started being scared of death, which is a pretty primal

Reprehensible

human fear. However, from about the middle of the nineteenth century, the Western world was held in the shonky grip of what came to be known as spiritualism. Two of the first practitioners of this phenomenon were a pair of sweet-looking, unassuming young girls who lived on a farm just outside New York.

In 1848, eleven-year-old Kate and her elder sister, Maggie, fourteen, told a neighbour a terrifying story. According to the girls, around bedtime each night the house would fill with otherworldly tapping noises from inside the walls and against the furniture.

The neighbour asked for a demonstration, so that night, in the room they shared with their parents, Kate and Maggie huddled under a blanket as their mother acted as a sort of master of ceremonies. Mum asked the spirits to count to five, and sure enough five loud taps were heard in the room. She then asked the spirits to count to fifteen, which the undead obligingly did. Then the spirit was asked the age of the now terrified neighbour, and the taps measured out an exact thirty-three, which was, of course, the correct answer.

It may come as no great surprise to realise that there was no intervention from the 'other side' – the two girls just had a knack of being able to crack their toes and ankle joints at an appropriate volume. When a particularly loud noise was required, they could even crack the joints in their knees.

Despite the fact that a relative of the girls, Mrs Norman Culver, signed a statement in 1851 explaining that it was all a hoax and that she had taken part in some of the 'séances' by tapping whatever number was required on one of the girls' thighs, it was too late. The two children had grown to become celebrities of the new spiritualist movement. They also had grown to become miserable, both with serious financial woes and drinking problems.

Even years later when they confessed that their line of communication to the dead was nothing more than an uncanny ability to crack their joints, people devoted to spiritualism refused to believe them, so great was their need for the comfort this chicanery delivered.

That's the thing with scoundrels – they know how to appeal to our most basic desires.

Now if you'll excuse me, I have to email all my banking details to some poor prince from Nigeria – it's amazing how generous he can be considering all that he has gone through.

There is No April Sun in Poyais

If you try to find the Latin American country of Poyais on a map, you will be unsuccessful. That is not because it no longer exits, it is because the place has *never* existed – except in the mind of Gregor MacGregor, also known as 'His Serene Highness Gregor the First, Sovereign of the State of Poyais and its Dependencies, and Cacique of the Poyer Nation'. He was also a soldier, a mercenary and one of the most notorious swindlers of the nineteenth century.

The fact that Gregor would end up as a soldier was hardly surprising. He was named after his grandfather, Gregor MacGregor, also known as Gregor the Beautiful, thus establishing a family penchant for self-promotion. He was also a famous warrior and

Reprehensible

one of the founding officers of the Black Watch – a revered infantry battalion of the Royal Regiment of Scotland. And his younger namesake started the nineteenth century off just as his grandfather would have wanted: serving with considerable distinction in the British Army.

However, in 1811, he boarded a ship to Venezuela; his plan was to seek fame and fortune fighting alongside the colonies seeking their independence from Imperial Spain.

His dashing nature proved to be an immediate hit with his local superiors, and he was granted a field commission by no less than the great revolutionary leader El Libertador, Simón Bolívar. Gregor rose quickly through the ranks, and by the tender age of thirty he achieved the title of General of Division in the Army of Venezuela and New Granada. He was so admired and beloved that not only did Bolívar decorate Gregor with the insignia of the Order of Libertadores, he also consented to the marriage between the Scotsman and his own beloved niece.

Sadly, this would be MacGregor's high-water mark.

When the Spanish withdrew their hold on Venezuela, things began to go awry.

Needing new battles and more glory, MacGregor put together a small force and basically waged a one-man war against the Spanish wherever he could find them. This had mixed results; there were victories from Portobelo, Panama, to as far north as Amelia Island, which is now part of present-day Florida.

By the spring of 1820 he found himself pursued by the Spanish and hiding out in a part of Nicaragua that had the rather unfortunate name of 'Mosquito Coast'.

Its original inhabitants were the native tribe known as the Miskito Indians (yes, that's where the region's name comes from). Its primary purpose for Europeans had been as a hiding place for pirates and other brigands trying to escape the law, all attempts to colonise the place having failed.

It was here that MacGregor had his eureka moment. It was said that he persuaded the native chief to give him title to the land, a fact that he could never actually prove and most historians dismiss. He did however come up with a fictitious name for the area – he christened it Poyais, immediately declared himself the ruler and then boarded a ship to London. It was on the voyage home that his plans were solidified, and by the time he disembarked in London he was ready to hit the ground running.

His first task was to produce a guidebook and a series of pamphlets extolling the opportunities of his fictitious nation, making it sound as enticing as possible to potential investors. He wrote at length of the fertile soil, the wonderful weather and mountains covered in valuable timber from cedar to mahogany. Gold could simply be picked up from the ground and precious stones littered the landscape.

Then there were plantations of the most valued products of the age. Indigo, coffee, cotton and sugar grew in abundance, as well as exotic fruits and herds of what he described as almost morbidly obese cattle.

There was the glittering capital, with its royal palace and parliament. The streets were lined with mansions, dockside warehouses and, of course, a dazzling opera house. He went on to tell how, as regent, he would often take magnificent processions through his capital, flanked by a retinue of The Knights of the Green Cross (whatever that is) and his personal bodyguards, the Poyasian Lancers.

That might have been enough for your average megalomaniac, but MacGregor wasn't done yet. Apparently musicians had composed outrageously complimentary ballads about Poyais, and the engravings he commissioned depicting daily life in the newly 'discovered' paradise sold in their thousands in both London and Edinburgh. He was the talk of both cities and felt so emboldened that he had this letter printed and published:

> 'WE, GREGOR, extended the greeting of a brother sovereign to King George and appointed William John Richardson [one of Gregor's employees], Commander of the Most Illustrious Order of the Green Cross, Major in Our Regiment of Horse Guards, to be Our Charge d'Affaires in the United Kingdom of Great Britain.'

It may come as no surprise that there is no record of King George's response. But that didn't slow MacGregor down – within a year he had opened offices in Edinburgh and London.

Investment was pouring in, but there was a far more reprehensible plot about to be launched. Poyais needed not just investment, it needed *people*, and for four shillings an acre you could actually buy yourself your future home in the land of unlimited promise. Although there is something obviously wicked about ripping off wealthy investors, it is in the deception of solid trades people, farmers and shopkeepers that MacGregor shows his true bastardry. Even worse, the vast majority of these 'settlers' came from his home country of Scotland, where his family name was still held in high regard.

On 10 September 1822, fifty wide-eyed, excited folk sailed out of Leith on the *Honduras Packet*, a well-worn merchant ship, excited about the new life that awaited them on the other side of the Atlantic Ocean. They would be the first wave of migrants heading off to Poyais. That is, after MacGregor had finished fleecing them.

As well as charging for land and passage, he also gave some of the younger, more educated men lofty positions within the Poyaisian military and civil service. Some of these positions required uniforms, which MacGregor was more than happy to procure and charge for. But more insidious than this was the currency scam. The migrants were told that to make their life easier on arrival – and also to get a better exchange rate – it would be a good idea if they swapped their Scottish coins for notes payable at the Bank of Poyais. These notes were merely 70,000 worthless pieces of paper that MacGregor had secretly printed in Edinburgh only a few months before.

Even as the *Honduras Packet* was pulling away from the British coast, MacGregor realised that he was in dire need of more capital. Setting up such an elaborate scam had used up more money than he had expected. Also, the response had been far greater than even he had hoped for. There were ships to charter, agents to be paid and, well, why use your own money when you could use someone else's?

Reprehensible

With this in mind, he approached the venerable banking house of Perring & Company, situated in the financial hub of London. The head of the company was Sir John Perring, a man of extensive business experience in what was then the financial hub of the world. He had actually been London's Lord Mayor and a member of Parliament – surely he would see through this nefarious scheme?

Sir John lent MacGregor the enormous sum of two hundred thousand pounds (well over one hundred million pounds in today's money). Actually, he insured a bond issue where stockholders could exchange their bonds for freehold land in Poyais or sell them for the market value. MacGregor promised that the almost boundless resources of his kingdom would underwrite the bonds.

Perring would be bankrupt within three years.

But back to the *Honduras Packet*. After an uneventful voyage across the Atlantic, the new citizens arrived at what they had been told was the location of the capital of Poyais. Dressed in their finest, they assembled on deck and stared in disbelief at the uninhabited Mosquito Coast. Dropping anchor, they fired off a signal gun. Surely everything would be explained once the pilot boat came out to greet them.

Obviously, the pilot boat didn't come.

They made their way ashore, the general belief among the passengers being that they must have strayed off course. They unloaded their provisions onto the beach and a search party set off to find the errant capital of their new land. There was some urgency to this mission, for not only were they confused about where they were and had insufficient supplies but *another* ship from Scotland arrived – this one with one hundred and fifty passengers.

Suddenly a hurricane hit, and the two ships were carried out to sea. Alone in a hostile land, these poor folk clung to the beach, the fittest forming up search parties and leaving sporadically in a desperate bid to find help.

By the time news of their plight had reached General Codd, the British governor of Honduras, sickness had set in. He dispatched a schooner on a desperate mission to save them. Sadly, by the time help arrived, two-thirds of the passengers had died, mostly from a combination of malaria, yellow fever and starvation. Another contributing factor was, as one of the younger 'settlers' described, 'Not one was able to assist another out of such a number, and many of those who had newly come from Scotland were well advanced in years and had come here to end their days in peace and comfort.'

The next urgent undertaking for General Codd was to put as many ships to sea as he could muster. MacGregor had organised many more boatloads of newly persuaded Poyaisians, which needed to be intercepted before they suffered the same fate as the original victims of his greed.

It was a year's long effort to locate these boats and repatriate the victims back home. All up, seven ships filled with swindled immigrants set sail from ports all over Scotland and England. During this period, MacGregor and his cronies slipped out of London and were inflicting themselves on the good citizenry of Paris. By 1825 they had offices in the City of Light, selling

Reprehensible

investment opportunities in Poyais as well as organising more ships of colonisers. In September of that year at least one ship was due to sail from Le Havre on its way to the dreaded Mosquito Coast.

And yet, MacGregor *still* needed extra funds. Maintaining the lifestyle of a Latin American Regent obviously ate up a lot of money, as did fitting out ships and promotional activity – not to mention keeping his inner circle well paid and quiet.

To this end, he contacted another long-time, well-established London financial institution. Thomas Jenkins & Company had a reputation that rivalled Perring's. And, sadly, Jenkins performed just about as much due diligence. They underwrote a bond share of a staggering three hundred thousand pounds (over one hundred and seventy million pounds today) – one hundred thousand more than Perring's. This amount was secured against the goldmines of the non-existent region of 'Paulaza'.

By 1827 the French were starting to figure out that there was something more than a bit dodgy about this self-proclaimed Prince of Poyais, and MacGregor did what all good con men do – he legged it, fleeing back to London where he was promptly arrested. And just as promptly the charges were dropped! This may be due to the fact that many of the 'great' financial minds of London did not want to endure the embarrassment that a trial would bring them.

MacGregor then, strangely, returned to Paris, where he was once again arrested. This time he was taken to jail on charges of fraud. He even had the audacity to release a statement while in prison, complaining that he was 'suffering as one of the founders of independence in the New World', almost as if he was making claims to be some sort of political prisoner. Sadly, the case against him was pretty much botched by the French prosecutors and was eventually dropped, meaning that this master fraudster only ever spent three months in prison.

Seemingly chastened, MacGregor decided to keep his head down and lived in modest, quiet circumstances for almost a decade, until he had finally blown all of his ill-gotten gains. But he was never one to go without for too long – he simply petitioned the Venezuelan Government for help.

Fortunately, an old mentor from his days fighting against the Spanish was now an important man within the republic. MacGregor was to return to Caracas, where he was given his old rank of general and a healthy pension. He lived out the last six years of his life in comfort and respect before dying in 1845 of natural causes.

I suppose there is one thing we can be grateful for – at least the Prince of Poyais died well over a century before the internet and cryptocurrency. God only knows how much more damage he could have done with access to those money pits.

First, Choose Your Goat

By the 1930s, quack and drunkard John Brinkley was living the high life. He owned three yachts, a vast Los Angeles mansion with his name spelled out in its garden in flashing neon, a

Reprehensible

huge pool tiled with tiny swastikas (oh yeah, he was a fervent admirer of Hitler), as well as a two-storey pipe organ that he would hire the organist from Grauman's Chinese Theatre to belt out a few tunes on for his not infrequent soirées – ones at which the Duke of Windsor would often be found. Think of him as a creepy Jay Gatsby. His radio show *Medical Question Box* was a national hit, even though it was generated out of a tiny border town in Mexico, a town that Brinkley virtually owned, along with other stretches of land throughout the American Midwest.

Not bad for a self-taught surgeon . . .

Yes, that's right, I said self-taught!

I can admire a self-taught chef or artist, but I kind of think that when it comes to surgery you might want to have done a bit more study than skimming through a textbook. He was like most swindlers – extremely skilled in the art of separating money from the gullible . . . and to a lesser extent separating testicles from goats.

Brinkley was that classic pedlar of quack medical procedures, and he specialised in cures for erectile dysfunction, which has always been a boon to those who can claim to cure it and a cause of great stress to those who endure it.

Men have been concocting spurious cures for lack of sexual performance since, well, there have been men. These were mostly potions, diets, rituals and the usual spectrum of quack medicines and ointments. You have to be in a pretty desperate state of mind if you are willing to not even ponder of the question, 'You're going to do *what* to my scrotum?'

You see, Dr Brinkley's patented cure for male impotency was a simple procedure that was best described in the brochure as a 'goat testicle implant', and I must stress here that the important word here is 'implant' not 'transplant'. The goat's testicles were roughly installed into the patient's scrotum, on top of his pre-existing, under-performing balls. The poor patient had to cough up at least five hundred dollars for the pleasure of Brinkley's services (over eight thousand dollars today), and remember this was often a small fortune for these people.

But here's the really creepy bit – after signing a few papers, which I'm guessing were mostly waivers, the poor rube was asked if he wanted to go 'out the back' to visit the paddock behind the hospital, so he could choose which goat he thought might best suit his needs.

Apparently the only post-procedure care on offer were bottles of basically sugar water, which Brinkley sold with a thousand per cent mark-up.

Of course people died – you can't just whack a set of goat's nuts into a human body and hope for the best. Pope Brock, who wrote the fascinating life story of Brinkley in his book *Charlatan: The Fraudulent Life of John Brinkley*, describes him as, 'though perhaps not the worst serial killer in American history, ranked by body count alone he is at least a finalist for the crown'.

Fortunately for all involved (particularly the goats), Morris Fishbein, the editor of the American Medical Association's journal, could spot a dangerous fraud when he saw one. He attacked Brinkley in the journal and, like all braggarts and bastards, Brinkley took the bait and in 1939 he sued Fishbein.

Reprehensible

Dumb move, yet one that hucksters often fall for.

Under cross-examination his bogus qualifications were exposed, his dubious methods were held up for ridicule, and eventually the one medical qualification he had (which, by the way, came from an uncredited college and seemed to be based on the somewhat spurious herbal treatment known as 'Eclectic Medicine') was taken away from him. Within two years Brinkley was bankrupt, had a heart attack and lost a leg – he died soon after.

However, there is one bizarre legacy of the wasted life of Dr John Brinkley. His radio program *Medical Question Box* ran without commercials, and Brinkley would play country-and-western music in the program breaks. It was broadcasted from a radio station, which Brinkley just happened to own, on the Mexican side of the border. This is important because the station didn't have to comply with strict US broadcasting rules. Its wattage was huge, and as such its reach covered a vast amount of the American market.

It is said by music historians that he was instrumental in bringing country-and-western music to a wider audience. One music act in particular owed a great deal of their success to Brinkley's show – The Carter Family. And this was especially good news to a young boy in Dyess, Arkansas. His family called him J.R., but we all know him best as Johnny Cash. Years later he would go on to marry June Carter, and one of music's greatest love stories came into being.

That aside, John Brinkley was a reprehensible human being.

Don't Sports Meet Me in St Louis

If you were to ask an ardent sports buff what infamous event occurred during the 1904 Olympics held in St Louis, they might just answer that it was the winning of the marathon by American Fred Lorz, a runner who was subsequently stripped of that win during the medal presentation after it was discovered that he had spent some of the race as a passenger in one of those newfangled automobiles before alighting and crossing the finish line with not only a stupendous lead but hardly any signs of exhaustion. What is often not recalled is that the whole marathon itself was disastrously organised, to the point where some athletes almost lost their lives and Olympic officials even considered banning this cornerstone event from future Games.

Things did not get off to a good start for the first Olympics ever to be held in America. For one, they were seen as somewhat of a sideshow to the larger event going on at the same time: the St Louis World's Fair. There were a few runners in the marathon who were well known and recognised as legitimate athletics competitors. Then there were the ten Greek runners, none of whom had ever run a marathon before. I'm guessing that they were operating along the same theory my nephew once did when, as a young boy, he took to the ice for the first time, somehow confident he could skate because his mother was from Sweden.

From this theory, these sons of Hermes made the assumption that, *Hey, Greeks invented this distance, so obviously we must be good at it.*

Then there was the infamous Mr Lorz, who had never competed in a full marathon before either. Moreover, very few people had actually ever seen him run, mostly due to the fact that he trained at night, so as not to interfere with his day-job as a bricklayer.

The most flamboyant competitor was the retired Cuban mailman Felix Carbajal. He had funded his trip to St Louis by giving running exhibitions in his homeland.

He then sadly lost his funds shortly upon arrival on the US mainland in a dice game in New Orleans, and had to hitchhike and walk to St Louis. He cut a dashing figure on the starting line – all five foot of him in his beret, street shoes, long-sleeved shirt and trousers. His fellow runners would take pity on him and borrowed a pair of scissors so they could turn those trousers into shorts.

And yet no other runner has equalled his exploits in the race either before or since. During the event he playfully stole two peaches from some spectators; he then ransacked an apple orchard along the race's route before succumbing to stomach cramps and lying down for a nap.

Even more dangerous to the runners than gorging on rotten fruit was the race organisers' deliberate restriction of their access to water. There were only two water stops along the whole route: the first, a water tower ten kilometres in, and the second, a well at the twenty-kilometre mark. That left over half a race to go.

This was not an oversight but rather a conscious act of what can only be considered as perversion of the scientific method. James Sullivan, the chief organiser of the Games, had intentionally restricted the athletes' water intake to test the effect of dehydration on marathon runners. This was all done on a day with both soaring temperatures and high humidity.

Then there was the course itself, described by another official as 'the most difficult a human being was ever asked to run'. It was a street course that included seven punishingly steep hills, all through the city – but with no road closures. The runners had to contend with traffic and trolley cars, as well as railway lines, pedestrians and a mobile spectator fleet on bicycles, foot and in motor vehicles.

To make matters worse, the running surface had wilfully been made even more hazardous with rocks strewn across the road, which itself was also worryingly uneven and in most stretches had been covered in an inch-thick layer of loose, fine dust for reasons that no one would or could explain. This treacherous dust soon turned out to be extremely dangerous for most of those involved.

Thirty-two runners assembled on the start line that steamy August afternoon and, at 3.03 pm exactly, the starter's gun fired and Lorz broke out to an early lead. Fellow American Thomas Hicks soon passed him – not to anyone's surprise as he was an acknowledged marathon runner and the event favourite.

It was then that the growing dust cloud kicked up by the runners, their support vehicles and the spectator fleet claimed its first victim. Californian William Garcia went down hard, his oesophagus haemorrhaging. Another runner, John London, succumbed too and began vomiting and immediately withdrew.

Around about this time the South African competitor Len Tau was set upon by a passing pack of wild dogs that proceeded to chase him well over a kilometre off the designated course. I suppose just to mix things up a bit.

Reprehensible

By the nineteen-kilometre mark Lorz had unsurprisingly fallen away from the pack due to vicious cramps, and it is at this stage that he grabbed a ride with one of the spectator vehicles, where he would spend the next eighteen kilometres. When his cramps abated, he rejoined the race a considerable distance ahead of the rest of the field.

The crowd cheered him on as he entered the stadium and burst through the finish line. Alice Roosevelt (Teddy's daughter) even placed the winning laurel wreath on his head. And then a voice from the crowd rang out – one of Hicks's handlers had seen Lorz getting out of that infamous get-ahead car.

Lorz was booed, the gold medal was never actually presented to him.

Now Lorz, to his credit, immediately started telling anyone who would listen that it was just a prank – there was no way he would ever accept the title of Olympic champion. And, in his defence, there were certainly a lot of witnesses who had observed him waving and smiling at the crowd as he was driven past them. Surely these were not the actions of a duplicitous man.

But the crowd was not interested in Lorz anymore. They had turned their eyes back to the stadium entrance, trying to glimpse which of the distant figures they could barely make out through the dust cloud might actually be the man winning the damn thing.

The frontrunner slowly came into view . . . and, yes, it was the race favourite, Thomas Hicks, his body shattered by the harsh conditions, but now, having heard of Lorz's disqualification, running hard on nothing but grit and determination. Well, actually, nothing but grit and determination, and egg whites, and French brandy – oh, and some strychnine.

It was the first recorded incident of doping in Olympic history – not that strychnine was illegal back then, but the highly toxic substance was still extremely dodgy and not to mention potentially lethal. Taken in small doses, it can produce a stimulant effect, and anyone who's ever read a diet book knows that egg whites are pretty much the cure for everything.

His handlers *responsibly* held back on the brandy up until the last few k's, when they allowed him to use it to chase the strychnine and egg white measure. The thought was that it would help lift his spirits.

A race official by the name of Charles Lucas observed the change that came over Hicks during the home stretch, later writing, 'Over the last two miles of the road, Hicks was running like a well-oiled piece of machinery. His eyes were dull, lusterless, the ashen colour of his face had deepened; his arms appeared as weights well tied down, he could scarcely lift his legs, while his knees were almost stiff.'

I'm going to go out on a limb here and assume that Mr Lucas had never actually seen 'a well-oiled piece of machinery'!

As Hicks entered the stadium, the crowd roared, Hicks faltered, his trainers eventually ran down onto the track and carried him over the finish line. They even bothered to manipulate his legs, in a weird marionette sort of way to give the illusion of running.

Hicks was declared the winner, and the appalled Olympic committee gave Lorz a lifetime ban, which was subsequently lifted.

I guess they couldn't find any firm rulings on 'automobile-assisted marathon wins'. Actually, Lorz and Hicks competed against each other in the 1905 Boston marathon, which Lorz won completely unassisted.

The saddest thing about this whole silly tale isn't the cheating, or the doping, or the pack of wild dogs. It's the fact that it often overshadows the best story of the 1904 Olympics – the one involving the American gymnast, George Eyser, who competed with a wooden leg and won six medals in one day – three gold, two silver and one bronze.

Daddy Dearest

It is a curious fact that one of the greatest (and yet largely forgotten) literary scandals in the English-speaking world had its origin with an insecure young man attempting to find favour with a distant, bombastic father. The father was Samuel Ireland, an engraver with aspirations to be a writer. His son went by the name of William-Henry, and he too had hopes for a creative life, as an actor or perhaps a playwright. However, by his nineteenth birthday, in 1795, he was working a rather mundane job as what we would probably consider an assistant to a law clerk's assistant, in the offices of a friend of his father.

Poor William-Henry had once been described by a teacher as being 'so stupid as to be a disgrace to his school' – an insult his father frequently liked to repeat, not only to his poor son, but

Scoundrels, Both Dirty & Rotten

also to the many guests that came to their home. Samuel would entertain these guests by sharing his greatest passion, his collection of historical curios – a passion he never shared with other members of his family, to whom he paid scant attention. There were a few paintings by Hogarth and van Dyck; some rare, antiquated manuscripts and books; as well as a rag that he claimed was an actual segment from a mummy's shroud.

Then there was his most cherished item: a goblet that he insisted was made out of the famed mulberry tree that Shakespeare had planted in his home in Stratford-upon-Avon. Samuel was obsessed with the Bard, and as William-Henry would later recall, 'My father would declare that to possess a single vestige of the poet's handwriting would be esteemed a gem beyond all price.'

And that's how the whole damn mess got started.

In late 1794 William-Henry came across one of his father's books that contained a reproduction of Shakespeare's signature. He spirited the book away from his father's study to his office and, considering that his job was pretty much unsupervised busy work, he spent hours diligently tracing the signature until he figured that he could reproduce it with his eyes closed. His workplace also had the advantage of being filled with old documents that stretched back years.

So William-Henry forged – quite literally – a plan.

He cut out a blank piece of an old rent agreement, wrote up a deed and then signed Shakespeare's name. He then aged the parchment by holding it near a candle flame, exactly like a certain Year 7 student at Newcastle High would do over 170 years later to recreate a page from Captain Cook's journal. (Yes, I got an

A- for it, thanks for asking.) He then attached a wax seal, appropriated from another document lying around his workplace, and took his dubious creation home.

Later that evening, William-Henry presented it to his father, but rather than unbridled joy the cranky old bugger cast a less than enthusiastic glance over the forgery and said, 'I can certainly believe it to be a genuine document of the time.' It was almost as if Samuel could not bring himself to believe that anything this astounding could have provenance with his underachieving son. He was willingly admitting to its age but not yet ready to concede to its authenticity.

In hindsight, he probably should have gone with his gut instinct.

But the next morning he showed it to a family friend, Sir Frederick Eden. Now Sir Fred was a bit of a buff on old manuscripts, and seals in particular. And it was the seal that William-Henry had grabbed at random that was the clincher in Eden's estimation.

Eden explained that the seal contained a representation of a 'quintain' – a piece of medieval training equipment that jousters would level their lance at for target practice. Sir Fred then explained to Samuel that this was obviously a reference to something a knight would 'shake a spear' at. *Therefore*, it was a cryptic clue to the seal having been that of Shakespeare's, *ergo*, the document was genuine. (Seriously!)

Samuel was overjoyed and soon his study was crowded with his fellow collectors, all astounded by this miraculous find that William-Henry had stumbled across. They implored the young man to explain where he had come by such a treasure and, like most scam artists, William-Henry already had a vaguely plausible backstory ready to go: he had discovered it in an old trunk belonging to a wealthy and deeply private gentleman who only wanted to be known as Mr H.

Surely this would satisfy Samuel and his cronies, he thought. His father would be happy, proud that his now marginally less stupid son had procured this amazing relic, and everyone could move on with their lives.

It had the opposite result, whetting his father's appetite for further discoveries. Samuel theorised that where there was one Shakespeare document there must be others, and his son should go back and search for more.

William-Henry would later recall, 'I was sometimes supplicated; at others, commanded to resume my search among my friend's supposed papers, and not unfrequently taunted as being an absolute idiot for suffering such a brilliant opportunity to escape me.'

Samuel was never going to win a Father of the Year trophy.

So to oblige his demanding dad, and with the resources available to him at his place of employment, William-Henry did just that. Over the next few months, he forged letters both to and from Shakespeare, along with some contracts with actors. Emboldened by the reception these fakes received, he even went as far as to construct a love poem from Shakespeare to Anne Hathaway, complete with a lock of hair.

You would think that William-Henry might be tempted to stop while he was ahead and simply say that the fictitious trunk was now empty of any Shakespeare-related 'merchandise'.

Reprehensible

You'd think that, but . . .

William-Henry then turned to printed texts of some well-known plays and got back to forging, altering a passage here or a phrase there, to produce what he declared to be early, long-lost versions of Shakespeare's work. In short time, in his own 'Shakespearean' handwriting, he turned out an entire first draft of *King Lear*, which he followed up with a section of an early draft of *Hamlet*. Both forgeries featured ridiculous attempts at Elizabethan phrases and spellings, replete with way too many nouns ending in the letter 'e'. (For those of you old enough to remember, this was also a common occurrence in the 1970s when many a cafe stopped being a cafe and became a 'Coffee Shoppe'.)

Samuel was over the moon with these pages that, in his mind, showed an insight into Shakespeare's writing process, and soon his drawing room was overflowing with Shakespeare and antiquity enthusiasts, to whom he would proudly show off his latest discoveries. This was a bit of a double-edged sword for the Irelands. Increased attention also meant increased scrutiny, and not every visitor to the house was as willing to believe in these writings with the same fervour, or dare I say vain gullibility, as Samuel Ireland.

William-Henry was by now getting desperately nervous – surely it was time to bring the whole misjudged endeavour to a halt?

That would be one option . . .

Or you could do as William-Henry did and inform your father that you had actually discovered remnants of a hitherto *unknown* play by Shakespeare! Surely this must be the Holy Grail for any Bard 'scholar'.

William-Henry would later say, 'With my usual impetuosity, I made known to Mr Ireland the discovery of such a piece before a single line was really executed.' So he was forced to drip-feed his father a scene or two at a time from what would be titled, upon completion, the lost Shakespeare classic *Vortigern and Rowena*.

A tale set in the fifth century about a warrior king and his beloved young woman, William-Henry lifted most of his material from *Holinshed's Chronicles* (a source of old stories that Shakespeare had relied on) with some slightly altered extra plots and characters from a range of Shakespeare's tragic and historical works.

Seeing as he could not initially find enough old blank manuscript pages to construct this forgery, William-Henry wrote his opus, which was actually longer than the average work of Shakespeare, on contemporary paper. This would satisfy his father's impatience to receive the play. He told the old duffer that it was a transcript done in his own hand, and this ploy actually worked, giving him the time he needed to scrounge up enough aged paper to fully present *Vortigern and Rowena* in all its forged glory.

Oh, and just to put the cherry on the cake, William-Henry also forged a letter explaining why no one had come across this masterpiece before. In the letter, Shakespeare explains that *Vortigern and Rowena* was his greatest work, and he would not publish it until a printer would pay him what he thought it was worth.

Around this time, playwright and theatrical impresario Richard Brinsley Sheridan had expanded his Drury Lane theatre to 3500 seats. The writer of *School for Scandal* was looking for the

Reprehensible

right play – something newsworthy, something earth-shattering, something never before seen or heard.

I'm afraid you can probably guess where this is all heading.

Sheridan was known to be no great fan of Shakespeare's, but he reckoned that a recently discovered masterpiece might just be the play to put those 3500 bums on seats a night that he desperately needed to cover his massive debts. He was also a rather bad gambler, so he went to the Irelands' home and cast his eyes over the manuscript.

His first comment was, 'This is rather strange, for though you are acquainted with my opinion as to Shakespeare, yet be that as it may, he certainly always wrote poetry.' Then after more reading, 'There are certainly some bold ideas, but they are crude and undigested.'

Yet again we arrive at a point in this story where a giant red flag should have been raised ... but, sensing a box office hit, Sheridan announced that *Vortigern and Rowena* would have its London debut come April of the new year.

It was soon after this that Samuel Ireland asked his son if he could meet the reclusive owner of the trunk of wonders: the mysterious Mr H. William-Henry explained that such a request was impossible, but he could pass along his father's correspondence to the non-existent landowner. So Samuel and Mr H began exchanging letters, and not surprisingly a fair amount of the content of the notes from Mr H contained passages praising William-Henry as a bright and talented young man.

Things began to unravel just before Christmas 1795. Samuel Ireland actually published his collection of forgeries under the full title *Miscellaneous Papers and Legal Instruments Printed Under the Hand and Seal of William Shakespeare*. The London newspapers were not kind. *The Telegraph* even went to the point of writing a satirical version of the papers in the form of a mock letter from Shakespeare to his contemporary playwright Ben Jonson. The paper ridiculed the *Shakespeare Papers*' attempts to recreate Elizabethan spelling: 'Deere Siree, Wille youe doee mee theee favvouree too dinnee wythee mee onn Friddaye nextte, att twoo off thee clockee, eatte somme muttonne choppes andd somme poottaattoooeeese.' (That's the actual spelling in the mock letter, and over two hundred years later it's still pretty funny.)

The literary sharks could smell blood in the water.

Edmond Malone, expert and editor of Shakespeare's complete works, took aim, describing the published papers as a 'clumsy and daring fraud'. He took particular interest in a letter supposedly written to Shakespeare from Queen Elizabeth, dismissing the style and spelling as 'not only not the orthography of Elizabeth, or of her time, but it is for the most part the orthography of no age whatsoever'.

His 442-page annihilation of the fraudulent papers was not only an instant hit, but it also dropped on 31 March 1796. Two days before *Vortigern and Rowena* premiered at Drury Lane.

Opening night came with a full house, and thousands more outside unable to secure a seat. The play was rolling along – not being wildly received but there were no real problems – until the third act when a minor player, who had never been convinced of its authenticity, hammed up one of his lines and got a laugh.

Reprehensible

Then in the final act, the noted actor and lead John Philip Kemble (another cast member who had expressed his doubts) completely overplayed a soliloquy where Vortigern confronts Death, and most of the audience broke out into hysterical laughter and whistling. It was all the cast could do to actually finish the performance.

But complete it they did, and as the curtain fell it was announced that there would be a repeat performance the following Monday. This was greeted with disparaging howls, and then the first few rows – divided between cynics and true believers – broke out into a prolonged brawl that lasted almost half an hour. The only thing that would calm the audience down was another announcement *cancelling* the performance, saying it would be replaced by a revival of *School for Scandal*.

Samuel Ireland, who had earlier made sure that all were aware of his arrival at the theatre, apparently exited with considerably less fanfare. But what of William-Henry, who had spent the whole wretched night watching nervously from the wings? Years later he would write, 'I retired to bed, more easy in my mind than I had been for a great length of time, as the load was removed which oppressed me.'

A few months after the one and only performance of *Vortigern and Rowena*, William-Henry made a confession, to his mother and sister, and then to another history-obsessed friend of his father.

Sadly, his father refused to believe anyone who contradicted his belief in the genuine nature of his beloved Shakespeare papers. He even expressed that there was no way a dull-witted man like his son could have perpetrated such a scheme – and definitely never to the level where he, himself, could have been fooled.

He clung to this delusion for the last four years of his life.

However, for William-Henry, the fact that his father could not even contemplate that he had been the source of the forgeries was the final insult. The two men had a vicious argument and the son stormed out of the family home forever.

William-Henry would continue to pursue a creative career, this time creating original work in his own name. He even managed to publish a few novels and books of poetry, though sadly not to much acclaim or financial success.

He and his father never reconciled.

Too Young to be Papal?

These days when we think about Popes we think about old men – sometimes extremely old men – but this wasn't always the case. There have been young Popes, and in the middle of the tenth century there was one particularly young Pope whose papacy was unbelievably disastrous.

Pope John XII (born Octavianus) was either seventeen or twenty-four when he became pontiff. The lack of a clear date of birth is due to the fact that two women are credited with being his mother. They were either his father's wife or his concubine – no one can give a definitive answer, so his age varies in accordance with whoever claims to have given birth to the little stinker.

Reprehensible

What is certain is that the father, Alberic II of Spoleto, was an incredibly powerful man who saw himself as a sort of patriarch of Rome. So when Octavianus was a young boy, Alberic was in the perfect position to ensure his son's ascension to the most powerful civic position in Rome, but also that he would become the most powerful man in Christendom.

So in May 964 AD after Alberic and Pope Agapetus II had died, Octavianus became not only Pope John XII, but he also took on the secular role of 'Princeps' of Rome (an old Roman term that roughly translates as 'most eminent' and is the word from which 'prince' is derived).

These were two roles which it became almost immediately clear he was dreadfully unsuited for, and not just because of his perceived youth and inexperience. This was a man who was described by the Holy Roman Emperor Otto I as one 'who passed his whole life in vanity and adultery'. And this was from the Emperor that the young pontiff had helped install. Also, it was one of the kindest descriptions of Pope John XII ever uttered. Trust me on this.

The tenth-century writer Liuprand of Cremona described him with these words while chronicling accusations levelled against the Pope at the 963 Synod of Rome:

> Then rising up, the cardinal priest testified that he himself had seen John XII celebrate mass without taking communion. John, bishop of Narni, and John, a cardinal deacon, professed that they themselves saw that a deacon had been ordained in a horse stable, but were unsure of the time. Benedict, a cardinal

Scoundrels, Both Dirty & Rotten

deacon, with other co-deacons and priests, said they knew that he had been paid for ordaining bishops, specifically that he had ordained a ten-year-old bishop in the city of Todi.

Apparently this was true: Pope John XII had actually ordained a child as part of a political move for his family. And, yes, the rest of the crimes seem somewhat obscure and ecclesiastical, but Liuprand isn't finished with Johnny Boy yet:

> They testified about his adultery, which they did not see with their own eyes, but nonetheless knew with certainty: he had fornicated with the widow of Rainier, with Stephan his father's concubine [I should hasten to add this was not the same concubine that was rumoured to be the Pope's mother, so I guess he drew the line at incest], with the widow Anna, and with his own niece [I stand somewhat sadly corrected], and he made the sacred palace into a whorehouse.

Liuprand then goes on to list a few of John's more terrifying crimes, but just to keep things balanced, he also lists a few of the more mundane transgressions that the Pope stood accused of:

> They said that he had gone hunting publicly; that he had blinded his confessor Benedict, and thereafter Benedict had died; that he had killed John [there seems to have been a lot of Johns around his time] after castrating him; girded on a sword, and put on a helmet and cuirass [a type of upper-body plate armour].

Reprehensible

> All clerics as well as laymen declared that he had toasted the devil with wine. They said that when playing dice, he invoked Jupiter, Venus and other demons. They even said he did not celebrate Matins [a form of devotional vigil] at the canonical hours, nor did he make the sign of the cross.

Liuprand was certainly no fan of the young Pope – he actively hated him – but it's bizarre how blinding, castration and murder get casually listed along with all the other lesser crimes.

Liuprand was also preparing this report for Holy Roman Emperor Otto I, the same Otto who had given Pope John XII the description of being vain and adulterous. It was this tortured relationship between Emperor and Pope that was at the very heart of John's nine torturous years as pontiff. Well, that and the sex, and the killing, and the corruption, and the blasphemy, and the hunting. (I guess we can't leave out the hunting.)

The two men would often declare uneasy truces with each other. Then actual battles would rage between their two forces. At one point Otto chased John out of Rome and warmed his seat with a more suitable Pope. This replacement subsequently fled Rome when he heard that John and his forces were about to re-enter the city.

John was still Pope in 964 AD when Otto was once again plotting to get rid of him, then the pontiff did everyone a favour and promptly died.

There are two theories about how Pope John XII shuffled off this mortal coil. One is that he suffered a stroke while having sex with a married noblewoman. The other is that the aggrieved husband of a noblewoman beat John to death when he discovered him having sex with his wife. Take your pick.

You would think that this would be the only moment in history where a Pope died while shagging, but bizarrely enough his eventual replacement, Pope Leo VII, would suffer a fatal stroke while having sex barely a year after Pope John XII 'died on the job'.

I am fully aware that the papacy was a very different institution in the tenth century than it is today, and much of what we know about Pope John XII's behaviour is from writings left behind by his most bitter enemies. That being said, he was maybe the worst Pope in an era that wasn't that short on bad pontiffs.

Proto-Scrooge

You have to be something special as a miser if you are to be considered the historical figure around which Charles Dickens based the character Ebenezer Scrooge. But John Elwes was more than just a miser – he was also a toady, a misanthrope, and he literally stank. For some years he was also a member of the British parliament.

Born in 1714, his original name was John Meggot, and it appears that he learned his penny-pinching ways from his mother. Despite the fact that she was an extremely wealthy woman who had inherited around one hundred thousand pounds (over twenty million dollars in today's money), she denied herself even

Reprehensible

the most basic of life's necessities, to the point where she wasted away to death while John was still a young man.

A rather gadfly youth, John Meggot plunged himself into the usual extravagances you might expect from an orphaned chap with more money than sense. However, this seems to have been a brief period of self-indulgence in an otherwise miserable, miserly life. He soon realised that what he needed to do was ingratiate himself with his even wealthier uncle, the baronet Sir Harvey Elwes.

Now, Sir Harvey was just as much a tight-arse as John's mother had been, and he also had a considerably greater fortune. John, in an effort to suck up to his uncle, changed his surname to Elwes, and the two men would spend joyless evenings together mocking others for their free-spending ways while sharing a single glass of wine between the two of them, just to save money.

This toadying seemed to have done the job, because when Sir Harvey finally and fortunately breathed his last in 1763, the now rebranded John Elwes found himself the sole heir to a fortune in excess of two hundred and fifty thousand pounds (about fifty million dollars today).

By now, John's miserly habits had been well established. He was known for going to bed just before sunset to avoid the extravagance of lighting a candle. He would sit with his poor servants in the kitchen during winter to save the cost of lighting another fire. And the location of these kitchens would constantly change. John, who by then had a rather large property portfolio, preferred to have no fixed abode. Rather, he chose to live in whichever property had been recently vacated by one of his poor, long-suffering tenants – Elwes regarded property maintenance as nearly as wasteful as candles.

And can we talk about the smell? In an already stinky era, John Elwes reeked to a degree that few people could match or even understand. It was said he would wear the same clothes every day for at least a month – and not just of a day! He would also sleep in them. For a while he sported a wig that he said he'd found discarded in a hedgerow. No wonder tales began to circulate that people in the street would often throw him coins, assuming that he was a beggar as opposed to one of the wealthiest men in England. He would actually take *pride* in these stories.

Around this time, another rumour began to do the rounds: Elwes had snatched a rotten moorhen (a medium-sized water bird) out of the mouth of a rat and had it for dinner. It's probably not true, I say *probably* because he was well known for eating putrid fruit and vegetables that he had scavenged. And if it was made up, one theory suggests that it was Elwes himself who did it, just to bolster his thrifty reputation.

So pathological was his tightness that he even tempted fate with his own health. Apparently one night while walking home he fell and badly cut both his legs. He eventually visited the local doctor but made a somewhat disturbing wager. He stated that he only wanted the doctor to treat one leg, for which the man would be paid. Elwes would treat the other leg. If the self-medicated leg healed first, Elwes insisted that the doctor reimburse him his fee. Sure enough, the doctor lost. Considering the state of medicine at the time, it was just sheer luck that Elwes managed to keep not just one but both of his stinky limbs.

Despite his wealth, Elwes decided that he needed something else to occupy his time, other than stealing from rodents or making life-threatening wagers with people who should have known better. So in 1772 he found himself elected to parliament as the member for Berkshire – that is, after he had outlaid an astounding eighteen pence in election expenses. That's how you manage to make a 'rotten borough' even more rotten and cheap. This new job meant constant travel to London, and coaches were obviously a frivolous luxury as far as Elwes was concerned. Instead, he would set off for the capital on the back of a poor under-nourished horse, with one hard-boiled egg in his pocket to sustain him on his journey – a journey that would take him longer than most people, seeing as he would studiously avoid any roads, turnpikes or bridges that charged a toll.

His career in those chambers was something that could be considered somewhat less than stellar. He sat with whichever party he felt like on any given day, never once rose to his feet to speak in the House of Commons, and the running joke around the corridors of power was that no one could accuse him of being a turncoat, seeing as he only owned one suit.

After twelve years, the expense of regularly travelling to Westminster, as well as the thought of having to fork out another eighteen pence to get re-elected, proved too much and he quietly ended his pointless political career.

As he got older, Elwes slipped deeper into his miserly ways. He became more and more concerned with the delusional thought that he would die a pauper and could often be heard screaming at night, 'I will keep my money! Don't rob me!' Even in his last days he was so tight that his barrister was forced to write up his deathbed will by the sad light of a poorly stoked fireplace. Elwes wouldn't even pay for a candle to be lit for such a 'frivolous' purpose.

When he did die, his estate was well over five hundred thousand pounds, which went partially to his nephew and mostly to his two illegitimate sons, George and John. Well, he did owe George and John something, seeing as he hadn't deemed it worthy to pay for their education: 'Putting things into people's heads is the sure way to take money out of their pockets.'

But apart from having two sons out of wedlock, which means he must have had *some* pleasure in his life, John Elwes did indulge in one other bizarre form of fun. He loved visiting gambling houses – not to make wagers but to take pleasure in watching other people lose money. To this end he would do something extremely out of character. He would actually front his buddies so they could continue gambling and, as Elwes hoped, continue losing. He made these loans solely for his own entertainment, with no expectation of being paid back! Moreover, he considered it ungentlemanly to even ask that the debts his friends had accrued at cards and horse betting be repaid.

One time he loaned Lord Abingdon seven thousand pounds to wager on a horse that was racing at Newmarket. He even spent fourteen hours riding to the track to see the bet take place. When asked if he was hungry, he reached into his coat pocket and retrieved a pancake, which he proudly stated had probably been in there for two months but, in his words, was 'good as new'.

Greed, Graft and a Horse's Arse

Giles Mompesson was such a symbol of corruption in seventeenth-century England that his name actually became a synonym for greed. Those wishing to highlight the faults of the monarchies of both James I and Charles I often invoked his crimes and actions, and he was the inspiration for the lead character, Sir Giles Overreach, in Philip Massinger's 1625 play *A New Way to Pay Old Debts*, a scathing satire of avarice in the Stuart court.

Giles's story begins in Wiltshire, where he was born in either 1583 or 1584. Little is known of him until he enters Hart Hall, Oxford, to study law in 1600, but then he ends up back in Wiltshire a year later, with no degree and very few prospects.

But then Giles, like so many of his ilk, finds a way to begin his quick and slimy ride to the heights of power: marriage.

In 1606 Giles wedded Katherine St John, the daughter of the somewhat awkwardly named Sir John St John. 'Sir Double Johns' was a man of considerable power and means – not only in the town of Wiltshire but also in London. Through his father-in-law's influence, Giles became the Member of Parliament for the district of Great Bedwyn in 1614 – not bad for a failed law student!

However, the greatest boost to Giles Mompesson came when his wife's sister, Barbara, married Edward Villiers. Edward was the half-brother to George Villiers, who was not only a favourite of King James I but was also rumoured to be the king's lover.

This gave Giles a direct route to the king, and boy did he know how to exploit it.

In 1616, he saw a loophole in England's licensing laws – local justices of the peace licensed taverns, but inns on the other hand had no direct or unambiguous governing body. Giles suggested that there needed to be such a body, and that he himself should oversee it, along with two other commissioners. Fulke Greville, chancellor of the exchequer, was dead-set against the plan.

Mompesson, however, had George Villiers on his side, as well as Attorney-General Sir Francis Bacon. The king was soon convinced that this was a good idea, and in 1617 he made Giles one of the three commissioners overseeing the inns of the land, and he chucked in a knighthood just to give him the gravitas that his new position implied.

One thing that wasn't clearly implied was just exactly what powers *Sir* Giles actually had – which left him free to pretty much make them up as they suited him.

Any fines or levies that the inns might be charged were left to Sir Giles to decide upon, as were whatever licence fee he thought was appropriate for any establishment. Let's not forget that many of these inns had been operating for decades, if not centuries, so it was better to pay up than try to start again. The only rule that Sir Giles had to adhere to was that four-fifths of any income he raised was to go to the Crown; the remainder was his to keep. Anyone who has ever watched an episode of *The Sopranos* has a fair understanding of how this system works. It was basically a shakedown operation.

Like many a good mobster, Sir Giles was nothing if not entrepreneurial. Even though it was the local authorities who

Reprehensible

oversaw the taverns, Mompesson struck on a scheme where he would grant a new licence to any tavern that had been shut down for being considered of 'ill repute' – as long as they paid him a suitable 'licensing fee', or should I say bribe. And if a tavern hadn't actually infringed, Sir Giles was more than happy to give it a nudge in the wrong direction.

There was one story that involved his agents pounding on a tavern door late one night. They claimed that they were in danger and asked if they could seek sanctuary; they described it as an 'emergency'. The tavern owner took them in, and the next morning the agents charged him for running an unlicensed inn, seeing as they had found accommodation under his roof.

In the same year, Sir Giles proposed a scheme to Villiers where he would sell off decayed wood from the king's estates. He would do this for a one-thousand-pound fee for the first year and another one-thousand-pound fee four years later, to be paid upon the completion of the project. It would later be established that he had skimmed over *ten thousand pounds* from the sale of the wood, as well as pocketing his two-thousand-pound fee.

Not content with this scheme, he somehow managed to get himself appointed as an investigator into gold and silver thread manufacturing. There was a great deal of demand for the expensive thread at the time, and he readily took up the job of extorting goldsmiths for bogus fees and licences.

Then there was his scam involving 'concealed' Crown lands, which was land belonging to the Crown that over the years had become neglected or through a lack of royal attention might have been assigned for some random purpose.

Sir Giles was voracious in his application for surveys and titles to wrest as much land as he could back under the king's control. One of the main motives for his tireless efforts was that any land deemed to be worth less than two hundred pounds was his for the keeping.

And let's not forget the other schemes involving King James's New River Company, where Sir Giles oversaw the books (never a good idea) as well as the licences for the manufacturing of coke from coal.

What is even more astounding is that Sir Giles Mompesson managed to get this many nefarious schemes up and running in just three short years. However, by 1620 the tide was beginning to turn. Even with George Villiers's support and his father-in-law's efforts to get him re-elected to parliament, numerous investigations were beginning to close in on him.

It was discovered that Sir Giles had inappropriately prosecuted over three thousand inns, either on spurious claims or by digging up arcane and unused laws that dated back to the Tudor period. He was swiftly and soundly found guilty of extortion.

Sir Giles threw himself on the mercy of the court, although he did claim in his defence that it was partially Attorney-General Sir Francis Bacon's fault for finding his schemes legal in the first place. But it was too late – the Crown had turned its back on him and Sir Giles became one of the most despised men in Britain. On 3 March 1621, he fled to France. (I'm starting to get the feeling that for centuries the English Channel was teeming with cads, bounders and scoundrels 'fleeing to France'.)

A week later his sentence was announced – and what a sentence it was!

By order of the court, he was compelled to pay a ten-thousand-pound fine, relinquish his knighthood and – here's the best bit – walk down the length of the Strand 'with his face in a horse's anus'! Fortunately for the horse, a few days later this sentence was expanded to include banishment. Seeing as Giles was already overseas, the poor nag was saved the indignity of having to appear in public with the reprobate.

By then, Charles I was in power and Katherine was back living with her father, Sir John St John, where they both petitioned for Giles's return. He came back briefly, but was once again expelled from the country, this time by parliament.

Giles then goes back and forth for a while, visiting Charles a few times during the civil war to pledge his support – without ever actually doing anything about it. He then simply disappears from the public eye, living out the rest of his life on his father-in-law's estate, before dying some time around 1663, not with a bang but with a whimper (well, at least it wasn't a whine).

Rotten Tomatoes

Before I get started on this topic, can I just say that this piece has nothing to do with today's modern tomato health pills? I have never tried them and have nothing to say either for or against them. (There, that should keep legal happy.)

But back in 1837 I'm amazed that people were not even a little bit sceptical about the new wonder product on the market,

'Dr Miles' Compound Extract of Tomato', given that it claimed to cure a whole multitude of ailments, ranging from indigestion and constipation to syphilis and 'eruptive diseases'.

I mean, Mr Archibald Miles, pick one!

This was on the back of another quack, Dr John Cook Bennett, who, after a 'claimed visit' to Europe, announced that the consumption of tomatoes was something of a cure-all for cholera, dyspepsia, headaches and diarrhoea. I say 'claimed' because Bennett was pretty good at making up claims, research and qualifications, and there are still doubts that he ever left the US.

But at least he stopped short of any claims about syphilis.

Don't get me wrong – the tomato is a wonderful fruit, brimming with flavour and healthy vitamins. It's just that nineteenth-century North Americans were mostly unaware of that. If a household grew tomatoes, it was not in the fruit and vegetable patch; it was more likely to be found in a flowerpot. The simple reason for this is, despite the fact that Central and South America had long enjoyed eating tomatoes, as did most of Europe, horticulturalists in the United States thought tomatoes far too brightly coloured to be edible, so people grew them only for aesthetic reasons.

Despite that, Bennett had lit the vine-ripened blue touchpaper and Miles had come up with the pills and a massive distribution network – the tomato pill craze was off and running. This obviously meant that there would be competitors, and one in particular, Dr Guy R. Phelps, unlike the other two, actually had a verifiable medical degree from no less a hallowed institution than Yale University. Phelps launched his own 'Compound Tomato Pills' – and that's when the passata really hit the fan.

Miles either wrote under a pseudonym or had someone else write an article claiming that Phelps's pills were nothing more than a 'baseless imitation'. Miles went further, approving an editorial in the *New York Journal of Commerce* that branded Phelps both a 'quack' and a 'charlatan'.

Not one to back down, Phelps published a letter that snapped back about Miles, who had 'about as much claim to the title of doctor, as my horse and no more!'

Accusations continued back and forth around the theft of formulas and processes. At one point Phelps really threw down the gauntlet, calling Miles 'unjust and unmanly'. All up, the sparring and name-calling played out for over two years in the pages of the country's biggest newspapers.

Miles eventually published a piece claiming that the reason Phelps's tomato pills were cheaper than his was obviously because they did not contain any of the new wonder ingredient: tomato! On this point he was actually right – none of Phelps's tomato pills had ever been anywhere near a genuine tomato.

But then again, neither had any of Miles's pills.

Both products were remarkably devoid of any traces of tomato; they were just red-coloured placebos that *at best* may have had a mild laxative side-effect. And that is only good if you are actually looking for a mild laxative side-effect.

Just as quickly as they appeared, the two products faded from the American consciousness. There was, however, one indisputably good side-effect: Americans had realised that not only was the tomato extremely good for you but it also tasted absolutely wonderful.

Shakespeare's Hole in the Ground

It is somewhat odd to think that one of the world's worst acts of desecration of a historic site began with a pleasant picnic under a mulberry tree. But this was no ordinary mulberry tree. It stood in the garden of William Shakespeare's last home and was actually planted by the Bard himself. It was said that in his final days on earth, he had gazed out the window of his Stratford home, looking lovingly upon the tree that he had long nurtured.

The men at this picnic were no ordinary men. There was Sir Hugh Clopton, one of the wealthiest men in the Stratford area, who had recently bought Shakespeare's last home so that it could be a permanent memorial to the local who had forged such an impact on both the English stage and English language. With him were two young actors, Charles Macklin and David Garrick, the latter of whom would go on to become the greatest actor and director of his age. He would do more to popularise Shakespeare than any actor or director in the history of theatre.

But on this day, they were actually celebrating Garrick's theatrical London debut. He had just performed the lead role in *Richard III* and was already being hailed a genius. The day was glorious and the wine was flowing when Garrick leaped to his feet and declared, 'Sir, I propose a toast to Shakespeare's dear house, his dear garden and his very dear mulberry tree, planted by his own dear hand. May they never perish and remain forever a reminder of the people's poet.'

Talk about tempting fate.

Just nine years later, Sir Hugh died and *New Place*, as the house was known, had to be sold off to repay some of his considerable debts.

The new owner was the Reverend Francis Gastrell, a wealthy if somewhat ill-tempered man of the cloth who, apart from that failing, was almost hermit-like in his habits. He had bought the house in out-of-the-way Stratford to serve as a quiet country retreat. There was just one flaw in this tree change: Shakespeare's reputation as a local lad done good had been greatly enhanced in the past nine years by Garrick's conquering of the London stage. *New Place* and its celebrated mulberry tree had become something of an eighteenth-century tourist destination, to the point where hundreds of people a day were traipsing through the reverend's garden to sit beneath the tree and break off a twig so that they might pay homage to both the actor and the Bard.

These day-trippers incensed the new owner, to the point that in 1756 Gastrell fenced off his garden and had massive padlocks placed on the gates. Unfortunately, this didn't work, and theatre-mad sightseers were still constantly plaguing him. So he cut the damn thing down.

In a wonderful piece of poetic justice, he sold the wood to a local craftsman, who fashioned the timber into Shakespeare-themed souvenirs.

It was at this time that Gastrell's battles with the local council, who wanted to charge him with 'wanton vandalism', began. Enraged by the accusation – and the still constant stream of tourists invading his privacy – he fled Stratford and moved to another city, Lichfield.

This is where things got even more messy.

He left a few of his servants behind to manage *New Place*, but the council placed a special tax on all properties that were not occupied by the owner or the owner's immediate family for more than a month. When Gastrell became aware of this tax, he flew into one of his famous rages and, upon returning to Stratford, made the council aware in no uncertain terms that there was no way he would be paying the forty shillings that they said he owed.

When the council sent two bailiffs around to collect the tax, Gastrell chased them off his land, shouting threats of hellfire and damnation. It was at this point that the reverend finally did his biggest dummy spit. He ordered the house to be demolished, and he fled back to his other home in Lichfield, much to the chagrin of his wife, Jane, who had been enjoying some greatly needed 'me time' away from her quarrelsome husband.

Gastrell never returned to Stratford, and for the rest of his life his friends and family were forbidden to even utter the words 'Shakespeare' or 'mulberry'.

One unexpected result from the whole affair was that the hole in the ground where *New Place* had stood became an even *greater* tourist attraction once news of what the angry reverend had done was published and began to spread throughout the country. The council actually charged admission to wander around the hole and made considerably more money than they would have if Gastrell had paid his taxes in the first place.

Strangely enough, this wouldn't be the last time that picnicking would endanger a British heritage site. By the late 1800s, Stonehenge was on private land and in a bad state of disrepair. Tourists had chipped off souvenir shards and carved graffiti into the Neolithic blocks. One of the pillars had actually fallen over and a lintel was severely cracked.

Around this time it had become fashionable for the upper-class to picnic at the base of the stones. The idle rich had recently embraced the continental fashion of eating al fresco. Unfortunately, what they *hadn't* embraced was cleaning up after themselves. Their habit of leaving behind food scraps and wine bottles, along with other rubbish, attracted rats and rabbits. Realising that they were on to an easy feed, the animals started to make nests and burrows at the base of the standing pillars. This weakened their foundations to the point where they had to be propped up with wooden trusses, simply for safety reasons.

After years of campaigning, Stonehenge finally received the government heritage support it so badly needed. Now, of course, it is an exceedingly well-maintained World Heritage site.

Fortunately, the greatest danger to be faced on a day trip to Stonehenge now is being stuck on the bus next to some self-proclaimed druid. But it does go to reinforce a theory I have long held: nothing good comes out of picnics.

Scoundrels, Both Dirty & Rotten

No, Seriously, It Actually Happened

We are all aware of the stories of out-of-town rubes being suckered into buying the Brooklyn Bridge in the early twentieth century. It's such a well-loved part of American folklore that even Bugs Bunny had a crack at it. It's so outlandish, it's so over the top, it's so ridiculous . . . that, yes, it actually happened. Moreover, one particularly outrageous conman by the name of George C. Parker would later claim that at the height of his powers he had managed to sell the Brooklyn Bridge twice in one week.

Parker also managed to find gullible buyers for Madison Square Garden, the Metropolitan Museum of Art, the Statue of Liberty, as well as Grant's Tomb. For the last con, he would pretend to be the general's grandson who had fallen on bad times. Quite the ruse, but I have one burning question: just who actually thought that they could make money by acquiring the tomb of Ulysses S. Grant? But dressing the part was always in George Parker's repertoire. He once escaped custody in 1908 by simply donning the hat and coat of his arresting sheriff and then calmly walking out the front door of the courthouse in which he was about to stand trial.

Not that George had the whole Brooklyn Bridge market all to himself, of course.

It was not uncommon for the local police to have to remove from the busy bridge hucksters who had set up impromptu booths attempting to collect tolls from unimpressed New Yorkers. Then you had men like William McCloundy, who was also known as 'I.O.U. O'Brien', which you have to admit is one very revealing

Reprehensible

pseudonym. McCloundy was the first person ever convicted of selling the bridge, and after his arrest in 1901 he spent two and a half years in Sing Sing Prison for grand larceny.

However, Parker and McCloundy did not invent this particular hoax.

In 2005, a *New York Times* article by Gabriel Cohen, 'For You, Half Price', refers to Jay Robert Nash's 1976 book *Hustlers and Con Men: An Anecdotal History of the Confidence Man and His Games*. In the article, he cites Nash's interview with the notorious swindler Joseph 'Yellow Kid' Weil. Weil, who was long retired, recalled that the first time he'd heard about the bridge swindle was from the 1880s and 90s, and he attributes the con to two sets of perpetrators.

First, there was a certain Reed C. Waddell, and hot on his heels were two infamous brothers, Charles and Fred Gondorff. Cohen wrote, 'Perpetrators such as Mr Waddell and the Gondorff brothers were savvy. They timed the path of beat cops working near the bridge, and when they knew the officers would be out of sight, they propped up signs reading "Bridge for Sale".'

I know it seems unbelievable to us that someone would fall for something as simple as a hand-painted sign saying 'Bridge for Sale'. Surely no one would be that gullible in this day and age? To those people I have two words: 'Nigerian Prince'.

Nash takes up the story:

> The Gondorffs sold the bridge many times. They would sell it for two, three hundred dollars, up to one thousand. Once they sold half the bridge for two hundred and fifty because

the mark didn't have enough cash . . . By all accounts the bulk of the suckers were greenhorns, fresh off the boat. Swindlers used to approach the stewards of international vessels docked at Ellis Island and pay them for information about passengers who might have money and be interested in buying property.

Later historians have questioned this version of events, but what is most likely true is that swindlers had been selling off the bridge to unsophisticated 'investors' pretty much from the time of its completion in 1883.

What is not up for dispute is that Waddell and the Gondorffs were actual crooks plying their trade in New York at that particular time. The Gondorffs would belatedly achieve a certain amount of fame. Years after leaving New York they were in Chicago, where they invented the horse racing 'wire scam', where a conman convinces a punter that he has advance knowledge of a race result before news of that result reaches an off-track betting site. As such, they were part of the inspiration for the hit 1973 movie *The Sting*, starring Robert Redford and Paul Newman.

Soap Box Opera

In October of 1973, a rather strange, small article appeared within the pages of *The New York Times*. It contained three phrases that you would not expect to see juxtaposed within one piece of writing:

Reprehensible

'Skiing world jetsetter'
'Charges of contributing to the delinquency of a minor'
'All-American Soap Box Derby'

The jetsetter was Robert Lange Sr, a man who helped develop, engineer and manufacture the plastic ski boot revolution. The minor was his nephew Jimmy Gronen. The All-American Soap Box Derby was the All-American Soap Box Derby.

Now, this was not Mr Lange's first brush with scandal at the derby – an event that positions single-occupant, gravity-propelled vehicles at the top of a hill to see who can get down the fastest. There had been a question asked the previous year about the suspiciously amazing performance of his son Robert Jr's car, which eventually went on to take out the competition. These questions only got more serious when, instead of donating the car to the Soap Box Derby Museum, like all previous winners, the vehicle mysteriously disappeared. Witnesses at the time attested to the fact that they'd seen it half-hidden in Mr Lange's garage.

What alerted everyone to the fact that something was amiss was the rapid speed that the Langes' soap box would achieve from the starting line, especially for a vehicle supposedly relying solely on the gravitational properties of the hill.

So when Lange's nephew entered the derby the following year, and seemed to have the same acceleration advantages at the starting line, and went on to *win* the event . . . those questions grew even louder.

It was decided that the soap box should be thoroughly inspected. And the first thing they noticed was a small button built into the headrest. What could the button possibly be used for in a non-motorised vehicle, and why would Lange have placed it there?

To answer this question, you have to understand some of the mechanics of soap box racing. At the start of the race, the soap box cars are held in place at the top of a hill by a metal plate that rests against the nose of the vehicle. To start the race, the plate – or more correctly *plates* – are dropped away with considerable force. And this is where the headrest button came into play. Once the Lange soap box had been put through an X-ray machine at the local Goodyear tyre factory, the role of the mystery button was discovered.

The button was a switch that connected an electromagnet in the nose with a battery hidden behind the driver inside the body of the vehicle. Once he was on the starting line, young Jimmy Gronen would press his helmet back onto the button, thus engaging the magnet. When the metal plate dropped, the attraction between the magnet and the plate would cause the soap box to lurch forward, giving the driver a boost at the start, where it counted most, before the great equaliser of gravity took over.

Lange, in his subsequent defence, claimed that similar systems had been in place for years, a charge vehemently denied by the racing association. The charges of 'corrupting a minor' were later dropped, due to the fact that Jimmy had already forfeited both his championship and prize money once the magnet had been discovered.

This begs two questions. What, ultimately, was to gain? Lange was a wealthy man and the prize money (which included a scholarship endowment) given to the winner of the derby was an amount that would have been fairly inconsequential to him or his family, unlike the many other blue-collar contestants. And secondly, what sort of man coaches his nephew in the black arts of soap box derby cheating? I mean, my uncles taught me how to fish (which translated into beer and swearing before sunrise), net fishing for prawns (which I don't think was completely legal) and how to shoot at empty beer cans with a shotgun held together with electrical tape (!), but they would never stoop to cheating.

Also, I loved all my uncles, and never once did *we* end up either in court or in *The New York Times*.

Suggested Reading

As you might imagine, researching this book took me to some wild and wacky places. Here are some of the sources I found the most useful and entertaining.

Abbott, Karen. 'The 1904 Olympic Marathon May Have Been the Strangest Ever', smithsonian.com, 7 August 2012.

Admin, M. 'Hans Christian Andersen Was a Bit of a Pervert', knowledgenuts.com, 7 November 2013.

Alexander, Kristine. '10 More Historically Important Perverts', toptenz.net, 14 May 2018.

Allan, Victor. 'Gregor MacGregor, the Prince of Poyais', historytoday.com, 11 July 2018.

Andrews, Evan. 'The Cardiff Giant Fools the Nation, 145 Years Ago', history.com, 22 August 2018.

Baidya, Sankalan. '25 Interesting and Weird Sir Isaac Newton Facts', factslegend.org, 16 July 2014.

Baker, Russell. 'The Bald Truth About Julius Caesar', *The Baltimore Evening Sun*, 21 November 1991.

Ball, Graham. 'The Sordid Secret Life of H.G. Wells', *Express*, 30 March 2010.

Bolluyt, Jess. 'The Vainest Presidents of All Time (and How Donald Trump Compares)', cheatsheet.com, 6 October 2018.

Reprehensible

Braun, Adee. 'The Tomato Pill Craze', atlasobscura.com, 16 October 2017.

Bryant, Chris. 'Thugs, Scoundrels and Womanisers: the worst behaved MPs in history', *The Guardian*, 24 March 2014.

Bumbar, Micky. 'Ferdinand Magellan, the Explorer Who Spent More Money on Sherry Than Weapons', lordsofthedrinks.com, 3 June 2015.

Bumbar, Micky. 'Karl Marx, the Drunkard Who Laid the Foundation for Communism', lordsofthedrinks.com, 6 November 2014.

Bumbar, Micky. 'William the Conqueror, the First Norman King of England and Inventor of the "All Alcohol Diet"', lordsofthedrinks.net, 21 October 2014.

Burke, Matthew. '42 Debauched Facts About Historical Royal Scandals', factinate.com.

Carlton, Genevieve. 'History's Most Bizarre Duel Was Fought Between a Topless Princess and a Topless Countess', ranker.com.

Carlton, Genevieve. 'The Wild Life of Gouverneur Morris, the Most Mysterious Founding Father of Them All', medium.com, 26 May 2018.

Cawthorne. Nigel. *The Sex Lives of the Kings and Queens of England*, Prion, London, 1994.

Chalakoski, Martin. 'Peter III, Once Placed a Rat on Trial', thevintagenews.com, 4 June 2018.

Clark, Brooke. '10 Reasons You Should Be Reading Martial', partisanmagazine.com, 26 May 2016.

Crow, Jonathan. 'Isaac Newton Creates a List of His 57 Sins (Circa 1662)', openculture.com, 31 March 2015.

Cybulskie, Danièle. 'How to Kill a Medieval Zombie', medievalists.net.

Dantzer, Alexandra. 'Royal Women Used Professional Foot Ticklers in Rather Arousing Ways', thevintagenews.com, 19 January 2010.

Dash, Mike. 'John Brinkley, the Goat-gland Quack', *The Telegraph*, 18 April 2008.

Davis, Lauren. 'A Princess Once Dueled a Countess Over Floral Arrangements . . . Topless', gizmodo.com, 20 May 2015.

Suggested Reading

Dean, Michelle. 'Saturday History Lesson: Hans Christian Andersen as Charles Dickens' Houseguest', therumpus.net, 18 August 2012.

Dunn, Beth. 'The Turn of the Leg', wondersandmarvels.com.

Eschner, Kat. 'The Cardiff Giant Was Just a Big Hoax', smithsonian.com, 16 October 2017.

Falasha, Louis. 'Tesla's Pigeon: A Love Story', lazerhouse.org, 20 February 2015.

Flood, Alison. 'Ancient Greek Manuscripts Reveal Life Lessons From the Roman Empire', *The Guardian*, 11 February 2016.

Formichella, Janice. 'Top 10 Highly Successful Liars From History', listverse.com, 11 May 2017.

Fullerton, Huw. 'Did Queen Victoria Really Say "We are not amused"?', *Radio Times*.

Gilbert, Sophie. "Jingle Bells': A Racy Drinking Song (for Thanksgiving)', *The Atlantic*, 24 December 2015.

Gilsdorf, Ethan. 'J.R.R. Tolkien and C.S. Lewis: A Literary Friendship and Rivalry', literarytraveler.com, 1 October 2006.

Golgowski, Nina. 'Gymnophobics: The Feal-life 'Never-nudes' Who Live in Fear of Being Seen Naked (Even in Private)', *Daily Mail*, 18 May 2013.

Grabianowski, Ed. 'How Duels Work', howstuffworks.com, 22 June 2005.

Hanson, Sheila. 'Bicycle Face: A guide to Victorian cycling diseases', sheilahanlon.com, 4 January 2016.

Heaphy, Linda. 'The Bawdy Graffiti of Pompeii and Herculaneum', kashgar.com.au, 19 April 2017.

Henderson, Jon. 'The 10 Greatest Cheats in Sporting History', *The Observer*, 8 July 2001.

Howell, Helen Murphy. 'A History of Humanity's Disgusting Hygiene', owlcation.com, 27 March 2013.

Huffman, Zack. 'The Time a Pilgrim Was Executed for Having Sex With a Turkey', vice.com, 25 November 2015.

Hunt, Tristam. 'Eat, Drink and Be Communist', *The Spectator*, 15 April 2009.

Johnson, Paul. *Intellectuals: From Marx and Tolstoy to Sartre and Chomsky*, HarperCollins, New York, 1988.

Jones, Josh. 'In 1704, Isaac Newton Predicts the World Will End in 2060', openculture.com, 14 October 2015.

Junkies, Laurie. 'The Most Arcane State Laws in America', stories.avvo.com, 14 October 2011.

Kann, Drew. 'Eight of the Worst Popes in Church History', cnn.com, 15 April 2018.

Klein, Christopher. '7 Things You May Not Know About the Constitutional Convention', history.com, 31 August 2018.

Klein, Christopher. '10 Reasons Why Gouverneur Morris Was the Oddest Founding Father', history.com, 7 March 2019.

Kleyman, Katia. '11 Gross Facts About the Surprisingly Prolific Sex Life of Benjamin Franklin', ranker.com.

Knowles, Rachel. 'Hair Powder and Pomatum', regencyhistory.net, 12 January 2016.

Knowles, Rachel. 'The Rise and Fall of Beau Brummell (1778–1840)', regencyhistory.net, 14 November 2012.

Knowles, Rachel. '30 Beau Brummell Quotes and Anecdotes', regencyhistory.net, 21 November 2012.

Lampkin, Benjamin. '8 Things You Might Not Know About Chester A. Arthur', mentalfloss.com, 5 October 2015.

Lindsay, Jessica. 'Did Prince Albert Have a Prince Albert?', *Metro*, 27 April 2018.

Loomis, Erik. 'Anthony Comstock: American Prude', lawyersgunsmoneyblog.com, 15 February 2012.

Lovric, Michelle and Mardas, Nikifororos Doxiadis. *How to Insult, Abuse & Insinuate in Classical Latin*. Penguin Random House UK, 1998.

Luckel, Madeleine. 'Queen Victoria Made White Wedding Dresses Popular', *Vogue*, 15 January 2017.

Mackelden, Amy. '32 Royal Conspiracy Theories That Are Absolutely Bonkers', *Harper's Bazaar*, 29 July 2019.

Suggested Reading

Mann, E.H. 'This Week I Learned – the Coital Quandary of Louis XVI', ehmannwrites.com, 24 May 2018.

Marks, Anna. 'Victoria Con Men Faked the Middle Ages' Darkest Devices', vice.com, 18 June 2016.

Martin, Tim. 'The Scandalous Sex Life of H.G. Wells', *The Telegraph*, 2 February 2016.

McFadden, Christopher. '25 Extremely Embarrassing Architectural Failures', interestingengineering.com, 22 May 2017.

McMahon, Tony. 'Why Tsar Peter the Great Trashed a Famous Londoner's House', london-ghosts.com, 30 May 2018.

McNamara, Robert. 'Great Swindlers of the 19th Century', thoughtco.com, 25 May 2019.

McRobbie, Linda Rodriguez. 'The True Story of Roland the Farter, and How the Internet Killed Professional Flatulence', atlasobscura.com, 28 December 2015.

Micheletti, Ellen. 'Beau Brummell: The Ultimate Man of Style', allaboutromance.com, 12 May 2006.

Miharia, Akancha. 'From Orgies to Blowjobs, This Russian Queen Had Some of the Kinkiest Furniture You've Ever Seen', scoopwhoop.com, 27 July 2017.

Miller, Norman. 'John Elwes: Scrimper Who Inspired Ebenezer Scrooge', *The Telegraph*, 20 September 2016.

Misra, Ria. 'In the 18th Century, Wig-Stealing Bandits Roamed England's Countryside', gizmodo.com, 20 May 2015.

Modoo, Christopher. 'George "Beau" Brummell: The Originator of Dandyism', therake.com, August 2017.

Mohr, Melissa. *Holy Sh*t: A Brief History of Swearing*, Oxford University Press, Oxford, 2013.

Murr, Virginia. '10 Odd Obsessions of Famous Philosophers', listverse.com, 10 February 2014.

Nigro, Jeffrey A. & Phillips, William A. 'How Beau Brummell Changed Jane Austen's World', *Persuasions*, vol. 36, no. 1, 2015.

Nucilli, Ryleigh. 'The Biggest Feuds in the History of Science', ranker.com.

Reprehensible

O'Shea, Siobhan. 'Caca Dauphin: the Brief Craze for Prince Poo at Marie Antoinette's Court', interesly.com, 13 August 2018.

Oliver, Mark. '10 Insane Facts About Emperor Commodus Left Out of 'Gladiator', listverse.com, 18 September 2017.

Perry, Kellen. '12 Historical Figures You Didn't Know Had STDs', ranker.com.

Philippas, Ann. 'Hans Christian Andersen: The Eccentric Guest', dickensmuseum.com, 10 November 2016.

Pinsky, Robert. 'Dissed in Verse', slate.com, 26 April 2006.

Roberts, Kayleigh. 'Here's the Scientific Reason We're All So Obsessed With the Royal Family', *Marie Claire*, 2 September 2018.

Rodriguez, Linda. 'The History of Farting for Money', *New Republic*, 31 December 2015.

Schneider, Gregory S. 'The Mother Who Made George Washington – and Made Him Miserable', *The Washington Post*, 12 May 2017.

Scott, Kate. 'Dungeons & Deadlines: The Kinky Sex Lives of 8 Great Authors', bookriot.com, 16 February 2016.

Selin, Shannon. '10 Interesting Facts About Napoleon Bonaparte', shannonselin.com.

Simonovski, Nikola. 'Robert Cornelius: The Man Who Took the First Selfie in the World in 1839', thevintagenews.com, 9 December 2017.

Smallwood, Karl. '10 Crazy Things Done by Egyptian Pharaohs', toptenz.net, 23 March 2017.

Smith, Lassie. 'James Joyce Had Some Pretty Specific Sexual Desires', medium.com, 16 May 2018.

Spurr, John. '"Damn your blood": Swearing in Early Modern English', historyextra.com, 29 June 2018.

Stepko, Barbara. 'The Most Ridiculous Duel in History – in a Hot-Air Balloon!', thevintagenews.com, 1 August 2018.

Sterba, James P. 'Soap Box Derby Mystery of '72 May Stay Unsolved', *The New York Times*, 6 October 1973.

Stewart, Doug. 'To Be . . . Or Not: The Greatest Shakespeare Forgery', *Smithsonian Magazine*, June 2010.

Suggested Reading

Stockton, Richard. '7 Napoleon Bonaparte Facts They Don't Teach You in History Class', allthatsinteresting.com, 16 July 2018.

Stockton, Richard. 'Better Know a Pope: Stephen VI, The Grave Robber', allthatsinteresting.com, 22 May 2018.

Strauss, Bob. 'The Bone Wars', thoughtco.com, 14 January 2018.

Stromberg, Joseph. '"Bicycle face": a 19th-century Health Problem Made Up to Scare Women Away From Biking', vox.com, 24 March 2015.

Thorpe, J.R. '5 Historical Myths About Sex That People Actually Believed', bustle.com, 7 November 2015.

Thorpe, J.R. 'The Most Bizarre Sex Toy in History (Because Everyone Should Know About Bread Dildos)', bustle.com, 11 January 2017.

Thorpe, Vanessa. 'How Guest Hans Christian Andersen Destroyed His Friendship with Dickens', *The Guardian*, 10 September 2017.

Tourgee, Heather. 'How the Puritans Banned Christmas', newengland.com, 19 December 2018.

Valjak, Domagoj. 'Jean-Paul Sartre's Bad Mescaline Trip Led to the Philosopher Being Followed by Imaginary Crabs for Years', thevintagenews.com, 6 October 2017.

Veith, Gene. 'The Etiquette of Dueling', patheos.com, 30 March 2012.

Vorel, Jim. 'The 1800s: When Americans Drank Whiskey Like It Was Water', pastemagazine.com, 10 August 2018.

Walls, Jerry. 'Sinful, Scandalous C.S. Lewis, Joy, and the Incarnation', christianthought.hbu.edu, 9 December 2013.

Watson, Charles S. 'Sol Smith', encyclopediaofalabama.org, 19 July 2012.

Werbel, Amy. *Lust on Trial: Censorship and the Rise of American Obscenity in the Age of Anthony Comstock*, Columbia University Press, New York, 2018.

Williams, Brenda. *Medieval Secrets & Scandals*, Pavilion Books, London, 2013.

Winterman, Denise. 'The Man Who Demolished Shakespeare's House', bbc.com, 7 March 2013.

Writer, Steve Newman. 'The Rev Francis Gastrell Knocks Down Shakespeare's Last Home: New Place', medium.com, 10 June 2018.

Acknowledgments

There are a few people without whom this book would not have happened:

My manager and old friend Andrew Taylor, who said after the last book, 'So, you got another one in you?' Along with Tobie Newman, Heather Tyas and Julie Lawless, and all the team at More Talent.

Everyone at Simon & Schuster Australia for making me feel so much at home, especially Dan Ruffino and my editor, Brandon VanOver, who I regard as more of a co-conspirator than I do an editor, and he's damn fine company, which always helps.

And, as always, my eternally patient friends and family, who I've used as unpaid sounding boards during the writing of this book. I send you my thanks.